THE FALL OF THE NEW BABYLON

Frederick Guttmann R.

THE FALL OF THE NEW BABYLON, AND THE END OF FREEDOM

First edition. April 8, 2024.

ISBN: 979-8231451777

Written by Frederick Guttmann.

When the morning of September 11, 2001, the global media echoed the attack on the twin towers in New York, many of us immediately knew that the world we knew would never be the same.

The beginning of the suppression of civil liberties had begun.

The era of a new Nazism was emerging...

"We cannot solve problems by thinking in the same way as when we created them."

(Albert Einstein)

The Fall of New Babylon

Frederick Guttmann R.

2017-2021

258 pages

www.frederickguttmann.com[1]

frederickguttmann@gmail.com

1. http://www.frederickguttmann.com

Content

INTRODUCTION

The arrival of the industrial age was the beginning of the American era. The young nation was beginning to leave behind the great empires that until then had sustained great hegemonies. The Jesuits saw in this American continent a unique opportunity to reestablish Catholic power, but European oligarchies also wanted to use these lands to expand their power and influence. The US was the ideal fertile and prosperous land to run a new world government from there.

With the rise of the powerful North American empire, both in the Bible and in recent - and not so recent - visions, clear references were seen to a decisive stage in our history at the hands of this nation. This country, starting by promoting biblical values, would become the mother of the most putrid forces that operate on our planet. A den of thieves, lair of hateful spirits, greedy, avaricious and unscrupulous men, souls sold to power and wealth, prostitution and degradation at their highest levels, nameless aberrations, and the most sinister of all this, hidden from the eyes of the town, ignorant of everything that takes place behind the scenes.

As in a cunning game of chess, sometimes the queen is sacrificed for a greater purpose; Sometimes the fall of a major head in the power game can mean the rise of an empire, one greater than has ever existed on the face of our globe. In this thesis I will expose what many of us are clear about is the destruction of the United States of America - as we know it - as a master strategy of the Masters of the World, to raise the last great empire of our time. We are talking about the rise of a dictatorial world government based on surveillance technology, police force and mass mind control. A system that the Bible itself called the Thirion, or 'The Beast'.

In this investigation I will explain to you why the book of Revelation prophesies about the power behind the USA, that 'Deep State' that the 'Q Anon' movement has propagandized; that shadow power that is known in Christianity under the name of 'the Great Whore' or 'The Great Babylon'. We are not talking about the suicide of the Deep State, but about a sum of events that push the cataclysm of the US as its headquarters to make way for a world government.

I.

THE METAMORPHOSIS OF ROME

« Then I lifted up my eyes and looked, and behold, four horns. And I said to the angel who spoke with me: What are these? And he said to me, These are the horns that scattered Judah, Israel, and Jerusalem. Then Jehovah showed me four carpenters. And I said: What are these coming to do? And he answered me, saying, Those are the horns that scattered Judah, so that no one lifted up his head; But these have come to make them tremble, to pull down the horns of the nations that lifted up the horn on the land of Judah to scatter it. (Zechariah 1:18-21, The Bible – RVA Translation 60)

Important empires rose in ancient times, several of them causing serious damage to the then nation of Israel. One of those kingdoms still prevails, but not in the way it existed back then. At number 4 is Rome, which absorbed Greece, and is the last great empire that still exists today, only hidden under other names, other leaders and other geographical locations. The prophet Daniel also tells us about 4 beasts, a description that some have seen in our 'political, military, economic and religious' structures, while others only like those 4 empires of antiquity, reaching as far as Rome - or the perspective of David Brennan, of the UN, USA, European Union and Russia. But there are also other interpretations, such as seeing here the US, Russia, China and Europe – something that I also thought until recently – or directly the last Global Government. It is logical that the symbology that Daniel observes is codified, but the first description that is seen seems to evoke a winged lion, that is, a griffin or shirdal, which is a type of sphinx. According to the Greeks, the griffin was sacred to the god Apollo, and I do not think it is a mere curiosity that the name Phoebus itself was originally so similar to that of the 'well of the abyss'.

The other monster is like a bear - so characteristic of Soviet heraldry - but the third seems strange (a leopard with 4 heads), except if you notice that in Hebrew it says Narmer (tiger). The tiger, as well as the dragon and the panda, are characteristic animals of China. However, this 3rd being or creature has the '4' in its representation, which has no relation to said country, unless it is intended to evoke the Chinese economy. The 4 heads would be 4 kings or governments, and this does not agree much with China, even though, in fact, the US, Russia, China and Europe are the axis of the current world. Daniel's vision, relating to the 4 beasts, fits more precisely with the references of the sibyl and other prophetic visions of this nature, which describe 4 kingdoms, one after another, with Rome being the 4th and last. In the 'First Apocalypse of Baruch', or 2nd Baruch, the scribe narrates several dreams he has about the end of the Century, and in chapters 39 and 40, he tells how he sees '4 kingdoms' fall until the Messiah appears and judges the leader who will remain at the end of that 4th kingdom. Baruch refers that "this kingdom that in our time destroyed Zion will be destroyed, and it will be subdued by the one who comes after it. Again that one will be destroyed after a time and a third will arise that will also dominate in its time and will be destroyed. After this a fourth kingdom will rise whose tyranny will be harsher and worse than that of the previous ones. He will rule for a long time.

The Vatican has existed since 1929. In 1534 the Pope commissioned Ignatius of Loyola to found the Jesuits to destroy Protestantism and take control of all the world's classes. When the United States was founded in 1776, the Jesuits were already infiltrated in politics and the economy. The Jesuits were the promoters, precursors and to this day, owners of Hollywood and the film, artistic, music and media industries. Papal power was in Rome (specifically in the Vatican from the space that Mussolini gave them), but its executive, media, corporate, financial, logistical and political power passed to the US over more than 240 years (because They had already motivated the wars of independence and revolutions before, like all wars until today). While the bishop of Rome is the pope of the Vatican and the front for the world, the cardinal of New York is the pope of the United States, and both are pieces relegated to the Superior General of the Jesuit order, who directs the Military complex. US Industrial

The "Holy See" is only a city state if you look at it from a geographical perspective. We are talking about the city-country that controls the Earth. We are talking about the elite, about the power in the shadows, about what some call 'Illuminati', about the seat of economic power (Wall Street), about the political Babel (the UN, in Manhattan), about the headquarters of the global influence of media, cybernetics, fashion, music, cinema, etc. (California), of the velite headquarters (the Military-Industrial complex that invades and destabilizes all countries), of the one who overthrows democratic or opposing governments this axis (through its covert CIA agents) and motivates wars, guerrillas and terrorism (also through their secret agents).

Vatican-Rome – not in the geographical but logistical sense – has operated for at least 240 years from the US. Vatican was established by Musolini in 1929. One is talking about the Roman Empire (27 BC), be it called ' Rome' before, 'papacy' after, or 'USA' today. And that power came from what was previously a senate (8th century BC), and what was previously the power that Macedonia exercised through Alexander, and if we continue we reach the tower of Babel. All this, as many historians and books explain (such as William Bramley in 'God's of Eden', or RA Boulay in 'Dragons & Flying Serpents'), comes from the Nephilim dynasty, which is related in the Greek myth of the maiden. Phoenician (from Tyre) Europe and the bull.

The history books that deal with the subject explain how Rome lost unified power since the religious independence of England (Anglicans), Greece (Orthodox) and Turkey, as well as Ethiopia some time before, and even Egypt (Coptics), but continued to control the rest of Europe with the moral and psychological burden of religion, where they made people believe that they were the representatives of God, and consequently their word was like the word of God himself. When Luther contradicted them, he not only gave freedom of knowledge of the Bible (which until then was only read in Latin for a minority who knew Latin in Rome) starting with the Germanic language, but he began a spiritual revolution, which, with its pros and cons, changed European society. So from 1517 the split began in the hegemonic and ideological power of religion (predominant in Europe), so Pope Paul III accepted the project of Ignatius of Loyola in 1534 to, instead of more wars with the Protestants, use a control strategy through all levels of society and popular influence. As at that time the campaigns towards the Americas began, an opportunity was seen in that new continent.

Protestantism entered there with the settlers and groups and families that began their religious movements, so the Jesuits did the same, but going directly to take total power of the "new" territory. While the US Declaration of Independence was being signed in 1776, in Europe another Jesuit (Adam Weishaupt) founded the Masonic order that would begin to take global power (the Illuminati Order of Bavaria). In those 240 years, one group has controlled from Europe and another from the US, but their plan was to unify the world in a single government controlled by the "holy see", but without it seeming that it was a Catholic thing, nor of the Pope, nor of Rome, nor of the Vatican, but of the diplomacy and decisions of each free country.

Vatican City has been behind, from the beginning, the founding, structuring, wars of independence and laws of the United States. Few know of its secret war against Protestantism and its passage of power to the United States. working from there. All of the descriptions given in Revelation chapter 17 deal with a shadow government controlling the nations. In this research thesis I maintain – along with many others before me – that the Roman Empire has been evolving, changing facades, structures, strategies, names, government system and location, and has raised the US to be its executive hand and new den.

It is the cradle of a global government. At the moment it seems that there are independent countries, but the elite is the same. Before Rome, power was seen in particular kings in their empire, but since Rome, a global government system began that has been mutating and going through multiple phases of change of all kinds, taking power in more and more ways. intricate. As time has passed and we reach the 20th century, this power has controlled everything from the shadows, starting from the financial monopoly. Since 1917 (100 years ago), banking control and the Zionist plan skyrocketed the agenda, accelerating it beyond proportions, the likes of which had never been seen before.

In the visions of the prophet Daniel, where he mentions 4 beasts, the 3rd fits with what would be Ancient Greece, which was the mother of what would later become Europe. This is already known from the ancient myth of the Phoenician maiden Europa who was snatched away by Zeus (transformed into a bull), who took her to the island of Crete, and which Herodotus seems to have interpreted as a kidnapping by the monoic people (being that precisely the Minoans come from King Minos, son of Europe). The myth of the bull is key to this story and its hidden symbolism, but the most important thing is that Europa became the 'first queen of Crete'. Therefore, from 'Tyre' would have come the royalty that entered ancient Greece, and that is also significant, since the name Tire appears again and again related to the designation of beast (Thirius, in Greek), as reflected in Revelation. Billy Meier seems to refer to said 'beast' as a 'minotaur'. Homer, in the Iliad, affirms that Europe was the daughter of the Phoenix, which is another important symbol in the occult iconography of Freemasonry, evoking suicide in order to rise again rejuvenated (this also goes for the 'economy').

According to the myth, Europa had three children of Zeus, known as 'judges of the underworld', and King Asterion - who took that woman - adopted her three children. His son Minos banished his brothers from the throne after the death of Asterion three generations before the Trojan War. This whole story is much longer, but it must be mentioned that Pasiphae (Minos's wife) fell in love with a bull that Poseidon had sent for sacrifice, since Minos did not want to sacrifice it. Poseidon made her lie with the bull and conceive the Minotaur. Minos' daughter Ariadne ('Liber' to the Romans) married the hero Theseus and then the god Dionysus (god of wine). To all of these, it is believed that the symbol of the bull and Europe are those that represent the European continent, and it is from the ancestry of this maiden that the monarchy came.

Especially in the prophecies of the Sibylline oracles, a calamitous destruction for Rome is mentioned, which can be on several fronts and in various ways. We literally talk about the city of Rome, and we also talk about logistical Rome (USA), which is not an entire government or an entire structure of the nation, but an elite and power pyramid per se, what we know as Deep State. According to the prophecies, this "great city" – which receives various names, or epithets – collapses before or during the beginning of the government of the Antichrist dictatorship. To differentiate it from the kingdom of the Beast, this other "creature" is often described in Revelation as a woman or a city. This means that the fourth beast identifies a set of power systems, one of which currently sits upon it, but which the final beast itself will undo.

Through the Q movement we have information that points to this power structure as a dark network full of pedophilia, satanism and abominable rituals. Apoc. 18:2, when reading that 'it has been made a habitation of demons', it is usually understood that it is as a result of its destruction, but the original form of the wording is not intended to imply that, since 'Egenetus' is 'made' in continuous tense, not in future tense. For this reason, "the great Babel has fallen" is a phrase that is completed with an explanation: "made the abode of demons", not since it is destroyed, but rather it is destroyed having been 'the habitation of unclean spirits'. Isaiah explains it as well, telling the world that "Yaheveh is angry with all the nations, and indignant with all their host." (Isa. 34:2, R60)

But let us clarify that 'his army', in Hebrew 'Tzabaam', encompasses the military, as well as the social (hosts, people), but also the 'forces', which often identify the powers of evil. Whether it be armies, people, or spirits of darkness, "he will destroy them and hand them over to the slaughter." This is not something past, but the same thing we have already been talking about: "their dead will be thrown away, and a stench will rise from their corpses; and the mountains will be dissolved because of their blood. And all the host of heaven will be dissolved, and the heavens will be rolled up like a book; and all his army will fall, as the leaf falls from the vine, and as the leaf falls from the fig tree. For my sword will be drunken in heaven..." (Isa. 34:3-5, R60) Here also applies 'armies of heaven' in terms of the generality of the powers that are above, not precisely the good ones, but the structure itself, where good and evil rule these heavens. And in this chapter, speaking of all these spiritual forces in a metaphorical sense, he adds that this will occur as the "day of vengeance of Jaheveh, a year of retribution in the dispute of Zion." (verse 8)

He then adds how the world will be ravaged by dark spirits (although one seems to read that he talks about 'animals'). All of these come together, because that is the will of God, but not forever, but only at that end, when everything comes to light. The Bible in this sense reaffirms that the height of their 'Adikímata' (injustices, iniquities) is such that it has come before God. For this reason, twice as much evil will come to him: "give him torment and weeping" (verse 7). Her pride is such that she believes she is the invincible superpower, "because she says in her heart: I sit as a queen, and I am not a widow, and I will not see tears." Who is your husband? On the contrary, "in a single day" (a very short period of months) "their plagues will come; death, crying and hunger, and it will be burned with fire; for the Lord God is mighty, who judges her. The rest of the nations will see "the smoke of its fire" from "far away for fear of its torment." And this is imperatively a matter linked to money (prostitution, markets, luxuries, wealth, banking, etc.): "the strong city [...] the merchants of the earth weep and lament over it, because no one buys its merchandise anymore." ; merchandise of gold, silver, precious stones, pearls, fine linen, [...] horses and chariots. [...] in one hour so much wealth has been consumed.

And furthermore, he knows that it is the one that mentally and economically controls humanity, making them "slaves", dominating the "souls of men" (verse 13). The hidden power of this Roman elite that operates from the US – mainly – will be punished: "The light of a lamp will no longer shine in you, nor will the voice of husband and wife be heard in you anymore" (verse 23) . Everything they achieved was forged thanks to the dark powers of their satanic rituals: "for by your sorceries all nations were deceived." (Rev. 18:1-24) Sorcery? The original Greek passage says 'farmakeia'. Yes, pharmaceuticals, drugs, pharmaceutical industry. She is the one who is responsible for harming the majority of humanity. We can see that there is a clear analogy here between witchcraft, or the occult and demonic, with legal drugs, and the corporations that promote them. This pyramidal web is directed by a puppeteer; a demagogue who uses a scheme of 7 leaders to exert his control over our world.

The episodes that point to an individual who gets humanity into trouble and produces a schism between man and God is what concerns the story of Lucifer. There are also many coincidences with other texts (Sumerian, Scandinavian, Egyptian, Arab, Hebrew, Christian) that speak of an individual who worked for certain gods on Earth and tried to take the power of the main god who ruled in Mesopotamia at that time, with the same individual they describe as the serpent from the garden of Eden. These coincide with the Targum and the texts about Job from Qumran, which mention the Nephilim being judged and him being with them. Those three matches are pretty strong to assume that they are the same individual. However, over time, the idea of opponent, slanderer, leader of demons, ancient serpent and dragon became generalized for everything that had anything to do with this movement, way of thinking and ideology and all those who, in any way, , place, time or race, personified her.

That is why Revelation speaks of a dragon with 7 heads, but Satan is not septiccephalic (7-headed), but rather 7 individuals represent that ancient concept of Satan. At this point, the prophet Daniel announces that all this would be the case until what was to come was decreed upon 'the one' who 'made desolate' his people - that is, the Romans. It is precisely in this period of time when John the Apocalypse is referred to - where the 'sentence' against the 'desolator' is concluded, which is the last power that will rise on Earth. The Sibylline prophesied: «But when Rome also rules over Egypt, ruling always, then the greatest kingdom of the immortal King must appear over men. And a holy Lord will come to hold the scepter in every land to all ages of rapidly accelerating time. (Sibylline Oracles. Book III. Verses 55-60)

This mention that Rome will be the last kingdom on Earth, and that it will fall with the appearance of Christ, is constant. The fortune teller of the oracle said more about those kingdoms: "But then time rolled around there arose the kingdom of Egypt, then that of the Persians and the Medes and the Ethiopians, and Assyria and Babylon, and then that of the Macedonians. , the Egyptian once again, then that of Rome.» (Sibylline Oracles - Book III. Verse 190) It is necessary to understand that we must study the history of Roman power to reveal the hidden plot in this, not looking at the area of Italy, but at the very structure of the hidden power that has been maintained, and who eventually migrated to the US.

And in this respect the sibyl concludes her exposition on the powers that will govern the Earth, and in another part she says it again: "When the great tower fell and the languages of men were separated into many languages of mortals, first it was established the royal power of Egypt, that of the Persians and the Medes and also of the Ethiopians. And from Assyria and Babylon, then the great pride of Macedonia boasted; Then, fifth, the last, the famous lawless kingdom of the Italians shows many evils to all mortals and must endure the hardships of men of all countries. And he will lead the kings of the untamed nations to the West, make laws for the people and subdue all things. (Book VIII. Verses 5-17) What did the sibyl mean by "leading the kings" to the "west"? Where did Christopher Columbus, Hernán Cortés and all the other conquistadors come from, and who sponsored them? As researcher John Phelps explains, the United States was founded through the Jesuits, an order of knights created by Ignatius of Loyola with the protection of Rome, to destroy Protestants from the world (although this took them centuries to achieve).

But the description of its location gives two curious details: 7 mountains on which it sits. Both Jerusalem and Vatican City are surrounded and basically situated on 7 hills - but this is not conclusive. It says that the mountains (or mountains) are 7 kingdoms, but currently there are 194 countries, so one could assume that it would be a kind of 'G-7' (Germany, Canada, United States, France, Italy, Japan and United Kingdom). The issue is this: it says that "five have fallen", that is, they are no longer, and that "one is" (in the time of John), and another "will come and go to perdition." Consequently, it seems to allude more to a government directed by threads that transcend time. By John's day, "power" was in the hands of Rome, and this has continued until today, except that by the 5th century AD. C. his power was no longer known openly, while today he works politically from the UN; geographically and militarily from the US; economically from Wall Street and the City of London, although its headquarters are still in Rome (in Vatican City, more explicitly). It is true that 5 major empires fell before Rome (Greece-Macedonia, Media-Persia, Babylon, Assyria and Egypt), and that another power must arise after 'Rome-UN-Babel'.

If we are talking about a structure, and this 4th Beast is Roman, its 7 heads, how can they be the previous kingdoms if those had already been identified as 'beasts'? In John's day, 'Rome' was being ruled by its 11th emperor ('Domitian', last of the 'Flavian' dynasty), and this apostle continued his work in Ephesus during the rule of Nerva (Rev. 10:11), and perhaps even at the beginning of Trajan's. But there is more: Rome was built on the basis of all the peoples that preceded it, mixing the cults, ideas, beliefs and myths of all of them. For this reason they also consider it 'Babel', since it represents the combination of all philosophies in the world. Someone would say that it is not really located around 7 mountains or hills (Aventine, Capitoline, Celio, Esquilinium, Palatine, Quirinal and Viminal) in a geographical sense - if we talk about the Vatican - but rather the location of 'Rome' itself (in fact, ironically, between the 7 hills and the Vatican City it spans the Tiber River and the so-called 'Field of Mars'). These seven hills figure prominently in Roman mythology, religion, and politics; Traditionally, the original city is believed to have been founded by Romulus and Remus on the Palatine Hill (Collis Palatinus). The early seven hills were: Cermalus, Palatium, Velia, peaks of the Palatine Hill, Cispius, Fagutalis, Oppius, peaks of the Esquiline Hill, and Sucusa. Initially, the seven hills were occupied by small settlements that grouped together and formed a city known as "Rome."

The 7 kingdoms are the 7 mountains that have progressively ruled the world after the flood. Basically: 1. Babel (with Nimrod's tower), 2. Egypt, 3. Babylon, 4. Assyria, 5. Persia-Media, 6. Greece (Macedonia), 7. Rome. The 7 mountains are 7 kingdoms. 5 have already passed (Egypt, Assyria, Babylon, Medopersia, Greece). One has been from before Jesus until today (Rome) and another is almost completed (that of the beast). Rome will fall while the beast completely rises.

The citizens of the seven hills began to participate in a series of religious games that began to unite the groups. The city of Rome was therefore born once the settlements began to act as a group, draining the marshy valleys that separated them and turning them into markets and forums. Whoever studies the real core of Rome and Freemasonry sees that all its bases belong to Egyptian, Assyrian, Babylonian, Persian, Greek, Israelite and Roman culture. They do not adopt elements from America, Africa, Scandinavia or the Far East. Its principles consist of the mixture of these 7 kingdoms. The elements of Christianity were really Hebrew, and therefore it is Hebrew Christianity that represents this other absorbed principle, and in fact, Ieshua was born under the rule of the 'first Roman emperor', Caesar Augustus, and will return under the rule of the last ruler of this empire.

Just look at the characteristics of the Beast: "he was like a leopard, and his feet were like a bear's, and his mouth was like a lion's mouth." (Rev. 13:2, R60) Like a leopard with the feet of a bear and the mouth of a lion? What were the first three beasts that Daniel saw like? "The first was like a lion, [...] another second beast, like a bear, [...] another, like a leopard..." (Dan. 7:4-6, R60) It is evident that all of these are analogies: the 10 horns of the Beast will be the 10 supernations, and its 10 diadems (small crowns) will be its sub-emperors; The 7 heads of the Dragon are 7 demigods, and the 7 of the Beast are 7 demigods, whose other analogy is the 7 mountains of Rome and the 7 empires on which it was established. The fallen '5' are not only the empires, but the 'demigod' who directed said empire behind the scenes in the corresponding period.

The apostle John is told that "the beast that you saw was, and is not; and is about to rise from the abyss and go to perdition; and the inhabitants of the earth [...] will be amazed when they see the beast that was and is not, and will be." (Rev. 17:8, R60) And he adds that "it is also the eighth; and is from among the seven..." (verse 11) 'It was and it is not'? Did it exist and no longer exist? Was it and is it no longer? Which one is 'that one' that is one of the 7? Few of us have stopped to analyze that the description of chapter 13 speaks of a beast similar to a leopard, a lion and a bear, which has 10 diadems and was wounded, but the description of chapter 17 speaks of a scarlet beast and the prostitute on it. , which is not mentioned in chapter 13.

Although, we know that 5 kingdoms – which also conquered Babylon (Babel) – existed before Rome ("one is", they told John in his day, during the period of Roman domination), which were Egypt, Assyria, Babylon, Persia and Macedonia. So, one more to go up and be the last empire. Consequently: «The beast that was, and is not, is also the eighth; and it is from among the seven" (Rev. 17:11, R60) That is, this 7th empire is that of the Beast, which in turn represents all the previous ones. That is why it says: "These have the same purpose, and will hand over their power and authority to the beast" (Rev. 17:13, R60), since there will be a distribution of the world into 10 regions, but a global super-headquarters. , that of the Beast himself.

Currently, certain American researchers see many analogies between aspects of the scarlet beast that appear as a prostitute woman and the power mechanics of the Deep State, operating from the US. Following that thread, the same thing that we would observe in the Beast of the Antichrist that will fall before the beginning of the Messianic Millennium, also the Roman-American harlot would use the same structural model. The matter of the figures with 7 heads, 10 horns, etc. For example, I read a certain analyst see this model of the 10 in the US gubernatorial system. Aside from Malloy and Brandstad, the other 8 advisors were Jay Nixon (D-Missouri), Matt Mead (R-Wyo.), Brian Sandoval (R-Nev.), Bill Haslam (R-Tennessee), Steve Bullock (D-Montana), Mark Dayton (D-Minn.), Terry McAuliffe (D-Va.), and Rick Snyder (R-Mich.) .

Currently, the main characters of the entire emergency apparatus of said country are 7, who are advised by the 10 advisors, and they are: Ashton Carter (Secretary of Defense), Jeh Johnson (Secretary of National Security), Lisa Mónaco (Assistant to the President for Homeland Security and Counterterrorism), Valerie Jarrett (Assistant to the President for Intergovernmental Affairs and Public Engagement), Admiral William E. Gortney (Commander, USNORTHCOM (or 'US Northern Command')), Admiral Paul F. Zukunft (Commander of the Coast Guard) and General Frank J. Grass (Chief of the National Guard Bureau).

On December 2, 2016, Donald Trump chose retired Marine General James Mattis as Secretary of Defense. Days later, on December 12, Trump chose General John Kelly as Secretary of Homeland Security (who would have replaced William Gortney as Commanding General of the Northern Command, ending this exercise in February of last year). For his part, since August 2012, the Chief of the National Guard Bureau is Joseph L. Lengyel. Although, since no modification has been communicated, Lori Robinson is the current Chief of the Northern Command, elected in mid-May of last year. Robinson is "the woman with the most military power in the world" and "is a four-star general (the maximum that can be achieved in peacetime), in the US Air Force." (Stated 'ElMundo.es', in a report). His rank also assumes that "he is responsible for guaranteeing the security of the United States from the North Pole to the border of Guatemala, Belize and Mexico, as well as a large part of the Caribbean (excluding Cuba). Robinson also assumes the role of commander in chief of Northern Aerospace Command (NORAD)."

II.
THE CORE OF BABEL

One of the great enigmas hidden in the biblical book of Revelation is the mystery of Babylon. There has been speculation for a long time about the nature of this city mentioned there, stating that it would be the Roman Empire, Jerusalem, the Vatican or the United States. This "Babylon" is defined as a "city", taking the Greek word 'pólis', from which terms such as "politics", "police" or "controversy" are born. The term refers to "many people," encompassing the idea of a metropolis. In the Hebrew language it is 'Aír' or 'Iír', which also translates agitation, village, watchman or donkey (which may recall the symbol of the Democratic Party of the United States). In addition to this, 'Iír' is the linguistic root for the Hebrew voice 'Eirom' (naked).

In the first instance, if we could define the "big city" with mere epithets, and without more information, it would not be crazy to consider that the cryptic message spoke of a place with many people, a place dominated by politics, a place of a lot of control. police, a place of much controversy, a place of much agitation, a place of much surveillance and a place without shame (where nudity is sold to the world). Clearly that couldn't be Jerusalem or the Vatican, but something on the scale of New York or Los Angeles. But let's assume that it is just a speculation, and let's go back to merely analyzing the root of the name of the "polis" itself: Babylon.

Although the text of Revelation appears in Greek, and in that language and references it is called 'Babylon' (where the name in English comes from, and the later Spanish 'Babylon'), the truth is that the word is of Sumerian origin: ' Babili' (BAB-ILI = 'Gate of God', or 'Gate of the Gods'). The Jewish historian Titus Flavius Josephus, records in his work 'Antiquities of the Jews' (volume I) that in the plain of Senaar (Shinar, Sumer), a ruler called Nebrodes (Nemrud, Nimrod) instigated the peoples who had united as one to build a great tower as a symbol of global unification (the first attempt at globalization in the history of our world). He adds that «The place where they built the tower was called Babylon, because of the confusion of the languages; because in Hebrew babel means confusion." (verse 3) But at first they were not confused, for the sound 'Babili' gave rise to the Semitic 'Babel', which means, first of all, 'mixture'.

The Greek Sibyl also narrates this around the 2nd century BC. C., telling in his book III (verse 120): «When in the land of Assyria they built a tower; - (And they all spoke one language, and resolved to ride high in the starry sky; But the [...] Immortal caused a mighty force, and then he snaked from above, bringing down the great tower, and stirred up the mortals to cause quarrels among them, therefore men gave that city the name of Babylon); - Now, when the tower fell and the tongues of men returned to all kinds of sounds, immediately the whole earth was full of men who were divided and [into various] kingdoms..." (Sibylline Oracles).

Why would they call the great prostitute of Revelation 'Babylon'? If you are evoking an analogy, on the one hand we have a "mixture" of all the people from all over the world, which on this planet we could locate in New York. In that city is the office of the United Nations Organization (the headquarters of leaders from around the world), there is also the main economic center (Wall Street). If it weren't New York, the closest thing to these characteristics would be Los Angeles, where the global cyber center is located and also the main driver of the music, television series and film industries (even XXX (fornication), which is the most It is sold worldwide, and millions get drunk from its "prostitution" wine).

The story of the tower of Babel is, however, fundamental to decipher the mystery of Babylon in the book of Revelation, since by comparative analogy and analysis of the historical record we can see that the city of Babel (Babylon) was established as the first metropolis of the Earth, like the great capital, bringing together all its people under the same ideal, the same language and a single leader. If we must find a comparison between then and the present, the closest thing on a political level would be the UN, although today our planet has globalized in such a way that at any moment a world leader could rise and be hailed as a planetary ruler. , if it achieved ideological unification and peace. Furthermore, we see that there are predominant languages, where English reigns in number for international affairs and is the most taught everywhere after the mother language of each country. There are also other aspects such as the economic one, where to a large extent everyone still depends on the US dollar (from the FED, or Federal Reserve Fund), for deposits and financial movements. It is important to focus on these details even if they seem redundant.

It could be considered a crude coincidence, but the Greek phrase "Babilon i megali" (Babylon the great), is numerically 129, just as in Hebrew it is 'Seder Olamei Hadash' (New World Order). For those of us who consider that man is constantly guided by invisible intelligent forces, it is not surprising that these same "beings" have encoded messages everywhere for those who wanted to discover the "mysteries." It should be added that 129 computes the Greek definitions 'Pligi' (plague) and 'Sfájosin' (they massacred), both of which also appear in the Apocalypse, and even in contexts related to the fall of New Babylon, or a previous "pandemic." said event (which marks the beginning of the biblical Great Tribulation). But could all this be mere nonsense?

Gematria allows us to use various systems to find numerical values in letters, and in the case of Greek, just as 'Babylon i megali' is 129 in the short system of analysis, in the long one it is 1,380, which is the same for the name in Greek for 'George Bush', and is just below 1,381, which is the count for 'iesouíti táxis' (Jesuit Order). But could there be a relationship between the great Babel and the Jesuit order? For many researchers , the Jesuits are the most powerful organization in the world, and the fact that they come from papal power and are its main defenders supports the thesis that assumes that imperial power from Rome passed to the United States through the Jesuits. If not, why were people like the then president of that country, George Bush, present at the funeral of the order's top cardinal in the US? That cardinal was the most powerful man in the United States, according to some researchers, and the Bush family is a key part of the Illuminati elite, mainly in North America.

What is really happening? To understand this we must refer to the famous prophecy of the "destruction of Babylon." I have already commented on this in previous publications and in the 'Remote Viewing' books, but it is important to understand that the word 'Babylon' is Greek, and represents the linguistic adaptation of the Semitic word 'Babel'. This word has two meanings, one as 'mixture', since it evokes the Mesopotamian city Babel, which was the metropolis of that time that united all the great towns in one.

Its other meaning, as 'confusion', came after the failure of the famous 'tower': «When God saw them working like crazy he decided not to destroy them completely, since they had learned nothing from the destruction of previous sinners; Instead, he caused confusion among them by making them speak in different languages so that they would not understand each other. The place where they built the tower was called Babylon, because of the confusion of the languages; because in Hebrew babel means confusion. The Sibyl also mentions the tower and the confusion of languages, saying: "When men all spoke the same language, some of them built a tower of great height, as if they wanted to ascend to heaven for 4%, but the "The gods sent wind storms and tore down the tower, and made everyone speak a different language. That's why that city was called Babylon." (Antiquities of the Jews, Titus Flavius Josephus. I century. cap. IV, 3)

For most researchers, the prophecies about the destruction of a contemporary Babylon refer to the United States. Although it is in Revelation 17 and 19 that it mostly speaks of its punishment, some have found in Jeremiah 51 a clear earlier allusion to said punishment to that nation: "Behold, I raise up a destroying wind against Babylon, and against its inhabitants who rise up against me." (Jer 51:1, RVA 60) The concept of 'wind' in Western languages comes from the Eastern conception, which designated something invisible, and is translated interchangeably as 'spirit', in this case, understood as 'spirit of destruction' against said country. He adds: "And I will send fans to Babylon to fan her, and they will empty her land; for they will be against her from all sides in the day of evil." (Verse 51:2) The rhetoric and symbology used with the Chaldean analogy has made it appear for centuries that it was a prophecy about the Babylonian empire of the lineage of Nebukanetzar (Nebuchadnezzar), although historical objections could be enumerated that prove that These words were not addressed to that remote empire, and, however, they have not yet been fulfilled.

It would be very extensive to quote and clarify each word and verse of the 64 that cover this entire chapter on the old prophecy, but there are examples such as the tremendous similarity of one of the verses with another from the book of Revelation announcing the destruction of such a great harlot or great Babylon at the end of time: "Flee from the midst of Babylon, and save each one his life, so that you do not perish because of her wickedness; because the time is for Jaheveh's vengeance; He will give you his payment. (Jer. 51:6, KJV 60)

Note the similarity: «And I heard another voice from heaven, saying: Come out of her, my people, so that you do not share in her sins, nor receive part of her plagues; for their sins have reached up to heaven, and God has remembered their iniquities." (Rev. 18:4-5, KJV 60) Verse 7 recalls the power and influence of the United States in the land, and the testimonies that record that this country rose to support Israel: "Cup of Babylon was gold in the hand of Yaheveh, who made the whole earth drunk; The people drank of his wine; "Therefore the nations were stunned." (Jer. 51:7, R60) Once again an allegory with the words of the apostle John: «Another angel followed him, saying: Babylon, the great city, is fallen, is fallen, because she has made all nations drink of the wine. from the fury of her fornication. And the third angel followed them, saying with a loud voice: If anyone worships the beast and its image, and receives its mark on his forehead or on his hand, he also will drink of the wine of the wrath of God, which has been poured out pure. in the cup of his wrath..." (Rev. 14:8-10, KJV 60) With a little patience you will be able to do an analysis yourselves with these chapters and see that it speaks of the same city-country.

The Scarlet Woman

The apostle John described in Revelation a woman dressed in purple and scarlet, sitting on a Thirion (beast). Many fans of conspiracy theories relate it to a media idea, and since they delight in searching for and interpreting the symbolism expressed in films, television series or video clips - analyzing cryptic occult, satanist, freemason and apocalyptic messages - they see in This figure is a fundamental element of shadow power after much comparison and investigation.

One of these theorists is the Muslim who used the pseudonym 'Abdulla Hashim', from 'WakeUpProject', who even infiltrated meetings of Raelians and Yahweh sects, and participated in freedom marches in Cairo and television programs in Iran, to expose all kinds of dark organizations. The “woman in red” was one of her works in the HashemFilms series, 'Dajjal Shape-Shifter' (the Metamorphic Antichrist). In his thesis he showed how the music, film, magazine and fashion industries were moved by satanic threads and used social mind control programs to condition society, especially American (you can go deeper by studying the Monarca project). The Woman in Red was represented as an icon of occult power operating on the subconscious of youth – especially – preparing a docile people to receive a false Illuminati savior and immorally perverting society (see example in the first part of the saga The Matrix, when a young programmer creates a program of a blonde woman in a red dress who distracts Neo in a simulation).

Pay attention, because from now on AI (artificial intelligence) and 7D holograms will increasingly take over the horizon, every street, every building and every home, to the point that you will not know how to differentiate between reality and virtual reality. This was announced by the Hebrew prophet Ishaiahu (Isaiah) 2,600 years ago, warning about this digital Scarlet Woman: holograms in the atmosphere, holographic three-dimensional slogans representing the leader of the global government... below is an excerpt from this manuscript copy that was not incorporated in the Bible:

“...these are the days of the end of the age [...] Beliar the great prince, the king of this world, will descend [...] at his word the sun will rise at night and will cause the moon to appear at the sixth hour. [...] all the people in the world will believe in him [...] And they will sacrifice themselves to him and serve him saying: "This is from God and there is no other next to him." And a greater number of those who have joined together for the purpose of receiving the Beloved, who in turn, [leave] him aside behind him. And there will be the power of his miracles in every city and region. And he will set his image before him in every city. And he will rule for three years and seven months and twenty-seven days. And many believers and saints will have seen it, who will have hope in him who was crucified, Yeshua ha.Mashiach ha.Adonai, [after I, Isaiah, had seen him who was crucified and ascended] and also those who were believers in Him - of these a few in those days will be left as His servants, as they flee from desert to desert, awaiting the coming of the Beloved. And after (one thousand) three hundred and thirty-two days, the Lord will come with his angels and with the armies of the saints of the seventh heaven of the glory of the seventh heaven, and he will drag Beliar into Gehenna and also his armies." (Ascension of Isaiah chapter 4.1-14)

Now, Hashim's work is just one more portion of the pieces. The interest shown by many who wish to discover the truth of the "mystery" of Babylon and try to share it with the world is broad, a great awakening despite the power of ethical and educational corruption carried out by the harlot (especially today through the news media and television programs). These individual efforts – testimony of our awakening of planetary consciousness – aim to bring to light the shadow power behind the puppets of the globe and the horrifying influence that Luciferian Freemason occultism infers on humanity from corporate media, marketing, banking, fashion, music, cinema, television, the pharmaceutical industry, the educational system and an almost endless list of more branches – or "harlots – that wash people's brains and damage their biological organism.

Rome (the first phase of the 4th beast described by the prophet Daniel) has changed its facade and strategies from the beginning, and used the rise of the US to continue controlling the world from there, so that the Vatican would not be identified as the source of power and influence. All the power of Rome, through the Jesuits, passed to the entire establishment of the US over more than two centuries, and one of the platforms it used was the Jesuits to build the industry that operates from Hollywood. When we read chapter

17 of the book of Revelation, it adds that that woman in red is "THE MOTHER OF HARLOTS AND ABOMINATIONS OF THE EARTH." (verse 5, RVA 60) She maintains that she is the mother of all the others (the one who has given birth to them and nursed them and raised them), not strictly their spirit of influence. From it derive the rest of the prostitutes of unfair wealth, sexual abominations (such as the rituals of secret societies) and all the moral, ethical, ideological and cultural putrefaction that has spread throughout the world, especially since the last 100 years, and in exponential increase.

Who are those other whores who are your daughters? If they were extraterrestrials, it would be impossible to specify them or clarify their methods, but on Earth there are those who know them or have heard about them. Simple examples of these "whores" are the CFR, the Trilateral Commission, the Round Table, the Club of Rome, the Bilderberg Club, university fraternities (such as Skull&Bones or Scrolls&Keys) or Rosicrucian or Freemason memberships (such as the Bohemian Groove, the Order of the Garter, Prince Hall, the Roshanaya, the Knights of Malta, the Knights of Columbus...), the Mafia, the House of Windsor, the Zionists, the Crown Council of 13, the Committee of 300, the Think Tanks and Banksters (IMF, World Bank, FED, BIS), the Royal Institute of International Affairs, the UN, mega corporations... and the list goes on.

Let's look at other comments that John makes in his book: "Another angel followed him, saying: Babylon the great is fallen, because she has made all nations drink of the wine of the wrath of her fornication." (Rev. 14:8) What is this 'wine of the wrath of her fornication'? He has dedicated himself to bringing adultery and degradation everywhere, and now the consequences of that will not only affect the 'city' but the world he has perverted - since practically almost everyone has participated in his bad influence and has lived in "sin" because of the structure of thought and behavior that it has implemented and promoted. The New World Order is led by Jesuits and all their organizations, and with them the 13 families that control the world (who are related to the 13 ancient monarchies of Europe), the Round Table of billionaire Cecil Rhodes, and all the affiliates under them , be it the banksters, the mafia, the secret services, the UN, the CFR, the TC, the Bilderberg club, and so many secret societies, as I have said. Then with them are the mega rich who want to play the Illuminati role by doing great work, like Bill Gates. Let's not rule out the Zionist movement, but it is not the one on top, and like all the others, they are tendencies used by the elite to promote their interests.

Why describe this city as a "woman dressed in purple and scarlet"? In Greek, scarlet is 'Kokkínin', and is referred to only a few times in Scripture (the part of Rev. 12 that speaks of a "scarlet dragon" is a translation error, since it actually says "red dragon" or "reddish"), but what is its meaning? In ancient Hebrew culture they called this color 'Toreát Shaní' (red worm) or just 'Shaní' (see 2 Sam. 1:24), and it is known that both the bright dyes of purple and scarlet represented luxury and wealth, and were, therefore, the colors used by kings and emperors. This value came from the market cost of these dyes (the purple usually produced from snails and octopuses, and the scarlet from kermes insects), so the attire of said woman denotes a power of royalty and/or wealth. Whether you are identified as a woman, and not a man, depends on the added component of the description. A woman represents the life that is conceived, produced and nourished in her childhood, but a woman with added characters of whiteness, virginity or youth denotes purity and holiness.

However, a woman identified with these colors and jewels represents lust and greed. If we add to that that they call her 'Pornion' (prostitute, harlot), it becomes clear that it is because she is "sold" in exchange for benefits (from the word itself comes 'pornography'

= images of prostitutes). It strikes me that the colors he uses are typical of monarchy or emperors, because he is from a royalty from which Belial is said to come (the Antichrist, Armilius, Dajjal, false prophet, wicked, son of iniquity, son of perdition, etc.). In Louis Lefebvre's short film, 'I Pet Goat II' (at minute 1.35-40), Barack Obama is stepping on what looks like a golden coin with the seal of the British monarchy and is seen sweating, while the apple of 'Alice' comes to him and a lotus flower is produced from her. All the symbology of this video revolves around the gestation, birth, growth and manifestation of the Antichrist.

Now, John describes that the merchants or merchants have become 'enriched' thanks to the "power of their lust", or "sensuality". We have two elements that this evokes: gold, fornication (sexual rituals) and demonology. That is why it will be burned, looted and destroyed. He does not speak of something simply on a spiritual level, but rather a physical one - and he even warns his people to 'get out' of there, so that the punishment that is coming does not fall on them as well. In other words, there are geographical places where the nerve centers of this organization are located, and there are moral and principled people who live there. He does not tell them not to be part of his structure, but rather not to 'participate in his sins', that is, in his moral corruption, and consequently receive "part of his plagues." In other words, this corrupt and immoral “city” perverts people and will be devastated by fire, plagues and devastations (or the sum of all of them if the context of 'plague' and also 'fire' is understood).

The apostle John tells us that, "The waters that you saw where the harlot sits are peoples, multitudes, nations, and languages." (Rev. 17:15, R60) The book of revelation identifies the great Babel as a prostitute, however, the mother of all prostitutes on Earth, and only with the epithets of Babel, prostitute, woman in scarlet and purple , and drunkenness, it is clear that it is a power above all powers. For many, this is the true face of the 'Statue of Liberty' - or 'Libertinage' -, the main icon that represents the United States. A statue given by the French Freemasons to the gringos, and stands on Liberty Island, off Manhattan. Ironically the statue alone measures 45 meters high, and in the Kabalah the 45 represents man. Manhattan is in the middle of water, and in Manhattan there is Wall Street and the Rockefeller building of the United Nations. From there the entire world is dominated, but the statue itself is completely in the middle of the water and has a crown with 7 rays (7 seas, 7 continents), alluding to the control of the world. Even the symbol of his torch is another hidden allusion to the fire of Prometheus, who gave it to men, that is, conscience, awakening and truth, but not in the way of spiritual freedom but of the nakedness of man himself. Prometheus (Eosphorus in Roman mythology) is called Lucifer in Christianity.

The text of John also states: "The seven heads are seven mountains, on which the woman sits..." (Rev. 17:9, R60) The Greek term 'Ori' encompasses a predominant geographic place with respect to a level plain. of the sea, whether mountain, mountain or continent. This is applicable to a plain on an island type. As seen on the crown of the Statue of Liberty (the goddess Libertas or Liber, also known in fiction as 'Columbia'), the 7 points represent the 7 continents. The 7 continents have an analogy with 7 kings, but the Greek word is not limited to a particular or individual king, but to a kingdom. Although, we know that 5 kingdoms – which also conquered Babylon (Babel) – existed before Rome ("one is", they told John in his day, during the period of Roman domination), which were Egypt, Assyria, Babylon, Persia and Macedonia.

So, one more to go up and be the last empire. It is important to know that the deity Mithras, in whose cults the Roman soldiers were initiated, was usually represented with a crown of rays, and both the crown and the context of the figure were identical to that of the Statue of Liberty. Ironically, the Catholic Church names the bishops' cap that way, and it is evident that it comes from the form of headdress worn by the Egyptian pharaohs and with which the Indo-Aryan god Mithras was often portrayed. Likewise, this deity had a headdress of rays to represent the sun, since Mithras was a symbol of solar victory (the Unconquered Sun), and almost the entire Catholic cult was based on the Mithraist cult. So the statue's rays are a form of solar iconography, and the figure possibly an emulation of Mithras (considering that it appears hermaphrodite, since although it is clearly a female representation, it has the face of 'Michelangelo's David', which evokes to the biblical king David, from where he sees the heir to the throne, or the Messiah).

Seeing a statue with the crown of Mithras, a hermaphrodite face that could also be combining the Egyptian Isis and the Greek Apollo, and that holds the torch of Prometheus, is key to understanding the nature of this Freemason symbol. The Greek deity Apollo was the god of the Sun, coinciding with this cult of Mithras, but more remotely it seems that these attributes had not been added to him, but that he was simply the divinity of symmetry, art, song and music. By adding the idea of Apollo here we go even deeper into the rabbit hole where "Alice" fell.

How did Apollo become such a relevant deity for Freemasonry? According to the Oahspe (1882), a demon called Daeva or Daveas (possibly the same Daeva that gives rise to the demons of Hindu culture), after the withdrawal of Apollo - when he left the First Heaven of Earth to return to his kingdom -etheric world -, Daveas usurped his name, and since then he deceived the world by posing as Apollo. In short, Daevas (the false Apollo) was exiled by Usir (Osire, Osiris), but his judgment would come at the end of this era, when it is understood that he will return once again to deceive the world. Experts in the field agree that this figure of Apollo is analogous to the idea of the Antichrist. Hence Apollo's play on words with Apollyon (the angel of the abyss mentioned in Apoc. 9.7-11) or

Apolonion, which in Greek means 'perdition' or 'destruction', and which in the Hebrew language is the equivalent of the name of the abyss. , Abaddon.

But what would Isis have to do with it? The original Isis, sister of Osiris and mother of Horus, nothing. In fact, originally Isis symbolizes Sophia, the creator of this universe, and therefore also Mariam (Mary), the biological mother of Yeshua (Jesus), and also represents the Isis of Yeshua's time, who was his companion. and best student - also called Mariam -, who went to preach in France, where the capital city had been named Paris (which in ancient Egyptian meant 'the House of Isis'). No, it is the opposite idea, as seen in the antagonistic form of the painting of the 'Venus de Milo', known as 'Birth of Venus', by Botticelli, which appears in the stills of 'I Pet Goat II' (min . 3.15-20), at the time when the thermonuclear bomb that would trigger World War III is illustrated. It is the false idea, the Masonic one, that does hide a great hidden value. The Freemason name 'Isis' reflects the false ideas of Virgo-Mary (the Catholic deity par excellence), whose origin dates back to many cultures, especially Babylonian.

It is the same as the Greek Aphrodite, goddess of love, who came from Phenicia, from the Canaanite cultures, where she was known as Astarte, Ashtoret, Asherah, Ashtaroth and other derivations of the Akkadian Ishtar, from which comes the Castilian word 'star' and 'astro', or the name 'Esther'. This deity was first known in Sumer as 'Inanna', the goddess of war. The most important thing about Inanna is that she was the main patron saint of Babylon, competing for her post-flood title with the famed Marduk, and she was not only the goddess of war but, ironically, of love. What a mix, but that is explained in the transformation of the bloody Egyptian goddess Sekhmet into the beloved Hathor. Their cult started from sexual ritual and prostitution. Her Egyptian counterpart – the way she was known there – was the first 'Sekhmet' (Sejmet), the terrible one with the face of a cat, goddess of revenge and war, cause of the universal flood, of the appearance of the desert and goddess of power and strength. For some reason she changed and transformed into the loving 'Hathor', but not before betraying Ra and forcing him to leave planet Earth.

Combining the cult of the most representative deities of antiquity is incorporated with the cult of them, which is associated with the priority of provoking wars and all types of prostitution (money + sex) to honor these deities - or demons - and receive their favors and support to achieve their goals (rituals and worship that Catholics called "paganus"). Many American pastors (and some non-Americans) have spoken of dreams, visions and revelations where it is made known to them that the great Babylon, the great whore of the Apocalypse, is their own country. This has also been said by high-ranking officials of the United States, and they themselves also find many strange things in the symbology of their country, from their banknotes, the way their cities are distributed, the emblems national and emblematic buildings, all very close to mythology and the cult of deities outside of Christianity.

If the scarlet beast is Rome, and it mutates or perfects itself by getting rid of its prostitute "mother," could this be a reference to the 'deadly wound' that Revelation also speaks of? One of the key signs of the beginning of John's Revelation seems to be precisely the destruction of this city-country, and if we tried to look at current geopolitics, and consider a nation that encompasses these characteristics, we would take the United States, a and again, but how was the US going to suffer all the calamities that the Apocalypse warns of? According to the text, this "empire" will suffer invasion from its enemies, internal calamities, natural disasters and chaos. What could cause all this to the point of grounding such a nuclear power?

If the woman in purple and scarlet is the hidden power, she is the same one who "has corrupted the earth with her fornication," and is also guilty of the death of God's 'servants' (Rev. 19:1-2) – another piece that suggests that it does not speak of a single era, nor a single centralized government, nor a single geographical place (the servants referred to include the prophets, and as Isaiah explains, it was Belial who has instigated their murders, and foresees future persecution of Christians). The aforementioned city has the ability to negotiate with ALL the leaders of the world, since they "have committed fornication" with it (Rev. 17:1). This word is translated from the Greek 'Epórneisan', relating to prostitution (paying for sex or selling oneself sexually). And "the inhabitants of the earth have become drunk with the wine of her fornication." What does this intoxication consist of? Degradation and living in deception. But he not only deals and sells, but he controls them, he dominates them. What city does that?

The closest thing is New York, or what country could fit this description? The United States of America. Even the previous kingdoms, those that have preceded him, fit the symbology of the 7 mountains: 1. Egypt, 2. Babylon, 3. Assyria, 4. Persia, 5. Macedonia, 6. Rome and 7. The New World Order . Babel (the elite that uses the US now) is based and sustained by all of them, just look at its iconography (look, for example, at the eagle, which was already used by the Nazis, the Romans...).

Added to the point above is the verse that holds: "And the woman whom you saw is the great city that reigns over the kings of the earth." (Rev. 17:18, R60) How can a city reign over the "kings" of the Earth? Although specifically here he does not say the 'great city', but rather 'Babel the great', he does describe it as 'polis i megális' (great city), but not as 'great country'. If it is not a country or government, but a mere city, this center of power has a supranational character. The 'city' represents a location, whether geographical, strategic or logistical. The great harlot sits on the beast, so she is part of its structure, she is the one who initially controls the Beast. If the apocalyptic Beast, Bull or Minotaur represents the global government, then it is the renewed system that tries to get rid of the previous system, and that assault occurs on its entire "wealth" structure and its physical stability or support base.

That is, it also affects a geophysical place. What he is telling us with all this is that a new model of government overthrows the one that until then was controlling him, but the root is the same, and currently this is based on the monetary infrastructure of the Federal Reserve Bank and the US dollar that puts North America at the head of the world. If the dollar collapses, the US collapses, and the world economy collapses. This can only mean a restart of the planet's economy, but this time no longer with physical material but digital: a global cryptocurrency system, centralized, but not under the power of the US.

He further adds: "I saw the woman drunk with the blood of the saints, and with the blood of the martyrs of Jesus." (Rev. 17:6, R60) Decidedly all supporters of the theory that the great Babel is New York-USA. We agree that this reference, rather than applying to the past, when the US was still Rome (since Rome – not the Italian capital but the Roman Empire – now runs from the US), anticipates an event to come, which is martial law in the US - and on the American continent in general, and which will also be seen in Europe and many other countries - We already know that police and other law enforcement agencies are being indoctrinated into the fact that Christians are considered potential enemies of the state and terrorists, and now also those who do not observe the control measures determined by the WHO on viruses that are "out there."

It should also be remembered that the FEMA REX-84 facilities, although created to house immigrants, are said to be vacated by Donald Trump to be used as concentration camps for Christians, activists, preppers and anti-establishment people. The categories of individuals that the NSA has considered a priority will be killed immediately, without trial or lawyers, and Christians are in the eye of those lists. However, at the same time that the city-country is scourged as a nation, it will itself scourge itself and fall, even though this seems incredible.

Between 1870 and 1929 the pope had no physical territory at all, and the Vatican was under Italian sovereignty. The Italian leader Benito Mussolini finally resolved the crisis between modern Italy and the Papacy, when in 1929 'Vatican City' was founded, to which 44 hectares of the city of Rome were allocated in the area of the 'Papal Historical Buildings'. '. Since then there have been 8 popes until today. In the book of Revelation this Beast is spoken of as a 'mother' and her 'son' - I say, in a comical way - because the one who dominates is seen above as a prostitute, and below the one who is dominated, as a beast. or wild animal (like the maiden Europa sitting on the Bull). However, the animal loots, strips and burns the one who controlled it. It is interesting that the subject of the 'great prostitute' is said to be a 'mystery', considering that it is something hidden or secret; So search and investigation must be resorted to in order to discover the "mysterious" and intricate ins and outs of this "great prostitute."

That is to say, its identity is not clear to the naked eye, much less to those who are not initiated in dusting off and studying "mysteries" and "secrets." He is talking about an organization that exercises power over the structures of nations, and yet its name (in Hebrew it refers to "identity") is a "mystery" (even many researchers find similarity between this word and the synonym of 'conspiracy'). Therefore, he is talking about a shadow government. He says that he 'murders' the faithful and seekers of the truth, something characteristic of the famous 'elite', since he is not so shameless on a social level. He is not a president or general or director of a secret service who orders someone to be murdered and everyone knows it openly. Talk about 'undercover' things.

This "prostitute" controls all nations - says Juan - and this idea is identified as "waters" that "surround" her. It is clear that this cannot be Jerusalem, neither by the literal description of the water, nor by the symbolic concept (it could only be applied by the mention of 'murdering their prophets'). For its part, the Vatican is not crossed by water either, although the Tiber River passes nearby. Instead, Manhattan is surrounded by water, and the UN is in Manhattan, next to the Queens Midtown Tunnel. The desolation that the great Babel will receive is, in my opinion, the fall of both the United States and the Vatican (its mother); but especially the desolation, looting and destruction of the structure and power of both nuclei.

As far as Manhattan is concerned, it will be erased, starting with the financial collapse of Wall Street, then martial law in the US, followed by the attack they will receive from Russia and China, and then a tsunami that will sink New York (and then the West Coast and the Silicon Valley region). Apocalypse says that it is a "city", not a country, which still calls into question whether it can only be the Vatican. Since the Lateran Pacts in 1929 (between Cardinal Pietro Gasparri, Vatican Secretary of State on behalf of Pope Pius XI, and by the Prime Minister of Italy Benito Mussolini), it is considered an 'Independent State', rather than simply a city. (one of the 6 European micro states). For its part, New York City is not only a city, but is often considered 'the axis of the world'.

The US would be the 'new Rome' and through there the Vatican would control the world. This is known by many other researchers of history and secrecy, such as William Bramley himself, who in his book 'God's of Eden' describes the tools of the Jesuits to seize power. Furthermore, Adam Weishaupt, founder of the Bavarian Illuminati order, had been a Jesuit, and the current pope – Francis – is also one. The destiny of the world is governed from the West, be it military

(US Military Industrial Complex), economic (because they control a large part of the world's oil, especially with their military forces in export countries, and because they have the headquarters world financial, and the Federal Reserve began the bank debt), political (since both Wall Street and the UN are in Manhattan) and influence (music, film, television, fashion, computing, etc.). Therefore, the entire structure will fall (the true elite that is above the US and Rome, and after them all those under them will be destroyed).

III.
THE AMERICAN PHOENIX

In addition to telling us about the power of Great Babylon, various prophecies warn us of its fatal destruction. If the most accepted thesis (that said "city" is figuratively an allusion to the United States of America) is correct, the mystery could be solved, but let's add more reasons. Dark powers have been ruling our world since ancient times, raising empires, one after another, and directing their leaders. Symbolized through goats and rams, lion, leopard or bear beasts, wings of a great eagle, even as heads of the last great beast that will rise and dominate the entire planet. All of these kingdoms and their shadow organizations and elements are maintained to this day through the context better known as "Illuminati", and its countless branches.

The last phase of the elite's plan is to erect the greatest power that has ever existed on Earth, which Apocalypse calls 'Thiriou' (the Beast), but what will be the masterstroke to complete the puzzle that leaves his tan ready? longed for - and for thousands of years studied - project? According to much of the information that is known – at least to a certain degree, and by those of us who study these matters – the elite must bring down the world's economy, causing an unprecedented financial and banking crisis. Since the US dollar is the basis of this, it is important to keep in mind that this country would be seriously affected by this collapse, even more than the rest of the nations that depend on transactions and exchanges with their dollar. If it were possible, another point to achieve would be the elimination of national borders, creating only 10 super-nations. If this were achieved, there would be a global government based on 10 sections with only 10 "princes" over these regions (something similar to the 10 FEMA sections into which the US is secretly divided).

Another stratagem starts from subduing the entire society, but since this could not be achieved voluntarily on a global level, they must reduce the population, leaving a minimum of people on the planet (thus being easier to control), starting with social conditioning. massive that makes them vulnerable to their governments. For this they would have already been using several master pieces - but not at an exponential level - for which the aspect of war and virulent disease would be combined with that of hunger. The spread of transnational, civil and inter-power wars would destabilize all countries and eliminate millions of people through war, and would maintain a state of priority desire for peace among the masses. The use of epidemics spread throughout large population centers, large cities, would spread rapidly, bringing mortality everywhere in a matter of days. Added to this, the factor of economic collapse would cause misery in each place, and would cause the absolute dependence of civilians on the government apparatus, to receive food rations in exchange for services: selling themselves to the government. Thus the entire society would be a slave to its nation and political establishments.

It could be said that to achieve these plans it would not be necessary to eliminate country borders, but could all nations agree to use the same method? Even if this were the case, the border division, the various languages, flags and mother countries would continue to exist. How can we get countries to accept a single world government? The laudable options are a global nuclear war that ends the structures of the powers currently established and the countries under them; a common problem that transcends national property, and for this we could talk about an unstoppable and relentless epidemic that will wipe out almost all of humanity, a cybernetic enemy that will bring down all the systems of the largest cities on the planet, a large-scale environmental disaster that could be activated with a geophysical weapon, and even the invasion of extraterrestrials, even when it did not have to be true and it was only necessary to be invented through the media; Or simply the mixture of two or more of the above, or all of them combined.

However, none of this implies the priority given to the destruction of the "great Babylon", alongside the destruction of the rest of the countries in the world, unless its fall is not exactly part of the plan established by the entire elite. That is, we could be talking about an internal plot to betray the then head in power, which would add to the "divine punishment" hanging over her. This gives two options: either the elite intends not to depend on this harlot, or her fall was not part of their project and was something caused "by God." A third option could be forged, and be very plausible, which is the sum of both possibilities if the powers that be themselves already know what is coming about it. In other words, if the shadow power wanted to perpetuate its legacy, wouldn't it use all its resources and means at its disposal to study all future possibilities against it? Much has been said that the elite also studies and knows the prophecies, even that they use them to anticipate events, try to avoid or distort them, or, even, in the worst case scenario for them – knowing that they have no other alternative and His punishment is inevitable – planning his own 'death and resurrection'. However, a very plausible probability is that the US would finish its task, and now it would be the turn of the Global Government of "the Beast", for which it would be imperative to remove from the chess table the pieces that now hinder that vision.

Why did the dark shadow power of Freemasonry intend for the US logo to originally be a phoenix and not an eagle? The phoenix (the Egyptian Bennu) represents suicide in incendiary combustion to be reborn again in full vigor from one's own ashes: "Thereafter, when the limit of the time of the Phoenix will come around, there will be a race of peoples coming to plunder, confused tribes, enemies of the Hebrews. Then Ares will go to plunder Ares; and he himself will destroy the haughty menaces of the Romans. So [that] the power of Rome perish then while it was in its flowering; An ancient queen with cities dwelling around her, no more will the fertile land of Rome prevail, when out of Asia one must come to rule with Ares. And when he has done all these things, then he will come to the city. (Sibylline Oracles, Book VIII. Verses 180-195) Could this already be a premeditated idea that assumed that at some point that nation would burn and be reborn stronger from its own rubble?

Many prophecies have the component or "asterisk" that gives rise to a certain variation, or even not being fulfilled, but this does not seem to happen with what is described in Revelation, which makes it clear that it is a master plan that goes beyond any other. destination that could be expected or modified. This is the thing about the fall of great Babylon: it is inevitable. Revelation seems to give us a description of this by saying: "I saw one of his heads as if it were wounded to death, but his deadly wound was healed. The whole earth marveled after the beast..." (Ch. 13:3, KJV 95) Their heads? In Latin 'head' is 'Capita', where the word 'capital' or 'cedes' comes from. Verse 12 adds that the Antichrist will motivate and persuade "the earth and its inhabitants" to "worship the first beast, whose deadly wound was healed." This reborn beast would no longer have to be like the previous one with a world destroyed by misery, hunger, ruin, virulent plagues, desolation, depopulation and, above all, without competition, since the great nations and nuclear powers would have all destroyed each other (or at least would have been "disabled").

Yeshua (Jesus) warned that this would not be the end, but only the BEGINNING of what is commonly called 'Apocalypse' - something that is quite consistent with the signs that are seen in the world today and that also seem to be glimpsed in a the horizon, and not for a distant time but very close -: «But when you hear of wars and rumors of wars, do not be disturbed, because it must happen that way; **but it is not yet the end** , for nation will rise against nation and kingdom against kingdom; and there will be earthquakes in many places, and there will be famines and riots; These are the beginnings of pain." (Mark 13:7-8, RVA 95) Outside of interpretations and assumptions, it is notable that these warnings are not something generic to all of history, but rather the prelude to the end of this era before the beginning of what has been interpreted in Christianity as "reign of Jesus Christ" in his "second coming": "all this is only the beginning of sorrows." (Matt. 24:8, KJV 95)

There will be a mix of grave events, called the 'Great Tribulation', then a brief reign of the Antichrist followed by the War of Harmageddon, and then the return of the Lord. Furthermore, a clear sign of this is the same description that the Hebrew prophet Yoel (Joel) gave long before the apostle John when speaking of the use of thermonuclear weapons – and emphasizing that it will not be the end, but the beginning of all this. transition -: «I will do wonders in heaven and on earth , **blood, fire and columns of smoke** . **"The sun will turn into darkness and the moon into blood** , before the great and fearful day of Jaheveh comes." (Joel 2:30-31, KJV 95) This is what the prophet Yermiahu (Jeremiah) was referring to when he stated: "Do not let your heart faint, nor be afraid because of the rumor that will be heard in the land; In one year there will be rumor, and then in another year rumor, and there will be violence in the land, ruler against ruler. (Jer. 51:46, KJV 60)

The component that adds allusions to earthquakes is complemented by other quotes and prophecies that add more details about the seismic phenomenon (key to the end of this era according to Mayan and Aztec prophecies), which will be the fury of nature rebelling against nature. humanity for what we are causing it and what we will cause it (we must imagine what the global scenario will be like after the outbreak of the imminent and unavoidable nuclear war, and the environmental consequences it will have). What might seem more disconcerting is that, if it is true that the US is the great Whore (great Babylon) and must be sacrificed for a greater goal of the New World Order, how will they defeat it? If we talk about an atomic paroxysm, who could defeat this super power? The most likely nation is the one at the forefront of global military power: Russia. The other would be the current main economy and one of the main nuclear powers: China. The others, which are European (such as France, which is officially the 3rd world nuclear power), India, Saudi Arabia or Israel, are allies of the US, and only on the list could enemies such as North Korea and Iran, who are far from being able to represent a real threat to North America, at least if they are alone against it.

Ergo, what if the theory that the US will be self-attacking comes to life? It has happened before (let's not forget 9/11). A combination of two or more simultaneous events, such as an EMP (electromagnetic pulse attack), a cyber attack on the banking network or power grid, an invasion of Chinese troops on the West Coast, a biological or micro-nuclear bomb attack in densely populated centers of major cities, a civil war within the country itself and/or the imposition of martial law, or natural disasters, whether due to the Cascadia subduction fault or the eruption of the Yellowstone super-caldera. Certainly many of us believe that all of these scenarios will occur, and they will come to the US almost immediately (many simultaneously or within days, weeks and months).

This leads us to remember some of the many prophecies that exist about the destiny of the great Babylon (or directly about "USA", as those who claim to have received the vision or revelation say): «for from the north they will come **against** her destroyers" (Jer. 51:48, RVA 60) I will not cite each of the many announcers - even if they were the best known - since in the long run they describe almost the same thing with different words or details, coinciding with Revelation and the book of the prophet Yermiahu (Jeremiah chapters 23, 50 and 51), and which I have already addressed in the two volumes of my works 'Apocalypse, Remote Vision'. This is the case of verse 1 of chapter 51 of that Hebrew prophet: "Thus says Iaheveh: Behold, I raise up against Babel and against those who settle in it a **spirit of destruction** ."

The final word here, 'Mashchit' - in Hebrew - does not refer to Babylon (Babel) destroying others, but that desolation, destruction and escalating ruin will fall upon it, like a plague. In fact, the root of Mashchit is of the form Mashij (Messiah), that is, the spirit of the Messiah will come against Babylon, "I will send fans to Babylon to fan her, and they will empty her land; for **they will be against her from all sides** in the day of evil." (Jer. 51:2, KJV 95) Later other important details that the prophet tells us declare: "They will fall dead in the land of the Chaldeans and speared in their streets." (verse 4) Land of the Chaldeans? The word 'Chaldean', which identifies the people who gave rise to the Babylonians - and which shares roots with the Aramaic language -, is originally defined as 'Casdim' in Hebrew, or 'Kaldo' in Aramaic. What does this word mean? According to Zecharia Sitchin, "For generations, throughout the ancient world, the name 'Chaldean' was synonymous with 'stargazers', with astronomers." (The Twelfth Planet, chapter 6, 1976) At a global level, what organization stands out for its advances and preeminence in the study of space and the beginning of space travel? The US 'National Aeronautics and Space Administration', known by its acronym 'NASA'.

Apart from this, the Hebrew definition 'Casdim', although apparently of unknown origin, can also be read as 'Ka.Shedim', where the term 'Shedim' means 'demons', and 'Ka' stands for relative 'as ' (in the likeness of), from the noun 'because' (because) or of conformity, circumstance or multiplication (although in demotic it was the name that identified the spirit-energy or vital force of the being). Although, before the idea of demon, Shedim was understood as the concept of spiritual creatures, entities or beings of nature. For example, the jinn were something similar to a Shed or Lammasu (Karubu or Cherub), and the idea derived from the association with the same sound 'Shedeh', or Sedeh (field), from the Semitic form 'Shedu', same root of Shed. For this reason, the colloquialism or euphemism of 'Behemah ha.Sedeh' (beast of the field) or 'Ziím' (wild beasts) was often used to refer to spirits of nature, usually malevolent.

This would explain the section of Revelation that speaks of the 4th Horse (the brown one), which brings disease and mass death due to the combination of several factors mentioned above: "to kill with the sword, with hunger, with mortality, and with the wild beasts. " the earth." (Rev. 6:8, KJV 60) If the use of the word 'Chaldeans' in Jeremiah 51 is a cryptic message that evokes the great Babylon, it coincides with the apostle John's own vision: «... The great has fallen, the great has fallen . Babylon, for it has **become the dwelling place of demons** and the haunt of **every unclean spirit** , and the haunt of every unclean and hateful bird . (Rev. 18:2, KJV 60)

If the symbolisms you use are combined with other concepts within a context, they usually identify an association. There are so many biblical cases to highlight that it would be content for several books, but on this occasion it is clearly a description of all types of demonic entities (even the word that translates as 'bird', from the Greek 'Ornéou - instead of saying 'Poulí ' (bird, bird) -, is from the same cognate of Ornias, chief of the demons of Baal-Zebub, according to the secret texts of Solomon), a clear analogy with Jeremiah 51:37: «And Babylon will be heaps of ruins, a habitation of jackals, fear and mockery, without an inhabitant." Jackals? In Hebrew it is called Tanim, the same root as Tanin (dragon), both Hebrew euphemisms relating to demonic entities. Let us observe some other important analogies that link the great Babylon-Whore of Revelation with the Babylon described in Jeremiah 51 (and that from the description it is evident that he was not only speaking of the ancient Babylon of Nebuchadnezzar, but of the future, since he says that was "between many waters" - and that city had no sea - and that it was an empire that "desolated the entire Earth" - even though it only included certain kingdoms that were growing fertile -):

1. - « **Flee from the midst of Babylon** , and save each one his life, so that you do not perish because of her wickedness ; because **the time is for Jaheveh's vengeance** ; He will give you his payment. (Jer. 51:6, KJV 60); « **Come out from the midst of her, my people** , and save each one his life from the fierce wrath of Jaheveh.» (verse 45)

- «And I heard another voice from heaven, saying: " **Come out of her** , **my people** , so that you do not share in her sins nor receive part of her plagues !, because her sins have reached up to heaven and **God has remembered them." their evils** ." (Rev. 18:4-5, KJV 95)

2) – «... **made the whole earth drunk** ; The people drank of his wine; "Therefore the nations were stunned." (Jer. 51:7, KJV 60)

- "The kings of the earth have committed fornication with her, and **the inhabitants of the earth have become drunk** with the wine of her fornication." (Rev. 17:2, KJV 95)

3) - "You, who **dwell among many waters** , rich in treasures, your end has come, the measure of your greed ." (Jer. 51:13, KJV 60)

- "...I will show you the sentence against the great harlot, who sits **on many waters** ." (Rev. 17:1, KJV 95), "The woman was clothed in purple and scarlet, adorned with gold and precious stones and pearls " (verse 4)

4) – "... **their houses are on fire** , their locks are broken." (Jer. 51:30, KJV 60); "The fords were taken, and **the bastions burned with fire** , and the men of war were dismayed." (verse 32)

- "And when they saw the smoke of **its burning** they cried out, saying, 'What city was like this great city?'" (Rev. 18:18, KJV 95)

In addition to these brief coincidences there are many others, especially those that match the description of the USA today. That is the case of verses 12 to 14: «Raise a banner on the walls of Babylon, strengthen the guard, set sentinels, set up traps; for Iaheveh has deliberated, and will even put into effect what he has spoken against the inhabitants of Babylon. You, who dwell among many waters, rich in treasures, your end has come, the measure of your greed. Yaheveh Tzabaot swore by himself, saying: I will fill you with men like locusts, and they will raise a cry against you. Strengthen the guard? Post sentinels? Do you have traps? This is a STATE OF EXCEPTION. Will they raise a cry? Are you talking about mobs and mobs of protesters and protests?

He begins by talking about "walls" or "walls," which protect the border, which Donald Trump began talking about during his election campaign, but which later reminds us of the health dictatorship that was implemented since 2020, translated into quarantines, curfews. and greater control over the population. «Behold, I am against you, O destroying mountain, says Yaheveh, who has destroyed the whole earth; and I will stretch out my hand against you, and I will roll you off the rocks, and I will reduce you to a burnt mountain. [...] Raise a banner in the land, sound a trumpet among the nations, prepare people against it; gather against her the kingdoms of Ararat, Minin and Ashkenaz; point against it captain, make horses come up like bristling locusts." (Jer. 51:25-27) Mini and Ashkenaz? Those regions are currently Russian (they were annexed by the Soviet Union)

Many have said that God established the USA as a Christian nation and a support for Israel, but they have renounced the religion of their Founding Fathers and will no longer be a support for Israel (since prophecy warns that Israel will stand alone before his enemies): «Every man has become conceited, and has no knowledge; Every craftsman of his sculpture is ashamed, because his idol is a lie, he has no spirit. They are vanity, a work worthy of ridicule; in the time of punishment they will perish. (Jer. 51:17-18, KJV 60). At one time it was a tool of God, but over time it became more and more apostate from faith and truth: "Babylon was a golden cup in the hand of Yaheveh..." (verse 7) Then he seems to cite the reference to the "deadly wound", which although it was healed, was not the same again: «We healed Babylon, and it is not healed; Leave her, and let us each go to our own land; because his judgment has reached to heaven. (verse 9)

It is also interesting that he says that each of those who were there "returned" to their own land, as if assuming that it was a multifaceted, multiethnic place or a world headquarters, essentially for immigrants. A verse that reminds us of the US Military-Industrial Complex is verse 25, which maintains: "Behold, I am against you, O destroying mountain, says Iaheveh, who destroyed the whole earth; And I will stretch out my hand against you, and I will roll you off the rocks, and I will reduce you to a burnt mountain. We know the number of invasions that the US has carried out, and the bases it has everywhere, but it is also worth noting the fierce and covert activity of the CIA and the CFR in each nation to destabilize it and subject it to US power.

Among the calamities that have been warned about the United States is that of great tsunamis hitting both coasts - eastern and western - coinciding with verse 42 of Jeremiah 51: «The sea rose on Babylon; It was covered with the multitude of its waves. And one of the most significant of all these predictions is the one that seems to evoke the tools that the shadow power used to keep society distracted, manipulated, deceived and programmed: its "stars." As he says, "Behold, the days are coming when I **will destroy the idols** of Babylon, and all her land will be ashamed, and all her dead will fall in the midst of her." (verse 47) Finally I will leave as a curiosity what could fit with a conspiracy theory and space missions, regarding the fact that the shadow government has more than just radio telescopes, space stations, shuttles and cosmonauts up there: " Though Babylon rises to the heavens and fortifies itself on high places , destroyers will come from me, says Yaheveh." (verse 53) This quote also recalls the program started with Ronald Reagan, called 'Star Wars', whose mission was the militarization of outer space, especially with intercontinental missiles armed with nuclear warheads.

We are watching how US states are starting to clash with each other. Although, some due to majorities of Democrats or Republicans, others due to disagreements over anti-covid measures, others due to covid vaccination laws, etc. This is the mere beginning, since both in the US and in the rest of the world everything would worsen as the economy and environmental disasters would suffer more and more. Will the process of change be through collapsing the US infrastructure, while that country is devastated by Mother Nature, civil war and foreign invasion (some other great world power)? From that incident the Beast reappears renewed and restructured, whose deadly wound is healed (Rev. 13:3, 12).

That is the Beast that Ezra seems to have seen, whose last 3 heads were destroyed between them, leaving only one. What three heads could they be? The description suggests that there are 3 super-powers that will be the last of the end of this era before the imminent arrival of the Messiah. It is notable that if we looked at this with modern eyes, the most coherent thing would be to assume that they are Russia, the US and China. But regarding that head that Revelation says will be " wounded to death " and will then be "healed," how and why? The quote from Apoc. 13 talks about the structure of said government, and regarding it he spends the following chapters "gloating" over the fall of the great prostitute, again and again. But even after beginning to mention the end of all this with the 7 golden bowls of wrath (Rev. 16), he returns to speak of the sentence that weighs on the great Babel (Rev. 17 and 18), and then he refers to the defeat of Belial and his armies. So, chronologically, first comes the judgment on the great Babel and then on the Beast.

IV.
THE DESTRUCTION OF THE USA

Below is a prophecy from September 1984 given to an Eastern European immigrant arriving in the US... Late one night, I couldn't sleep, the children were sleeping in the luggage. My wife and daughter were crying, I went out and walked. I didn't want them to see me cry. I walked around the building, crying and saying, "God! Why did you punish me? Why did you bring me to this country? I can't understand anyone. If I try to ask someone something, all I hear is "I don't know." "I know." I stopped in front of the apartment and sat on a large rock. Suddenly, a bright light came towards me. I jumped up because it seemed like a car was coming straight at me, trying to hit me! I thought the police Romanian secret had tracked me to the United States and now they were trying to kill me. But it wasn't a car at all. When the light got closer, it surrounded me. From the light I heard the same voice I had heard so many times in prison.

He said, "Dumitru, why are you so desperate?" I said, "Why did you punish me? Why did you bring me to this country? I have nowhere to lay my head. I can't understand anyone." He said, "Dumitru, didn't I tell you that I am also here with you? I brought you to this country because this country will burn." I said, 'Then why did you bring me here to burn?' Why didn't you let me die in my own country? You should have let me die in prison in Romania! He said, "Dumitru, be patient so I can tell you. Come up to this." I climbed onto something next to him. I don't know what it was. I also know that I was not asleep. It wasn't a dream. It wasn't a vision. I was awake like now. He showed me all of California and said, "This is Sodom and Gomorrah! All of this will burn in one day! Sin has come to the Holy One." Then he took me to Las Vegas. "This is Sodom and Gomorrah. In one day it will burn." Then he showed me New York State. "Do you know what this is?" asked. I said no." He said, "This is New York. This is Sodom and Gomorrah! In one day it will burn." Then he showed me all of Florida, "This is Florida." He said, "This is Sodom and Gomorrah! In one day it will burn."

Then he took me back home, to the rock where we had started. "IN ONE DAY IT WILL BURN! I have shown you all this" - I said, "How will it burn?" He said, "Remember what I am telling you, because you will go to the television, to the radio, and to the churches. You must shout out loud. Do not be afraid, for I will be with you." I said, "How can I go? Who knows me here in the United States? I don't know anyone here." He said, "Don't worry. I will come before you. I will do many healings in American churches and open the doors for you. But don't say anything more than what I tell you. This country." It will burn!" I said, "What are you going to do with the church?" He said, "I want to save the church, but the churches have abandoned me." I said, "How did they abandon you?" He said, "The people praises herself. The honor that people are supposed to give to Jesus Christ, they take upon themselves. There are divorces in churches. There is adultery in the churches. There are homosexuals in churches. There are abortions. In the churches and all other sins that are possible.

Because of all the sin, I left some of the churches. You must shout out loud that they must put an end to their sin. They must turn to the Lord. The Lord never tires of forgiving. They must come closer to the Lord and live a clean life. If you have sinned until now, you must put an end to it and begin a new life as the Bible tells you to live." I said, "How will America burn?" America is the most powerful country in this world. Why did you bring us here to burn us? Why didn't you at least let us die where ALL the Duduman have died?" He said:

"Remember this, Dumitru. Russian spies have discovered where the nuclear warehouses are in the United States. When the Americans think it is peace and security, from the center of the country, some people will start fighting against the Government. The government will be busy with internal problems. Then from the ocean, from Cuba, Nicaragua, Mexico. "(He told me two other countries, but he didn't remember which ones they were)"... they will bomb the nuclear warehouses. When they explode, the United States will burn!"

"What will you do with the Church of the Lord? How will you save those who will turn to you?" I asked. He said, "Tell them this: how I saved the three young men from the fiery furnace, and how I saved Daniel from the lions' den, in the same way I will save them." The angel of the Lord also told me: "I have blessed this country because of the Jewish people who are in this country. I have seven million Jews in this country, but they do not want to recognize the Lord. They did not want to thank God for the blessing that they received in this country. Israel does not want to recognize Jesus Christ. They put their faith in the Jewish people of America. But, when America burns, the Lord will resurrect China, Japan and other nations to go against the Russians. They will strike the Russians and will push them to the gates of Paris.

There they will make a treaty and name the Russians as their leaders. Then they will unite against Israel. When Israel realizes that it does not have the strength of the United States behind it, it will panic. That is when she will turn to the Messiah for deliverance. That's when the Messiah will come. Then, the church will meet Jesus in the air, and he will take them back to the Mount of Olives. At that time, the battle of Armageddon will be fought." When I heard all this, I said, "If you really are the angel of the Lord, and everything you have told me is true, then everything you have said must be written in the Bible. ". He said, "Tell everyone to read Jeremiah 51:8-15, Revelation chapter 18, and Zechariah chapter 14, where

Christ fights against those who possess the earth. After His victory," said the angel, "there will be one flock. and a Shepherd. There will be no need for light. The Lamb of God will be the Light. There will be no illnesses, tears or deaths. There will only be eternal joy and God will be the ruler. Only one language. Just one song. And you don't need a translator! ...

And, Dumitru, "continued," a word of warning. If you hide anything from the American people that they tell you, I will punish you severely. ""How will I know that this is real, that it will really happen? ", I asked for." As a sign that I have spoken to you, tomorrow before you wake up, I will send someone to bring you a bed, and at noon I will send you a cart and a bucket of honey. After which I will send someone to pay the rent. "The next day, someone brought Dumitru a bed, and at noon a car arrived with the bucket of honey. He also paid the rent, as God had promised him (see chapter 10, page." THROUGH THE UNBURNED FIRE ".) Then the angel left. End of story.

On May 4, 2016, certain media echoed another news story about warnings from Orthodox Jews: «Rumors about the imminent coming of the Messiah are abundant today. The latest of these is that of Riminov Rebbe, a Hasidic rabbi who lives in New York. 'Israel Today' reports that while visiting his followers in Florida, the rabbi urged them to leave the US as soon as possible. According to the Orthodox website 'Behadrei Haredim', on the seventh day of Passover the rabbi urged his listeners to make a diaspora to Israel: "Listen to me carefully, dear Jews," said the rabbi, "he who has it in his hand to get up and go and return to the Holy Land of Israel do it as soon as possible while it is still possible, this includes leaving much of South America and most of Europe... also the USA will be a place of danger in the war and It is still too early to say that settlers within the US will survive, but many parts will be destroyed and poisoned, even civil war will break out in the US and the states isolated from the Federal Government... the land of "Israel will be the safest place to survive the war, although there will be terrible difficulties there too."

All these imprecations and exhortations are repeated over and over again, as several chapters of Revelation maintain about the fate of the great Whore, because of the evils she causes and the lack of ethics she sponsors: «A judgment will strike the United States while Obama is still in power... a gigantic wave will wipe out and flood Florida, New York and Washington [...] the US will be paralyzed and will never again be the powerful nation it once was... there will be great anguish in the nation, and all of this will happen in the last few years before I return... I saw a huge cloud of ash... buildings will collapse and there will be huge earthquakes... [...] the hills will start to shake, the stars will lose their brightness, your sun will start to emit flashes of radiation and the patterns climate will change... in the central planes there will be a great hurricane that will bring large amounts of rain. "The Russians will attack US infrastructure." (Patricia Green, 2015) The quotes about the fall of the United States and Rome are constantly simultaneous, one focused especially on religion and the other especially on financial matters.

In a post that I shared on December 14, 2020 (https://www.facebook.com/freddy.gutt/posts/10202446922251837) many points can be observed that clarify that the great Babel (great Babylon) or great prostitute (great harlot) are direct allusions to the USA; just as many others have been prophesying for years and revealing what has been told to them by the Holy Spirit (an example here, in Sherry Shriner's thesis: http://www.sherryshriner.com/spanish/america-babylon.htm, or the summary by Gary H. Kah: http://leondejudamins.blogspot.com.es/2014/05/new-york-la-gran-ramera.html [1]). They call this conspiracy theories

1. http://leondejudamins.blogspot.com.es/2014/05/new-york-la-gran-ramera.html

until they hear the statements of Stanislan Lunev, Glenda Jackson, Joanie Stahl, Tania Filloau, Alan Martin, Particia Green, Sara Hoffman, TD Hale, Chinese defectors, reports of UN militarization in the US ., police reinforcement, mass deportation, martial law, concentration camps, and other dreams and visions about invasion, civil war, nuclear war, financial collapse. US secret service agents and military generals of that country have LITERALLY acknowledged that their government knows perfectly well that they are the great Babel of the Bible, and it is not a new issue at all. To some of you it sounds new and you think it's just me because you probably haven't heard it before, but that's not the case. There are Christians in the US who talk about this in programs, interviews, blogs, articles... they tell how the Holy Spirit has explained it to them and the dreams and visions they receive.

Now, a somewhat longer and supremely detailed vision was transmitted to the priest Ezra in the 5th century BC. C. The scribe, who had lived in Babylon, among the exiles returned from captivity and resided in Jerusalem, and wrote several prophetic dreams and historical texts - in addition to the one known within the Tanak scroll, 'Ezra-Nehemiah'. In the book 2 Esdras (for others called '4 Esdras'), he explains in chapters 11 and 12 a vision about an eagle that "had twelve wings and three heads." Heads emerged from their wings and remained at rest, while the wings and their feathers ruled over the entire Earth. He adds that "there was no one to oppose it, no one among everything that has been created on earth." Ezra describes that at first "eight heads were counted like this," although the Syriac, Arabic-l, and Arabic-l versions read "These wings," and the Latin version translates "These opposite feathers." Then he says that one by one the wings came out to reign, but the second reigned like no other in the entire history of the governments of its wings. Starting in chapter 11:20, it says that "all his wings rose up on the right side, each one in its own time, to strengthen himself and reign;

then they disappeared. Among them there were some who rose, but without reigning.

After this, the twelve wings disappeared as well as its two heads. In the body of this eagle there were only three sleeping heads and six heads. In this sense, the final reference appears in the Latin, Syriac and Arabic-l versions as "His six ailerons", while the Arabic-2 version says: "He had only two wings left, in addition to the wing, so that "The body of the eagle had nothing but dumb heads." Already making a description almost at the end of the government of this kingdom, he comments that "then, two of these last ones separated, they stayed on the one that was on the right side and four stayed in their place. These four made the resolution to rise and reign. One stood up, straightened, and quickly disappeared. The same thing happened with the second, and it happened more quickly than the first. Then the two that remained made the resolution to rise and reign. While they were deliberating, behold, one of the three sleeping heads woke up: it was the middle one, the largest of all. Then she took these two heads with her. "He advanced with his companions and devoured these two heads that had deliberated to reign."

The other versions, instead of saying "two heads" in this last paragraph, say "two ailerons." And referring to this head, he notes: «This head occupied the entire earth, made those who inhabited it suffer all kinds of torments and oppressed the world much more than the wings that had risen. After this, this middle head disappeared like the others. Of the three, "two remained, and, like her, they reigned over the earth and its inhabitants. Then the head on the right side devoured the head on the left side. At that moment the Messiah appears and judges him, reproaching him for his role as the 4th tyrant or animal that reigned over the entire Earth, and then he kills him.

Now, he reports that "the head that had remained disappeared and the wings that had retreated towards it straightened and rose to reign and its claws waved." The translation here is strange, since the Syriac text itself seems altered, but it adds: "Then these disappeared; his body was consumed; "The earth suffered a violent shake, I myself was terrified by the greatness of my search and I woke up in great terror." This last part describes the end of the rule of the Beast, and in chapter 12:11 it is clarified, explaining the origin of the eagle itself: "The eagle that rises from the sea is the fourth kingdom that appeared to Daniel your brother, in dreams. But I didn't explain it to him like I'm going to explain it to you. Days will come when a kingdom more terrible than those that have gone before will rise upon the earth. Twelve kings will reign in it. He who will reign second will reign longer than the others. Here is the explanation of the twelve heads that you saw. Here, at the end, instead of "heads", the Latin, Syriac and Arabic-2 versions, describe "Wings". He is obviously talking about Rome, but he describes a succession of power at different intervals within the process of development of Rome over the last 2000 years (the senate or republic system, the imperial system, the system of dynasties, the time as a Byzantine empire, time of internal struggles, time alone as a religious establishment, etc.).

Later, when referring to the interior of the eagle and its voices in its bosom, he writes: "As for what you saw speaking, and the voice did not come from its head, but from the middle of its body: Here is what it is: Within this kingdom numerous struggles will arise; will be shaken to the point of falling; He will not fall at this time, but will remain in his power. As for the heads you have seen coming out of their wings. Instead of heads, the Latin and Syriac versions write "To the ends of their wings." And he continues: «Here is his explanation: Eight kings will arise whose years will be evil and whose duration will be short; Two of them will perish quickly at the appointed time.

Four will be preserved until the time of their end will come. The three sleeping heads that you have seen mean this: At the end of his days, the Most High will raise up three kings; They will make many innovations, and they will make the earth suffer. And to those who live in great terror, even more than to their predecessors; That is why they have been called eagle heads. For these heads of kingdom will be the end. Regarding the large disappearing head that you saw, it means that one of them will die in his bed, but in torment. The two that remain will die by the sword. And the last will perish by the sword. The Latin and Syriac versions have a different ending here: "One man's sword will devour his companion, but he himself will perish by the sword."

He continues stating about the "ailerons" or "heads": «The two heads that you have seen retreat near those on the right, here is their meaning: They are those that the Almighty keeps for the last days, in which the beginning of the final; there will be, as you have seen, a great commotion. This lion that you have seen come roaring out of the desert, speaking to this eagle and reproaching it for its faults, everything that you have heard, is the one that the Most High has preserved from the seed of David for the last days; It is he who will go out, come, speak (to men) about their sins, who will reproach them for their faults, and who will heap their retribution before them, who at first will make them appear alive at the judgment, and after having made these reproaches to them, "You will lose them." The Latin version uses the term "The Anointed One" when referring to "that one"; The Syriac version says "The Messiah", and the Arabic-2 version says "The King". It should be noted that the description of this dream speaks of a long-standing empire that, as its phases of change pass, "mutates" into new organisms, that is, Rome was first a senate, then an empire... there was a time of emperors and of Julio-Claudian, Flavian, Antonian and Severe dynasties, there was military anarchy, there was a readjustment towards the so-called 'Byzantine empire', and so on.

The same verse relates that the woman was "sitting on a scarlet beast full of names of blasphemy, which had seven heads and ten horns." (Rev. 17:3, R60) The indication assumes in the first instance that the woman is supported – initially – and maintained by that beast, which, as it appears in chapter 13, is a government that is to emerge on Earth, and that represents the Antichrist. Consequently, the prostitute relies on the government of the Antichrist, which as we know, will be manifest on Earth to control her. After describing her riches and adornments (luxuries, sumptuousness, elegance, avarice, etc.), he describes her as exultant and intoxicated in “fornication”, both in commercial dealings and in sexual pleasures: “she had in her hand a golden chalice full of abominations.” and from the filthiness of her fornication" (Rev. 17:4, R60). The relationship of this with international trade and also with "sexual freedom" (which we should more correctly call "free fornication" or "fornication" is evident). public"). I don't know what it will be like on other planets, but on Earth this comes from New York, with regard to the economy and the international market, and from California, with regard to moral degradation and sexual perversion.

It is enough to pay attention to the most characteristic phrases of these warnings... "it has become a habitation of demons and a haunt of every unclean spirit, and a shelter for every unclean and hateful bird." (Rev. 18:2, R60) This is not a figurative statement, but a literal one, since we know of the constant satanic rituals carried out by the elite and their pacts and evocation of demons. "all nations have drunk of the wine of the wrath of her fornication" (Rev. 18:3, R60) This passage appears as an explanation of why she "has fallen", as punishment from God. That is, the city is destroyed for corrupting the world, and never says anything about any place other than Earth. “the kings of the earth have committed fornication with it” (Rev.

18:3, R60) If that city is outside this globe, how do the kings commit fornication with it? Fornication is a sexual act of touching, whether metaphorical (Ez. 23:37) or literal. What these verses imply is that fornication has consisted, as I said before, of sexual pleasure (pornography, immorality and media degradation) and commerce (trafficking and international markets).

Let's go to those "the merchants of the earth have become rich from the power of their pleasures" (Rev. 18:3, R60) Merchants "of the Earth." The stock market. Then a voice says: "Come out of her, my people, so that you do not share in her sins" (Rev. 18:4, R60). Do not be involved, "nor receive part of her plagues." (Rev. 18:4, R60) If the servants are on Earth, and Babel was in another world, why would we suffer the plagues of that other planet? Refers to "part" of the plagues. That means that there will be isolated problems attacking the nation from different fronts, "because their sins have reached up to heaven" (Rev. 18:5, R60). And isn't the city supposed to be up there? If it reaches "to heaven", where does it reach from? And this is even more significant: "Give to her as she has given to you, and repay her double according to her works; In the chalice in which she prepared drink, prepare double for her. (Rev 18:6, R60) The Greek text is clearer, assuming that this city has done things to the servants that will happen twice as much to itself. And she adds that what she "prepared" will also be duplicated. When we analyze the whole issue of martial law in the US and everything that the elite with Obama are preparing against that country, we understand this verse perfectly.

He further adds, "in one day his plagues will come; death, mourning and famine, and it will be burned with fire" (Rev. 18:8, R60) Among the prophecies that coincide with each other, there is a great parallelism of this one with those of the great Tribulation: "nation will rise against nation, and kingdom against kingdom; and there will be pestilences and famines" (Matt. 24:7, R60) War is usually represented by fire, although this also identifies 'fire'; Hunger, scarcity and drought are another predicted event regarding what those of us who study the subject consider to be the death of the dollar; The plague, epidemic or plague is the same, as in other prophecies, announcing a bacteriological and biological war. What I explain in articles, books and documentaries, with multiple sources, coincides perfectly with all these biblical passages, because with the fall of the United States, both in its economy and in its structure (when it was invaded by Russia and China) international trade and markets will collapse.

We see even more that he quotes "the kings of the Earth", never kings or people from other places, whether from the sky or the stars. The text says that "they have lived with it" in delight, however, they have had part of the prosperity of the economy of that country, its capitalist system. Subsequently, "the merchants of the earth weep and lament over it, because no one buys their merchandise anymore" (Rev. 18:11, R60) Because there will be a systemic collapse of the markets: "merchandise of gold, of silver, of stones precious, of pearls, of fine linen, of purple, of silk, of scarlet, of every fragrant wood, of every object of ivory, of every object of precious wood, of copper, of iron and of marble; and cinnamon, spices, incense, myrrh, frankincense, wine, oil, fine flour, wheat, beasts, sheep, horses and chariots, and slaves, souls of men. (Rev. 18:12-13, R60) On this last point I must clarify that the Greek text says "even human body and soul", which we know has to do with the Illuminati and Satanism.

Other countries and business people will be seeing the fall of values, currencies and Wall Street... "The merchants of these things, who have become rich at the expense of her, will stand far away for fear of her torment" (Rev. 18 :15) And it speaks of the maritime transportation system that involves the majority of market traffic: "all those who worked in the sea stood far away" (Rev. 18:17, R60) The truth is that nowhere is it talked about of "stars", "heaven", "celestial abodes", "the heights" or something similar. Again and again he speaks of the "merchants of the Earth", and of a nerve center of finance: "What city was like this great city?" (Rev. 18:18) It speaks of contracts and covenants, which in biblical vocabulary is used with the connotation of marriage covenants or contracts: "nor will the voice of husband and wife be heard in you any more" (Rev. 18: 23, R60) Could it be that the institution of holy marriage given by God to man was fulfilled in a supposed diabolical city, seat of Satan?

So, are those merchants who see it from afar and complain, are they from this world or from another world? "your merchants were the great ones of the earth" (Rev. 18:23, R60) It clearly speaks of the great magnates who control the finances of the world. Among them are the owners of the pharmacological industries: "by your sorceries all nations were deceived" (Rev. 18:23, R95). The Greek word here is "pharmakeía", from which comes "drug", "pharmacy". Is he talking about drugs, the petro-chemical cartel (pharmaceutical industry) or magic, witchcraft and the occult itself? Any or all of these meanings are applicable to the elite and the US.

In addition to this he mentions the thousands who have been victims of the plots of these powerful ones, the multitude of victims and martyrs of the truth... "in her was found the blood of the prophets and the saints, and of all those who have been dead on earth." (Rev. 18:24, R60) are not prophets of the old style, but the prophets or informants of today. If it promotes wars, revolutions, coups d'état, overthrows, guerrillas, terrorism, murder of Christians and whistleblowers, missionaries, drug addiction, etc., we must go back to the powers of this world, which Even before the UN (since wars began all over the world, more than ever) they were already causing these misfortunes in every empire from which it has arisen.

If anyone doubts that "the great whore" is the one who "has corrupted the earth with her fornication" (Rev. 19:2, R60), they should rethink what they know about geopolitics and history, because pornography comes out of California for everything the world (thousands of films per year), the influence for the approval of all types of unions, supposedly marriages, and laws of all types of supposed genres. Not to mention the entertainment related in every sense, which is better not to mention. So, in the image of the 10 rulers who will control the world, which will be divided into 10 exclusive super nations (countries and borders as we understand them will not exist), the US is also divided into 10 FEMA sections at the time of collapse. As Rome controls the world through the infiltration of the Jesuits, the Vatican religion, Wall Street economics, UN politics and US military force, the beast will rise through 10 leaders, and not It will distribute its governments according to the form they have today, but in 10 supernations that will be the new geographical distribution of the Earth.

«The ten horns that you saw are ten kings, who have not yet received a kingdom; but for one hour they will receive authority as kings together with the beast. These have the same purpose, and they will hand over their power and authority to the beast. (Rev. 17:12-13, R60) The 10 horns are 10 leaders who will not take power until the Beast has done so. They will operate at the same time, and only for a short period (3 and a half years). When will that brief time be of his power? The text that will culminate with the coming of the Lord says: "They will fight against the Lamb, and the Lamb will overcome them" (Rev. 17:14, R60). This is how he explains it later when narrating the outcome of Har-Magedon: "I saw the beast, the kings of the earth and their armies, gathered together to make war against him who sat on the horse, and against his army. And the beast was taken, and with him the false prophet..." (Rev. 19:19-20, R60) The context tells us again and again of 3 and a half years of power of the Beast (Antichrist) and the false prophet (Antichrist), so the time of the 10 kings and the Beast will be 3 and a half years. Consequently "they have not yet received a kingdom." Why doesn't it say "they have not yet received power" but instead says "kingdom"? Because the distribution of those 10 kingdoms does not yet exist as such, but will be configured after the first part of the Third World War (when the Antichrist manifests).

«the ten horns that you saw on the beast, these will hate the harlot, and will leave her desolate and naked; and they will devour its flesh, and burn it with fire; for God has put it in their hearts to do what he wanted: to agree, and to give their kingdom to the beast" (Rev. 17:16-17, R60). The reference itself is quite clear in suggesting that these leaders will put themselves agree to destroy the great city, so that power passes to the Beast. As a result, what is seen is that the current superpower will be destroyed by the rest of the nations so that the Beast can take power, and at no time or place is anything spoken of from outside this globe.

The end of the Republic. The beginning of the Empire

What is the relevance of these 7 secretaries, admirals and generals, and their 10 advisors? The similarity with the biblical quotes about "the 10 horns" of the beast of Revelation. On other occasions I have spoken of other similarities between the 10 current monarchies of Europe and even the 10 super-nations in which the world of the Antichrist would be reconfigured, but on this occasion I have to highlight this outstanding analogy. The greatest relevance of this fact lies in the words of the apostle John, to whom they explain that "the ten horns that you saw on the beast, these will hate the harlot, and will leave her desolate and naked; and they will devour her flesh, and burn her with fire..." (Rev. 17:16, KJV 60). Previously we have emphasized the interpretation of 'the great whore' or 'great Babylon' as the USA of America; Also the close and direct relationship of its creation after the silent Roman empire, and protected by it. In this sense, the world government led by a satanic Illuminati elite uses all the control systems in the world and its many groups, from the UN, the CFR, the TC, the Bilderberg club, the Jesuit order, NATO, the Round Table , the Club of Rome, and, among many others, the banking mothers: the IMF, the WB and the BIS. This entire system or new World Order, increasingly consolidated, represents this biblical Beast.

What the prophecy seems to be implying, and fitting with other extra-biblical rumors, is that the Beast (New World Order) will betray the prostitute Babel (USA), and will use the Military-Industrial Complex for that purpose. . Although, the police apparatus and a UN army would be in charge of quelling civil revolts and imposing a state of emergency, arrests, blockades, checkpoints and checkpoints, raids, curfew, raids and executions, but the US military itself would be fighting abroad as NATO's main arm against Russia in Eastern Europe. We have spoken on many occasions about a Chinese and Russian invasion of US territory, but this would only be an additional component once the high treasonous action is carried out against the country itself (the US). Those are only two nations; Even if they were interpreted as two of the 4 beasts that the prophet Daniel saw, or part of 10 global nations, the context still does not fit. The Revelation passage says that "the horns" of the very "beast" on which "the harlot sits" will receive power at a certain time, and it also maintains that they will hate that harlot and destroy her. Being objective, the description is more in line with the martial law argument in the US.

To achieve a “planetary empire” the system of power must fall, and this is currently in the Whore (USA), and that includes too many obstacles and impediments due to civil, religious and bureaucratic liberties. Only a coup d'état could reduce these obstacles to nothing, but it still has obvious difficulties: 1) The military would have to agree (and by extension each and every patriotic American soldier who loves and reveres his nation); 2) The Senate would have to resign, which would only occur due to force majeure; 3) The people would rebel en masse (and Americans have guns under the freedoms of the Second Amendment of their Constitution, which would cause a bloody civil war with possible results similar to the Civil War).

Only a titanic conspiracy, perfectly directed and maintained in absolute silence, could triumph against these obvious impediments. The truth is that since the UN was established, plans to overthrow the US had already begun. Since the mid-1950s, Executive Orders and meetings of the House of Representatives began to promote laws of civil control and imperial absolutism. The Republican and Democratic political apparatus had to be motivated and/or pressured to participate in the legality of these presidential proposals (which, however, were not really the idea of the president, but of the elite above him). These 60 years of preparation have prepared a protocol for taking over government by the Federal Emergency Management Center (FEMA) that would be controlled by these 10 advisors and their 7 state officials (mostly military). The compartmentalization of the services is part of the compartmentalization of information, so that only a few, such as generals, colonels, admirals, secretaries of state or secret service would know what was really carried out at the federal level.

The reptile Barack Obama has been a key part of this destiny of the USA, and although it seems that he has disappeared from the scene, he only continues to play and maintain his charismatic character. This man is key to understanding the Apocalypse, as he has left the nation of the United States ready to collapse. However, everything indicates that he has a bigger plan in hand and does not want to damage his image. That is the role of Donald Trump, who will be in power for possibly only a few weeks, to finish Obama's work with the US on domestic affairs. Trump's character is perfect for what they want to do, since they must deceive American Christians, fuel social hatred towards Christians, cause riots and protests to give reasons to the federal government to take a heavy hand, must reduce the capacity of the people to counteract the police apparatus (that includes removing as many people as possible, especially those who may be belligerent, from the country), deceive the world by making it appear that the impending war was pacified (the UN Security Council made clear its interest against Israel, and Russian and NATO troops are facing each other in Eastern Europe), among other tricks.

As a Secret Service officer told a servant of Christ privately in December 2015: "Trump was already elected two years ago [...] once he carries out a mass deportation, he will begin a coast-to-coast [U.S.] arrest." "That will be martial law." Deportation is just the beginning. The lists of all people opposed to the government, branded as 'terrorists', will follow, from preppers (survivalists), ex-military and veterans, politicians, activists, Christians, Muslims... all those who are considered "theorists" of the conspiracy, who are easily tracked by the NSA (especially since they provide all their information openly in public through social networks, an invention of the FBI). In the US legislative apparatus, the limitation and idea of the concept of "terrorist" has been redesigned to include any person who thinks differently from the state, since they are considered an "enemy of the government." In addition, the laws have been restructured to eliminate legal processes or "prosecution", simplifying it into an arbitrary decision on the spot of the police department. In other words, the police force (whose powers will be expanded and almost unlimited) will be able to decide who is a terrorist and who is not, and execute them on the spot or take them to concentration camps, and said person will not be able to demand a trial or a lawyer (everything will be limited to the police officer's decision on the spot). These are the type of laws that have been established over these decades and that Obama has reinforced and made official.

Trump stated in 2016 that "after the border is 'secure,' immigration officials will begin to 'make a determination' about which undocumented immigrants will remain in the United States." (Cadena RT, January 20) Immigration officials? Yes, ICE. Shouldn't that be decided by the president himself? What "determination" should they make, if it has been Trump who has been behind the immigration propaganda since the beginning of his campaign? Are you saying that once you have expelled the immigrants (what he calls "securing the border", and which is interpreted as the construction of the border wall) it will be the ICE (Customs and Immigration Agency) who will make decisions on said issue? ?

An alleged ICE agent, who would have committed suicide in May of last year, precisely left some notes where he said: "If the American people knew what this government was planning, they would rise up and overthrow it, if I or anyone else in the country "If the federal government revealed what was coming, we would be killed anyway." He adds that "in federal law enforcement we have been working for several years to control riots and uprisings from a coming financial collapse and widespread banking failures. The exercises include life-size images of American men, including women and children, who we are told to shoot to "practice" and "get used to."

The official goes on to state: "We are told that the economy is terminally ill and will fail in 2016. We are also told that the banks are all insolvent and the FDIC does not have enough funds to bail out depositors. We are told that these events are inevitable and it is imperative that the government survive when the people rise above this. When the collapse occurs, the detention camps created under the FEMA REX-84 program in the 1980s to house the illegal aliens we were going to deport will be used to imprison American citizens who the government considers to be a "threat." . American citizens will be arrested without charge and imprisoned without trial for God knows how long. These camps have been equipped to carry out Hitler-scale murders! A true "purge" of American citizens by the same government that they themselves created and paid for! I can't be part of this.

The government knows the military will rise up to stop this, so our military is being deployed overseas, intentionally involved in foreign fighting, and deliberately downsized so they can't be here or help Americans! More than a billion rounds of hollow point ammunition have been removed from National Guard Armories at the state level, purchased by the federal government, the states themselves have been disarmed of military firepower so that they cannot defend themselves from the activities federal. For this reason, local police departments have been militarized and provided with armored vehicles and weapons of war.

He adds that "when the inevitable collapse begins to occur, electricity to the entire country will be turned off, as will all forms of communication. All banks will be closed immediately, no one will be able to get money because all ATMs will be offline. Credit, debit and EBT cards will not work. Everyone will be out of cash, they will have no way to get anything. The Emergency Alert System will be used to take over all broadcast stations and tell the public that this is the result of a cyber attack. But while the American people wait patiently for things to return to normal, the government will unleash raids on citizens they deem militant or dangerous. With all civil communications out, and all television and radio stations taken over by the Emergency Alert System, by the time what is happening continues, the government will already have the advantage. All federal prisons have been equipped with lethal gas systems. When things go wrong, all prisoners in all prisons will be placed in their locked cells. Prison staff will leave the facility, and a designated person will fire a lethal gas. All federal prisoners, regardless of their crime or sentence, will be gassed to death in their cells. "Once the gas is gone, the dead will be removed and the prisons will be used to house citizens fighting the federal attack."

Simultaneously, days before or days after the beginning of all this, international conflicts will break out once again. Although, Trump does not seem to play any role after carrying out the mega deportation. However, Obama does seem to enter the scene again, even having directly to do with international war, the push from World War III to the point of nuclear conflict. However, if there is war, economic collapse or a major natural disaster, FEMA comes into control of the US with those 7 heads and 10 advisors under absolute power. The power and role of the government section would be put on hold: there would be a vacuum in the presidential and senate power (the president of the country does not have any power). Given that it seems that after the great deportation the arrests will begin, it is understandable that the fall of the economy would be imminent, and this would be accompanied by civil war and the war against the Russians and Chinese. If this is accompanied by the prophetic natural disasters that will hit the world (with greater magnitude against the United States), it is logical that for several years FEMA will have all the power, and the legislative power will be annulled and suspended.

This is how the US will fall so that the new global government stands out, without dependence on the US. The only thing that would remain from the US would be the Military-Industrial Complex, which, in the opinion of many, comes to shape today Actually, NATO. Seen this way, we are assuming that the US military will stop being the defense of that country to be the strongest part of NATO, and as usual the most influential and representative involvement. On January 24, 'El Confidencial' commented in an article: «The geopolitical analyst Pedro Baños, General of Infantry and former military advisor in the European Parliament [said that] "We must not forget that NATO to a large extent means USA."..."

In his farewell address to the nation on January 17, 1961, former President Dwight D. Eisenhower said: "Our work, resources, and livelihood are all we have; This is the very structure of our society. In government councils, we must avoid the purchase of unjustified influence, whether sought or not, by the military-industrial complex. There is a risk of a disastrous development of usurped power and [that risk] will remain. We must never allow the weight of this conjunction to endanger our freedoms or democratic processes. Currently, annual US military spending represents approximately 47% of total global arms spending ($712 billion in 2009 alone). On December 23, 2016, Obama signed a defense law that authorizes providing $611 billion to the military in 2017. Why if he is not supposed to be playing any role in 2017, and that would be more of Trump's problem (Would even Trump simply repeal such legislation)? Ironically, through all this, Trump has said nothing about American armies in Eastern Europe or opposed that militarization, even though he is supposedly seeking to improve relations with Vladimir Putin.

Presidential Decrees

Consequently, if there is an economic collapse, a major natural disaster or war that affects the USA, the Council of Governors has the full right to put the police apparatus into operation with the Federal Emergency Management Center (FEMA). If that happens, the president loses power, and so does Congress and the House of Representatives. This situation could last, legally, for between 3 and 5 years, with a presidential vacuum and the country being controlled by FEMA and the Council of Governors (which respond to the Secretary of Defense, Secretary of State and Secretary of Homeland Security: https : //en.wikipedia.org/wiki/Council_of_Governors [2]). Through the legislation of the House of Representatives, opinions of senior military and secret service officials, and presidential Executive

2. https://en.wikipedia.org/wiki/Council_of_Governors

Orders, it is clear that Donald Trump has to finish a job that has been in the making for decades, and that is to destroy the United States alone. Look at some examples through the EOs (Executive Orders) signed by their presidents:

- Executive Order 13603 (https://en.wikipedia.org/wiki/Executive_Order_13603). Signed by Obama on March 16, 2012. It consists of "Preparation for National Defense Resources", based on policies and programs under the Defense Development Acts of 1950 (https://en.wikipedia.org/wiki /Defense_Production_Act). Its function is to take control of: A) "All articles and products that are capable of being ingested by humans or animals"; B) "All forms of energy"; C) "All civil means of transportation"; D) "All usable water from all sources"; E) "Health resources - medicines, biological products, medical devices, materials, facilities, health equipment, services and equipment"; F) Forced labor (or "induction," as the executive order delicately refers to military recruitment). The House declaration, HR 4079, puts into action ALL EXECUTIVE ORDERS at the same time, along with those related to the FEMA REX-84 concentration camp program (https://www.congress.gov/bill/ 114th-congress/house-bill/4079) and immigration prisons (https://es.wikipedia.org/wiki/Rex_84).
- Executive Order of July 1, 2016 (https://obamawhitehouse.archives.gov/the-press-office/2016/07/01/executive-order-united-states-policy-pre-and-post-strike-measures). Signed by Obama. Allows the US military and police to use force against its citizens as a preventive policy: https://www.washingtonpost.com/news/monkey-cage/wp/2016/07/07/obamas-new- executive-order-on-drones-means-the-us-may-still-violate-international-law/?utm_term=.b67ef913be86
- Executive Order 11051 (https://www.archives.gov/federal-register/executive-orders/1962.html). Details the responsibilities of the FEMA Office of Emergency Planning.

Authorizes the entry into force of ALL Moments of National Emergency declared by the President, increased Tension or Economic or financial Crisis (covers any conceivable national Crisis, but does not even mention war or attack) . http://www.disastercenter.com/laworder/11051.htm.

- Executive Order 10995 (https://fas.org/irp/offdocs/eo/eo-10995.htm). Provides for federal takeover of all communications and media.
- Executive Order 10997 (http://www.presidency.ucsb.edu/ws/?pid=58935). Provides for the federal takeover of all electrical, oil, gas, fuel and mineral facilities.
- Executive Order 10998 (http://www.disastercenter.com/laworder/10998.htm). Provides for federal takeover of national resources, primarily farms.
- Executive Order 10999 (http://www.presidency.ucsb.edu/ws/?pid=58937). It provides for the federal takeover of all means of transportation, control of highways, seaports, etc.
- Executive Order 11000 (http://www.presidency.ucsb.edu/ws/?pid=58938). It provides for the mobilization of all civilians and work brigades under the supervision of the Government.
- Executive Order 11001 (http://www.presidency.ucsb.edu/ws/?pid=58940). Provides for government takeover of the health, education and welfare system.
- Executive Order 11002 (http://www.presidency.ucsb.edu/ws/?pid=58941). Appoints the Postmaster General to carry out a national registry of all persons.
- Executive Order 11003 (http://www.disastercenter.com/laworder/11003.htm). It foresees that the Government assumes control of airports and airplanes.
- Executive Order 11004 (http://www.presidency.ucsb.edu/ws/?pid=58943). Establishes that the Housing and Finance Authority relocate the communities, and designate areas to abandon

and, likewise, establish new locations for the populations. This consists of depopulating green areas and overpopulating metropolises.

• Executive Order 11005 (http://www.disastercenter.com/laworder/11005.htm). It provides for the Government to assume control of railways, inland waterways and public storage facilities. All of the EOs up to Kennedy were combined under Richard Nixon into one huge Executive Order, allowing all of this to take place if the President declares a National Emergency, and it can be implemented by the head of FEMA, NOT EVEN BY THE PRESIDENT (the President already given that power under these executive orders). Executive Order 11490 combines all (https://en.wikipedia.org/wiki/Executive_Order_11490, http://www.presidency.ucsb.edu/ws/?pid=60479), and was reauthorized and expanded by Jimmy Carter on the 20th. July 1979. That is, Executive Order No. 11490 is the reaffirmation that a "national emergency" can be declared for any conceivable pretense.

• Executive Order 12672 (https://en.wikisource.org/wiki/Executive_Order_12672 and https://www.archives.gov/federal-register/executive-orders/1989-bush.html). Signed by Bush on March 24, 1989, delegating to the Director of FEMA powers that were conferred on the President by the Emergency Assistance and Disaster Assistance Act of 1988. Although described by the White House as simply a technical matter, in reality , the review delegates to the Director of FEMA direct responsibility for a large number of elements that were previously the sole prerogative of the President. That includes responsibility for Federal General Assistance, Emergency Assistance, Hazard Mitigation, Individual and Family Grant Programs, and the power to direct other federal agencies for an emergency. That is, all other federal agencies are under FEMA. These programs were rewritten in National Security Decision Directive 47 (https://www.hsdl.org/?abstract&did=462991),

which is in NSDD 47, and which was signed into law by President Reagan on July 22, 1982. It identified important areas to be as the nation's industrial base to maintain national defense and laid the foundation for the government's options to institute a police state (its title is 'Emergency Mobilization Preparation') and address legal limitations on the priority task that establishes the basis for the SUSPENSION OF THE US CONSTITUTION.

• Executive Order 10990 (http://www.presidency.ucsb.edu/ws/?pid=58928). Just like the rest of the EO before Kennedy, they were the first proposals, which were later vindicated by succeeding presidents.

• Executive Order 11310 (https://www.archives.gov/federal-register/executive-orders/1966.html). Grants authority to the Department of Justice to enforce plans set forth in executive orders, to institute industrial support, to establish judicial and legislative liaison, to monitor all aliens, to operate penitentiary and correctional facilities, and to advise and assist to the president.

• Executive Order 11049 (http://www.presidency.ucsb.edu/ws/?pid=58988). Assigns the emergency preparedness function to federal departments and agencies and consolidates 21 executive orders issued operationally over a fifteen-year period.

• Executive Order 11921 (https://en.wikipedia.org/wiki/Executive_Order_11921). Allows the Federal Emergency Preparedness Agency to develop plans to establish control over production and distribution mechanisms, energy sources, wages, salaries, credit and the flow of money in the United States and any financial institution anywhere indefinite national emergency situation. It also states that when a state of emergency is declared by the President, Congress cannot review the action for six months (https://fas.org/irp/offdocs/eo/eo-11921.htm [3]).

3. https://fas.org/irp/offdocs/eo/eo-11921.htm

• Executive Order 13757 (https://www.hsdl.org/?abstract&did=797652 [4]). Signed by Obama on December 28, it allows the Treasury (Secretary of the Treasury), under review by the Attorney General and the Secretary of State, to block or remove material related to operations on networks (whether computers, Internet access, access to accounts, etc.) to anyone considered related to cyber terrorism (this could include hacker communities).

• Obama's Executive Order referenced on October 13, 2016 (https://obamawhitehouse.archives.gov/the-press-office/2016/10/13/executive-order-coordinating-efforts-prepare-nation-space-weather -events). Pretext of solar activity for the intervention and reinforcement of electrical and energy systems through Civil Protection Services, NOAA and the Secretariats of Defense. The program deals with events that would prevent a national electromagnetic pulse attack.

As well as HR 4079, there is other legislation from the House of Representatives, such as HR 2749 (https://www.govtrack.us/congress/bills/111/hr2749/text), related to food. This is the Food Protection Act, and that affects the entire country, since it gives them the authority of the entire national geographic area, referring to all the states if they want, under food contamination guidelines. They can stop all forms of transportation in all states, and destroy vehicles, they can declare Martial Law, and they can shut down restaurants or whatever they see fit. Another case of these is HR 1274 (https://www.congress.gov/bill/114th-congress/house-bill/1274), as well as Obamacare Code ICD9E978 (http://beforeitsnews.com/healthcare/2014 /02/0000-guillotines-800-fema-camps-and-15000-russian-troops-whats-going-on-obamacare-code-icd9e978-execution-by-guillotine-666-mark-of-the-beast-2454424 .html) and the ICD E978 (http://www.centralx.com/diseases/icd889.htm),

4. https://www.hsdl.org/?abstract&did=797652

which consist of legal approvals to execute individuals. An example of this reinforcement is the '1033 Program', based on police reinforcement to control the civilian population.

I would like to conclude with some reflections on the words of the prophet Jeremiah: "Raise a banner on the walls of Babylon, strengthen the guard, set sentinels, set up traps; for Iaheveh has deliberated, and will even put into effect what he has spoken against the inhabitants of Babylon. You, who dwell among many waters, rich in treasures, your end has come, the measure of your greed. Yaheveh Tzabaot swore by himself, saying: I will fill you with men like locusts, and they will raise a cry against you. (Jer. 51:12-14) Strengthen the guard? Post sentinels? Do you have traps? This is a STATE OF EXCEPTION. Will they raise a cry? Are you talking about mobs and mobs of protesters and protests? «Behold, I am against you, O destroying mountain, says Yaheveh, who has destroyed the whole earth; and I will stretch out my hand against you, and I will roll you off the rocks, and I will reduce you to a burnt mountain. [...] Raise a banner in the land, sound a trumpet among the nations, prepare people against it; gather against her the kingdoms of Ararat, Minin and Ashkenaz; point against it captain, make horses come up like bristling locusts." (Jer. 51:25-27) Mini and Ashkenaz? Those regions are currently Russian (they were annexed by the Soviet Union)...

V.

GOG, FROM THE LAND OF MAGOG

What is Gog? It is a Hebrew term that means "rooftop" or a place located at the top of a place, or from the north. Magog is defined as the land Gog, and both are placed in a northern region, or simply ma-gog would be "where Gog is from" or "where the north is." Historically Gog was identified with the Baltic countries and the peoples who occupied the entire region from there to what is now Moscow. This fact has been used as an argument to interpret that Gog and Magog is Russia – as in the case of the Napoleonic invasion of Russia – coinciding with the passage of the biblical prophet Ezekiel who calls a principal "Rosh" (head), in Greek 'Rus ', that is, 'Russia'. What's more, the assessment says "rosh mesek" (Russia Moscow). At the time, the former president of the United States, Ronald Reagan, used this argument to point out the Soviets in the Cold War and legitimize the actions of the United States against said empire, during the invasion of Iraq. George H. Bush told former French President Jacques Chirac that "Gog and Magog work in the Middle East" and that he was fulfilling God's will by destroying the enemies of his people. He seemed to clearly say that the US was Gog and Magog and was deliberately eradicating Muslims. On the other hand, various eschatologists have assumed that the Har-mageddon war would be initiated by Gog and Magog, with Russia attacking Israel, although more recently they believe that Gog and Magog is Iran.

Others have assumed that the prophecy (from Ezekiel 38) must be understood in light of the mention given by the apostle John in Revelation 20:8, which alleges that Gog and Magog will attack Israel but after the Messianic Millennium. For others, like me, it is both: Gog will attack Israel at Har-mageddon, and he will also return against Israel after the Millennium. Historical descriptions of Gog and Magog coincide with Hebrew, and even Muslim allusions (although Islamic theologians have different interpretations of the identity of Gog and Magog, from the 10 tribes of Israel, the Jews, or even the communist empires of Russia. and China), although the catalyst for this attack is unclear. What would motivate Russia to attack Israel? They already tried it in the Yom Kippur War, in 1973, and they thought twice. The truth is that the vision of the prophet Ezekiel does not describe a nation but a coalition: "I will break you, and I will put hooks in your jaws, and I will bring out you and all your army, horses and horsemen, fully equipped, great multitude with flags and shields, all of them having swords; Persia, Cush and Put with them; all of them with shield and helmet; Gomer, and all his troops; the house of Togarma, of the northern borders, and all his troops; many towns with you. (Eze. 38:4-6, KJV 60). We know that Persia is Iran (and the prophet Enoch had also already prophesied, like the apostle John, that Persia (Iran) will attack Israel), and according to Bible scholars Cush is Ethiopia, Fut is Libya, Gomer could identify peoples of the Baltic , as well as Togarma.

Although almost all the data about Gog and Magog seem to describe an attack on a peaceful Israel (nothing to do with the current situation), the rabbis think that the coming of the Messiah and the war with Gog and Magog are a simultaneous event. Other prophecies that are not found in the Bible point out the decisive attack against Israel that will come from a leader who will motivate many nations against said nation and will precisely want to confront the Messiah, coinciding with the biblical references about the apocalyptic Beast: "And I saw the beast, the kings of the earth and their armies, gathered together to make war against him who sat on the horse, and against his army. (Rev. 19:19, KJV 60) If the beast represented the UN, that is, the planetary government or New World Order, what is its army? The United Nations army? It speaks of the kings of the earth and their armies, but also identifies the beast as part of the attacking side. Would Gog and Magog and the beast and the kings of the Earth be two groups that will unanimously attack Israel? If Gomer and Togarma are Baltic countries, what relevant troops are there? Well, the NATO army. We would be arguing that at a certain moment the UN and NATO armies would be directed by the Antichrist against Israel, while Libya and Iran also attacked it. Revelation points out that the beast, the false prophet (Belial or Antichrist) and the dragon will be the ones who incite the people beyond the Euphrates to call them to Har-magedon. The prophet Enoch also prophesied it, and clearly said "Persians" and "Medes" (Iran), and the peoples standing just before the Euphrates (Syria and Iraq), and that it stops are those of Iraq and eastern Syria (around to Mosul and the war zones with ISIS) and to Iran. If Ezekiel tells us that the Persians will accompany Gog, and Revelation says that those who will motivate them will be the forces of Antichrist, then this combination of UN and NATO troops with Libya, Iran, Iraq and Syria is evident.

Although, the passages seem to refer to the beast "instigating" the armies of the east (which could also refer to China), not to them directly cooperating together. However, it does not say that it incites the people of the north (which is not clear that it is Russia). Prophets such as Joel and Zechariah point out that in Har-mageddon Israel will be attacked by all the surrounding towns, and although it will begin with strength and advantage, at the end of the conflict it will be in danger and will be saved by the Messiah. But what happens with its great ally in America? The US and Israel are like older and younger brothers who have each other's backs and each has always supported the other. Isn't the US going to support Israel with its powerful army? Biblical Scripture shows that Israel must once again trust in God, not in its allies or its own strength, and be completely alone in the face of its enemies, so where is the US that will not help them, or why? wouldn't it help them?

Let's return to the Jesuits and the point that was left pending. As I said, at Cardinal O'Connor's funeral (after the Superior General of the Jesuit Order, he was the second most powerful man in the world) was the former president of the United States, George W. Bush, but why? that? According to experts in history, one of the most influential and determining families in the movement of the United States in the last half century are the Bushes. What's more, the great war that has occurred between the Bush and Kennedy families since the 1960s is not new (in fact, George HW Bush was director of the CIA shortly after John F. Kennedy was assassinated by CIA agents in Dallas (although they blamed Lee H. Oswald).

It must also be considered that according to leaks of Masonic activities, George Bush Senior himself - a member of Skull&Bones - was codenamed 'Magog'. The Bible speaks of a certain "Gog of Magog", who will be a key element in the end times, a leader who will move a great army to destroy Israel. Although it may seem far-fetched, in my opinion Gog may be a kind of conscience that possesses various leaders over time, and according to an Israeli boy in a vision he said he had several years ago, it was revealed to him that Gog was Barack H. .Obama. I cannot deny the number of coincidences – even if they may seem crude or forced – between the leaders of the US and Gog, and between Babel and American cities like New York or Los Angeles. But when we say the US we must remember that we are not simply referring to the country, but to the elite over said country, which controls the UN itself.

Another substantial fact is that biblical prophecy indicates that the end times will come with world conflicts everywhere simultaneously after the Jews return to their land. We already know more than well that many international conflicts have taken place after the founding of the UN (which was the same one that, after being established, signed by a majority the distribution of the land of Israel and the return of the Jews to Eretz Israel in 1947). 8), but only until the Crimean Crisis (2014) and the Syrian War, many countries had not begun to intervene in specific fights, much less to actively support opposing sides of the confrontation in a kind of New Cold War. However, these conflicts exploded with the Bush family's interests in the other, ancient Babylon: Iraq. It is known that the son of George HW Bush – also a former US president – owns several oil companies, and according to former US Naval Intelligence agent Milton William Cooper, in the 1970s and 80 he directed drug smuggling from South America (especially Colombia) to the US with US Navy ships and planes. He was chosen by MJ-12 for his ties to Skull&Bones, Freemasonry, hidden family networks and his leadership of 'Arbusto Oil' (or also known as 'Arbusto Energy' (arbusto in English is 'Bush')), a Texas oil company. The entire leadership of Bush's government was linked to oil companies.

The elite had already placed a CIA agent in Iraq to control oil from the Caspian, but that agent did not seem to want to continue cooperating with them and decided to lead Iraq to its former glory, and therefore was considered a dictator. Yes, I'm talking about Saddam Hussein. When Hussein betrayed US interests, the first war campaign of the Military-Industrial Complex was directed against him to regain power over the Middle East oil pipelines. This began in 1990 with operations like Desert Storm, but it did not secure the Bush legacy, so Bush Sr.'s son had to finish the family's work and, according to many researchers and testimonies, aided by the Mossad and directed by The CIA was aware of the self-attacks of September

11 to legitimize a new attack against Hussein. Some had already talked about the relationship between the death of John F. Kennedy and Bush Sr., even through the words of his brother Robert, who in front of a crowd yelled at him: "why did you kill my brother?" Curiously, months before the US presidential elections of the end of 2000, the favorite for the presidency, John Kennedy junior (son of JFK) strangely died in a flight accident, on the same days that George H. Bush disappeared without a trace for three days. After Kennedy's death, Bush's son reappeared. Bush's competition died, and he had to leave the prestigious magazine he had created, called 'George', and where he criticized the Bushes.

Many people know today that the main members of Bush Jr.'s cabinet (Condoleezza Rice, Dick Chenney, Donald Rumsfelt), who promoted the invasion of Iraq, had oil companies, but not many know that Osama Bin Laden was an agent of the CIA for Afghan military training against the Russians. The farce of the war on terror began with the use of the Muslim faith as a trigger and alleged weapons of mass destruction that were never found. Even so, Barack Obama did not order the place to be abandoned, but in one way or another combat forces remained there until Trump's mandate. What benefit did the US get from pursuing Bin Laden in Afghanistan? Keep the country's opium production under control of the US military. The most important thing with this is that the war on terror became an unprecedented international war that is still alive, and that has maintained control of the oil of Iraq (the ancient Babylon).

This has been the trigger for a series of conflicts in the region and the instigation of extremist Islamic armed groups with different general interests but with the West and Israel as a common enemy. Thanks to this, many revolutions and coups d'état have been unleashed in the Muslim world and terrorist attacks have been perpetrated even on European and American soil. It could be said that Babylon has awakened the monster of war worldwide, and that monster is becoming increasingly larger and more dangerous, and threatens the entire planet, as the biblical prophet Isaiah prophesied in his book, chapter "9-11." "...9-11? Yes, like September 11 of the fateful 2001...

Describes chapter 11 of Isaiah 9: "The buildings fell, but with hewn stones we will rebuild; The sycamores have been cut down, but we will replace them with cedars. Therefore Iaheveh raises up adversaries of Rezin against them, and incites their enemies, the Arameans in the east and the Philistines in the west, who devour Israel with their mouths full. With all this his wrath does not turn away, and his hand is still stretched out."

On the other hand, in Vedanta literature we also find mention of the interesting matter of Gogmagog. There he relates that [Dharma (Righteousness or Law) told Kalki] "Right now, infidels like Saka, Kamboja, Sabara, etc. They are under the control of Koli and that powerful Koli has defeated me by taking advantage of the influence of time. Godly men are being tortured and sent to the flames. That is why I have come for your protection." (Kalki Purana, III, verse 22) Thus, Kalki, surrounded by his allies, set out towards the desired place to conquer the infidels like Khasha, Kamboja, Sabara, Barbarians, etc.... The people living there carry out the orders of the women. Hearing that Kalki had come for battle, the angry Koli, along with his allies, sons and grandsons, arrived riding a chariot from the city of Bishasan. Seeing Koli, Kalki ordered his followers to engage him in battle. (Kalki Purana, III, verses 32, 33, 35, 36) Some see here an analogy with Revelation 19:19.

Lord Kalki, along with his soldiers armed with various types of weapons, participated in the war with Kok and Bikok. These two brothers are supreme demons, great fanatics and adepts in the art of war. These brothers are closely connected, powerful, difficult to defeat, and even feared by the gods. (Kalki Purana, III, verses 43 and 44) The elements of surprise here are the description of the war with the brothers called "Kok and Bikok", who are allied with Koli. Note the similarity to Gog and Magog described in the biblical book of Revelation and "Yajooj and Majooj" described in Islamic prophecies. They soon entered the city of Bishasan, the capital of Koli, and burned the city with a fire missile. Along with the city, Koli was also burnt down and his children and relatives were destroyed. (Kalki Purana, III, verses 9 and 10) Kalki's army entered the capital city of Koli called Bishasan (Babylon?) and burned the entire city along with Koli itself and its citizens. Similarly, Kalki's allies used various types of weapons and defeated the countries and their kings allied with Koli. Compare this to Revelations.

VI.

OBAMA, THE SNAKE'S TONGUE

Does Obama plan to stay for a third term? Tracing testimonies, prophecies, news and classified documentation, we can come across many convincing points that suggest that the US economy is about to collapse, and Barack Obama used that pretext – as well as an instigation of war towards Putin and a Islamic terrorist movement - to stay in office, presenting an unprecedented scenario with regard to presidential elections and takeover of government, and the fate of the world. People like Brian Carn, Hank Kunneman and James Bailey talk about a woman who will be in power in the US and carry out Obama's plans. Brian Carn said that it was specifically about Hillary Clinton, and these men who supposedly speak from prophecy or visions assume that there will be some kind of electoral reversal.

Another man who professes to have prophetic dreams commented on his blog: "I watched President Obama permanently leave the United States after appointing a woman to carry out the final stages of an evil plan to murder the American people. "They were planning to start killing us shortly after this woman took over, which led me to believe that they had conspired with foreign military forces to invade our land, although that was not part of the dream." (James Bailey, 2014) A key point, as also mentioned by the Canadian chaplain Tania Fiolleau in November 2016 – according to her visions – is that non-American troops are about to take said country (the UN for weapons confiscation, and the Chinese to invade). A Norwegian soldier, a member of the UN troops, shared on a preppers (survivalists) blog that they (UN units) were destined to enter the US between January or February to go house to house taking up arms . of the citizens, and anyone who opposed would be shot to death.

Both Brian Carn and Joanie Stahl, among others, spoke of key events before an imminent "end of the year", related to presidential elections. Carn said on December 4, 2015 that this would have to do with the distrust of the American people regarding the value of voting, which reminds us of the news that has been circulating since mid-November of this year regarding the election of Donald Trump . You should not give too much emphasis to the details, because in effect prophecies are not invariable warnings designed by the whim of a god or destiny, but rather mathematical convergences resulting from variables in the space-time continuum depending on the decisions of each and every person. one of the individuals involved in the processes of change in a place, and they respond, above all, to the thought system of collective consciences. This means that on various occasions there are things that are planned to happen due to the movements that are being carried out and according to the behavior of the critical mass of participants, but when one or more people involved who generate a greater impact on these processes change their attitude. , in the way of thinking and carrying out decisions in another direction, the space-time continuity is altered in certain variables.

Let's look at the case of the economy, assuming dates between the end of December 2015 and the beginning of 2017, before in 2012/2013, before in 2008, before in 2001. It is not that they were wrong, or not completely, but that the pawns involved in situations that would lead to substantial changes they did things that caused significant changes. 9/11 prevented the financial collapse that was coming, but it ultimately occurred in 2008-2009. It is not that things have to happen yes or yes, but that as long as the collective mass of consciousness of society does not modify its beliefs, emotions and ideas, there will be no significant variables that eliminate the destiny that they are marking with their vibrational processes. This is because vibration creates and modifies matter, however, it changes facts, it alters reality. In other words, as long as humanity does not change in the meantime in its mind and heart, there is no reason why the need for a Harmageddon to purify our planet will disappear.

Almost everyone who has spoken, prophetically or statistically, regarding final events related to these current months (and generally these last few years), has always incorporated the financial component, referring to an economic collapse, an imminent market crash, a catastrophe. financial. George Soros is one of those who has stated that the dollar will be devalued so that there is global financial "equity" (with a dollar, or strong currency, this would not be possible), although he did not say it in a prophetic sense. As was made known by the SuperStation95 news website, and other subsequent media, the New York police had found the ICE (Immigration and Customs Enforcement Agency) officer dead in the city's port in early May 2016. Said man had left suicide notes in his house, stating that the president would imminently take power of the country under the pretext of the fall of the dollar, and would use as an excuse a supposed 'cyber attack', presumably on the banking system (and let's look at how many accusations Obama has been making lately about Putin regarding issues of this nature). This would lead to martial law and domestic control protocols by FEMA (Federal Emergency Management Agency) coming into action as the military moves overseas.

Brian Carn stated that "a witch hunt lies at the end of Obama's reign because there will be an astonishing spectacle that will shock the souls of America and send the spirits of those who embrace the work of Presidential wisdom. An earthquake will come. There will be a forced conclusion that will come upon the White House. After this he said that the voting scandal will surprise Americans, and Hillary Clinton would be seen declaring victory. In the end it didn't happen, and the same with Trump, who should have won the presidency for the second time. Logically, the media play a leading role in having the ability to create a great influence on people and change their way of thinking, so that mass consciousness alters the space-time continuum .

A prophecy of the Sibylline Oracles, regarding the end times, maintains that a woman will lead world leadership in chaos – if the prophecy is correctly interpreted -. Some believe this could even apply to Kamala Harris, the US vice president, in case Joe Biden is unable to continue leading the country. Joanie Stahl had already commented in January 2016 that Obama would have an even more important position than president, to the point of possibly directing the United Nations itself, and Tania Fiolleau said that so far the American president has shown his charismatic face, But – as many people who have had premonitory dreams describe – Obama " is about to show his true colors ." According to Patricia Green, Jesus defined him as a "forked-tongued serpent," a demon who is about to show his true intentions. It is a very strange scenario that these people propose, with an annulment of the votes on Trump and the approval of the election towards Hillary, but with Obama being in power, despite all these setbacks. Obama certainly continues to be seen here and there from time to time, still being a possible candidate for a relevant place in this empire of the Antichrist that is on the rise.

Another point is that Stahl commented that a senior official in the US secret service, who works directly with Obama, would have told him that Trump would be elected, he would not be president, but he would be in the White House to take charge of a mass deportation. before martial law is established. Incidentally, another component that appears again and again in recent prophecies is the imposition of the imminent state of emergency in the US, along with the onset of a nuclear war. That nuclear war will be started by the US against Russia; China will help Russia and invade the US; Russia will attack the US with biological weapons... this scenario is graphically seen in the vision that Canadian animation designer Louis Lefebvre (who worked on the creation of 'Gollum' in The Lord of the Rings) captured in his film 'I , Pet Goat II' a few years ago, where you see Bush passing Obama, and with Obama the events of the great tribulation. Among them, once we have seen episodes such as terrorism and the invasion of the East by oil, we can see the Statue of Liberty being demolished (specifically the hand with the torch, a symbol of freedom), a child in whose eyes we see ' Markets Plunge', American B-2 planes shooting at an Islamic center (very similar to those in Turkey, such as Konya or Istanbul) and an atomic explosion. Then you see Chinese tanks crossing giant ribs and frames that assume war in Africa...

Steve Jackson, who designed roll cards, released a deck in 1994 where he showed many events that reveal the ideas of the world of secrecy and the shadow government, and among the most important (called 'New World Order') the one of ' Third World War', with the image of an atomic explosion in a city (in fact, David Brennan is another of many who prophetically warn of nuclear war where the US will also be attacked). Other similar letters announce an 'Energy Crisis', the Great Tribulation, the Blue Beam, the Rapture, martial law, the flooding of the US coasts, the nullification of laws and the activity of the Military-Industrial Complex.

All of these points come together and make more sense when we review the prophecies about the judgments that will come to the United States – which Rabbi Jonathan Kahn also warns of – such as those described by Sara Menet (1979) and many others. people, despite the fact that Patricia Green (May 2015) details them quite well, clarifying that they must have already occurred during Barack Obama's mandate. However, this has been postponed, according to some, such as Archbishop Viganó, due to a spirit of opposition that holds back the Antichrist, "until he is removed." It is my understanding that this force that is stopping the Antichrist is not just Donald Trump, as the archbishop interprets, but all of us, the resistance, who oppose the New World Order throughout the globe. Both in the Bible codes and in other dreams and visions of more people, this element of said man (Obama) and his role in the last days appears, as the Israeli boy Nathan points out in September 2015, when he says that Obama will lead the World War III, and will even be behind the armies that will later come against Israel. Could the American unconscious collective consciousness have prevented Obama's intentions several years ago?

In 1939, the psychic Edgar Cayce saw that the last president of the USA would be the 44th president (Obama), and he would be black, something that the Bulgarian psychic Baba Vanga is also said to have prophesied between the 70s and 90s. Let us remember the psychographies of Benjamín Solari, such as the one from 1938, when he stated: "the North American stove will be lit by the new black." In 1971, another servant of God, Alan Martin, dreamed of the same themes of martial law and disaster over the United States. .USA, looking at each of the presidential administrations. At that time he had no reference data to know when what he saw would happen, until in 1995 it became clear to him, and they showed him the name of the pattern, with which he saw the last administration that there would be over the United States, which would be the 9th after JFK, that is, referring to the case of Barry Soetoro (aka Barack Obama).

If we "set our sights on things above" and from there we look down, it is clear that things happen that we do not understand, and that one day they will be clarified. We will understand if Obama did not see it appropriate to do what he planned and/or the elites recommended that he let Hilary Clinton follow her strategy, convinced that it was in no way possible that Donald Trump would win. Once they saw that Trump won, and that it was a major obstacle to their plans, they accelerated their agenda with the COVID project and sabotaged the re-election to put a new pawn in his place: Biden. Furthermore, if we consider that the Bible had prophesied the fall of a great city or country, which it calls 'great harlot' and 'great Babylon', this makes even more sense. Most opinions of researchers and believers about the identity of this city-country confirm that it is New York, or in its context the USA, and that its time is now. An example of many are the cases explained by Sherry Shriner, Gary H. Kah, David Wilkerson, Christian John Price, Joel Richardson, Carl Gallups, Paul McGuire, Jonathan Kahn, Tom Horn, among many others, to clarify the "Mystery of Babylon." " and the New World Order, whose headquarters is the US.

Although it seems that there are contradictions in the way in which these events would begin in January or February of this year, what it seems is that there is a combination of situations. For example, Pastor Ken Peters, in 1980 - before "converting to Christ" - had a long, very detailed dream about the events of the great tribulation and the global rule of the Antichrist, and in it he mentions that it all started suddenly after a massive earthquake, after which laws immediately changed and cities became militarized. He defines Hummers and UN soldiers in a context that at that time he could not have known yet, but coincides with the data on national emergency that would facilitate the seizure of administrative power for the state of emergency in the USA.

Some speak of terrorist attacks (as especially mentioned by Glenda Jackson, who stated on TV that in a vision she saw that Obama was working with the Muslim Brotherhood to bring chaos and retain power in the White House), school shootings, an attack by electromagnetic pulse, an environmental disaster (earthquake, solar radiation or volcanic explosion), civil war (as has even been documented since 2014 by the Pentagon or politicians such as Ben

Carson (Republican presidential candidate in 2016) or Ron Paul (former congressman and also former presidential candidate, who is also fully convinced of the imminent fall of the dollar), the fall of the markets, a world war... however, one does not seem to contradict the other, but rather, precisely, these events will be combined or almost simultaneous as a start of the great tribulation that precedes the Antichrist.

An example is when on October 13, 2016, Barack Obama signed an Executive Order regarding supposed solar radiation, an illogical argument, given that not even the scientific parties that study solar behavior can foresee this, and even less so with the pressure that he defined : "they have 120 days to prepare the electrical systems..." Why 120 days? Were you expecting a maneuver with EMP (Electromagnetic Pulse attack)? A US lieutenant colonel, who worked on secret projects, gave Alexander Backman a lot of information regarding this matter. They spoke in an interview about the use of electromagnetic weapons and the plans of Russia and China to use them against the United States. They commented that for some reason they considered that the end of 2016 was a decisive moment to carry out these attack projects and of invasion of the US, so we would be within the time range that points to this. This was largely confirmed to the US government by former Russian Colonel Stanislav Lunev, when he defected from Russia in 1992 and immigrated to the US. Something similar was said by Dick Cheney and Tom Ridge, former advisor from the president of Homeland Security, who says that he was forced to leave his position because he could no longer handle such serious information. The issue of an EMP attack has been mentioned several times, even with very direct messages, such as in the new X-Files series, and it is a very clever masterstroke if they intend to blame the Soviets or Muslim hackers for restarting shutting down the network of the financial markets.

Also from prepper blogs one finds testimonies from war veterans and even American citizens, who speak of the exaggerated mobilization of foreign troops within the United States and also of heavy weapons. There is also talk of millions of combat ammunition purchased by the police, the militarization of police posts, maneuvers by UN soldiers within US territory and military exercises for operation within cities. Among these testimonies, a Texan commented that a Chinese man with whom he had an altercation yelled at him, telling him that his government (China) was going to soon invade his country. Many of these news and opinions from soldiers who have kept their names anonymous, say that it is true, and that the invasion will be in 2017 from the west coast, entering through California and Texas, and that the US will be abandoned to its own devices. luck. An example of this was the vision of Sarah Hoffman, talking about said invasion and how the US troops were not in the country to defend its citizens – something that the ICE agent who committed suicide also stated – but abroad, of So the civilians who will survive the tribulation will defend themselves against the Chinese with their own weapons.

The problems in Taiwan, the Philippines, Syria, Turkey and Eastern Europe are getting worse. A NATO war led by American forces is about to break out against Russia in eastern Europe. Operation 'Atlantic Resolve' has involved at least 3,500 US Army operatives, including 1,600 tanks, and not only American troops, but French, German and British troops. The great military mobilization has reactivated bases of operations and established new camp points in Poland, Romania, Lithuania, Latvia and Slovenia, without counting the thousands of American troops that are constantly moving and replacing in Syria and Iraq. An example of this incredible mobilization is the armed forces that arrived from the US through the United Kingdom and are being installed at the base in Bremerhaven (Germany) even during this month of January.

Is Barack Obama planning a false flag attack to activate the protocols that transfer state, local and federal power to FEMA? The truth is that at the executive level, if there was a natural disaster, a financial collapse or a war, the president-elect would only need his signature to be accompanied by that of the Attorney General in order to legally impose martial law and suppress opinion and power. of Congress for up to 5 years. Everything that has been moving since Ronald Reagan with executive orders is clearly the establishment of the bases for a mobilization of federal power in the hands of military power. Once that has occurred, what would determine the end of said event to reestablish power? federal of the nation? If, as some suspect, this is the "death wound" from which the beast survives, however, the government would be restored, but by then subject to the parameters of the new global government, the kingdom of the Antichrist.

Pastor TD Hale related, on December 28, 2011, regarding the USA, seeing in a dream: "...suddenly, I began to see bombs that had fallen everywhere. The country was totally destroyed. It seemed like things were totally just erased, grass, trees, everything. Everything was gone, burned. There was nothing left. There was nothing in the trees. It wasn't just a total disaster. [...] There was no food. There was not any water. I could see babies crying, adults, men all crying, holding on to their families. They were asking God for mercy. As I moved along I saw people running, looking for their loved ones who had completely disappeared and calling everywhere, [...] Madness had taken over. I could see people throwing themselves off bridges, to commit suicide. [...] I saw the mass hysteria, riots and all kinds of things that broke out in the city streets [...] I didn't see them grab things like televisions and electronic devices. They were grabbing the food. [...] They were grabbing water.

They were grabbing everything they could get their hands on to sustain their lives. It was about survival. I realized that this was different from the riots that had been seen in the past. [...] I saw them pushing some shelves and leaving the electronics aside... They were seriously trying to get the food, the bread, the boxes of water. [...] The protesters were fighting among themselves. I saw a man take a gun out of his pocket and shoot another man right in the head. [...] I found myself standing on the back side of the White House. [...] I saw the president of the United States, President Obama, standing on the balcony and I saw a shotgun in his hands. [...I heard a scream] When I turned my head to see where the scream was coming from, what I saw flying high in the air was a majestic eagle flying in the air around Washington DC [...] I suddenly saw the president of the United States point with the shotgun and shot and killed the eagle and it fell to the ground. When he did I looked back at him and he just had a smile on his face. And [...] the words I heard in the dream, "I've done it and I'm not going to have to deal with this in my administration." Then there was dead silence. Then I heard a voice saying, "Tell the people that what has been done is my will, that this comes from my hand, this is the hand of the Almighty, both in the generation of the righteous and the cursed. The righteous will find their I walk and they want to know what to do. The damned one will wander around without a compass because the cup is full."

What is clear is that if all these forecasts, prophecies and data – which they also complement with more information that is very long to provide now – rule Donald Trump out of the scenario (except to deport a large number of immigrants), they insinuate that Hillary could considered the winner after a review of the presidential elections and they categorically put Obama still in power, against all odds, we then have that the sum of information makes it seem that this Kenyan Muslim, Barry Sotoro (his real name) who is still in The White House will take advantage of an event that he himself has secretly motivated, to bring chaos to the US and activate the Executive Orders and HR protocols that have been signed since the mid-1950s. In this way he will be like a dictator. , and will not only sell the US on its own in the face of its enemies and the country's internal cataclysm, but will also use foreigners themselves to deal with a war against Russia from Europe. That means that Obama would begin the Apocalypse, and this will be clear in a few days.

Thousands of UN Troops await an Order

«Base operators refused to confirm, deny or discuss these sightings. Lately, rumors and reports about the presence of foreign troops in the US working with our armed forces have been hitting the public conscience. Originally government sources denied these reports, but now official reports are confirming what eyewitnesses had been reporting. "Russia itself confirms that the Obama administration has requested 15,000 Russian troops to train with FEMA in the event of a 'SHTF' scenario, particularly in the Washington DC, Maryland and Virginia area." You might be wondering what 'SHTF' is. In the preppers vocabulary (of survivalists or prepared for the end of the world) it is an equivalent to 'Doomsday' (day of final judgment) or the 'Kill Shot' (decisive blow), referring to some type of catastrophic event (natural disaster). , terrorist attack, financial collapse, nuclear war) that would trigger the Apocalypse.

These types of reports state: "It appears that foreign troops are working with US troops, in the practice of urban warfare, civil unrest and civil unrest scenarios. In Colorado, rumors that Russian troops practice to deal with terrorist attacks and martial law scenarios have been proven correct by our own military. Peterson Air Force Base in Colorado is another base that is used. Located in Germany is the Marshall center [...] Right now, the 'Department of Defense' is holding classes on counterterrorism. Of course, the definition of 'terrorism' belongs to the proponents of the 'new world order'. According to the definition used by the New World Order, a terrorist is one who opposes a takeover of his nation. "That would make all NWO resisters and/or anyone who does not agree with the new world order seen as potential terrorists."

"The problem with foreign troops that are trained to intervene on American soil in 'SHTF' scenarios, which could occur here, is that they have no loyalty to our Constitution, they have no loyalty to the inherent rights that have always been ours as American citizens. , and have no basis for restriction in any action they may perceive to be necessary, without regard to our laws. They have no constitutional right to intervene in the internal events of our country. NATO and the UN have the same goal, mission and function: to subvert the sovereignty of the US and the rest of the world, so that they all become a fascist world state. Our government officials have proven time and time again here lately that they are not to be trusted. "Congress is nothing more than a rubber stamp that the government wants, it is not the representative body of the citizens as it should be." A clear example of these US takeover maneuvers called 'Jade Helm 15', which "were based on the eponymous US military training exercise that took place in several US states in the summer 2015 [...] Approximately 1,200 soldiers were hired during the exercise." (https://en.wikipedia.org/wiki/Jade_Helm_15_conspiracy_theories [1])

1. https://en.wikipedia.org/wiki/Jade_Helm_15_conspiracy_theories

VII.

FROM DEPORTATION TO MARTIAL LAW

The US Congress, in its 110th resolution, established a 'Council of Governors' for cases of national emergency and advice to federal generals. It consists of the National Defense Authorization Act of 2008 that George W. Bush signed on January 28 of that year, and that Barack Obama officially established through Executive Order 13528, issued on January 11, 2010. These governors and His generals control – and with greater power they would control – the entire US, but not in the form of 50 states, but in 10 regions. These extensions are called 'FEMA Regions'. The military power of the US, whether individually or in the participation of NATO and/or the blue helmets (UN army) is a latent danger.

FEMA regions are numbered according to their "mega-cities" that are estimated as reference frames. The 10 FEMA regions and their base cities are: Boston (I), New York (II), Philadelphia (III), Atlanta (IV), Chicago (V), Denton (VI), Kansas City (VII), Denver (VIII), Oakland (IX) and Seattle (X). Before the election of Donald Trump, the body was established with the members that had been there since approximately 2010. The council of governors has two co-presidents (until then the Democrat Dannel Malloy, of Connecticut, and the Republican Terry Branstad, of Iowa) and the group advises the main secretaries of the federal apparatus: the Secretary of Defense, the Secretary of Homeland Security and the

White House National Security Council on matters related to the National Guard.

Those who followed the electoral campaign between Joe Biden and Donald Trump, outside of manipulated sources, learned that Biden was helped by various institutions, powers and world leaders to win, even when Trump had swept the votes , and it still continues to have a majority of supporters, both outside and inside the US. The last US presidents have been in the eye of the hurricane as they were the stones chosen to push the fall of said country. When Obama decided he would not use force to position himself for a third term, Trump was supposed to do his part. When it became clear that Trump's intentions were opposed to the Illuminati, they chose Biden for the dissolution of the USA

Americans' lack of support for Biden is unique in American history when it comes to the popularity of a president. Although, at a constitutional level Biden is not really president, but that is another topic to discuss that will not be the case in this book. Biden has played his role as a destabilizing piece of the federated states of the union. In mid September 2021, he announced measures that the Ministry of Labor should take to force the American population not to work if they were not vaccinated. 21 states of the union responded in opposition to his audacity. The vaccination agenda not only has the components that I talk about at length and in detail in my work 'COVID, The Greatest Conspiracy in History', but also the discriminatory social pressure that leaves millions of people around the globe no more chance. to have to resign from their jobs. Not only are these world leaders bribed to do such an outrage to their own compatriots, but in systemic terms of the economy and work they are a priority.

As I explain in my recent work, we are entering the Fourth Industrial Revolution, the era of robotics, artificial intelligence, super computers and drones, so there are millions of people who have no place to locate them, since it is not It is not possible to continue giving them a salary nor is it possible for them to continue pretending that their employment is functional. Strictly speaking, more than 70% of the jobs that still exist in the 21st century are not viable. They will not want to tell this truth to the population, so they make themselves resign. Just considering that more money has been printed in the current two years of the plan-demic than since the change from the gold standard to the petrodollar, the inflation bubble is growing at full speed and ready to burst at any moment . The more help they offer to people, the bigger the snowball becomes, because the GDP does not increase, on the contrary, it decreases and everything is becoming more expensive. If production does not increase, where does the money they are giving to society come from?

Reports from alternative US media have been reporting massive movements of UN troops within the US in recent years. Sometimes these maneuvers are not very common, but in certain periods of suspicious movements at the US level, internationally, this is observed more frequently (http://govtslaves.info/un-troops-landing-at-us-air-force-bases/ [1], http://www.thecommonsenseshow.com/2016/06/28/ why-are-un-troops-on-american-soil/ [2], http://www.thecommonsenseshow.com/2016/08/22/can-us-citizens-defeat-un-troops-on-america-soil/ [3], http://viralliberty.com/breaking-first-texas-now-virginia-un-troops-mobilizing-across-america-happening/ [4],

1. http://govtslaves.info/un-troops-landing-at-us-air-force-bases/
2. http://www.thecommonsenseshow.com/2016/06/28/why-are-un-troops-on-american-soil/
3. http://www.thecommonsenseshow.com/2016/08/22/can-us-citizens-defeat-un-troops-on-america-soil/
4. http://viralliberty.com/breaking-first-texas-now-virginia-un-troops-mobilizing-across-america-happening/

http://allnewspipeline.com/
Preparation_For_The_Event_Accelerates.php [5],
http://allnewspipeline.com
/UN_Troops_Across_America_Why.php [6]).

An example, from the 'Bk Hyland' website, states: "There have been several sightings of strange civilian planes landing at US Air Force bases, all of them carrying UN troops and/or having UN markings (or no badge). My husband, a Vietnam veteran, has been going to and from the 'VA Medical Hospital-Overton Brooks' three times a week this month. Barksdale Air Force Base, one of the most secure SAC (Strategic Air Command) bases in the nation, has observed unusual flights of 'C-130' or 'C-136' flying at Barksdale Air Force Base and on the ground at all hours. [...] The interstate runs past the front of the base and is clearly visible without restrictions. Barksdale is where President 'George W. Bush' landed on 9-11, and it is a well-protected facility. These flights have been reported by other citizens and several of the soldiers working inside the base have reported that UN troops are supplied to the US, having labels on their clothing and military names. When our soldiers question this, the soldiers are told that they did not see what they just saw.

Death wound

If the 'Roman Babel' - which was disguised as 'North American Babel' (in terms of focalization of hegemony) - is replaced by the 'global Babel', this "internal war" could be where the general structure itself is hurt: «And one of his heads as if wounded to death, and his plague of death healed. And all the earth marveled after the beast..." (Rev. 13:3) The phoenix symbol of Freemasonry hides this mystery. No one before or after explains what that "plague" (in Greek 'Pligí') consisted of that practically caused that "head" to die - or it did, but put another way. The Beast has settled on 7

5. http://allnewspipeline.com/Preparation_For_The_Event_Accelerates.php

6. http://allnewspipeline.com/UN_Troops_Across_America_Why.php

mountains (governments) and on 7 kingdoms, but it is assumed that by this time the 6th will have fallen and the 7th will replace it. Unless he who "is," who would represent Rome-USA, falls, and is restored. So the government that "rises from the ashes" is the perfected version of the previous one and with the entire model updated. Therefore it is still the same beast, only with internal changes and changes in appearance.

The chess player sacrifices the queen - if necessary - to win the game. That kingdom sacrifices itself to achieve a greater objective, and thus separate itself from the Vatican and any remnant of Christianity that may still exist. That is the phoenix of the new economy, it is the phoenix of the new USA (then it would be the number 1 head of the global 10, which would no longer be the USA as such, but a 'section' that would encompass what still today they are Canada, the USA and Mexico). The text does not say that it is 'one of the horns', but 'one of its heads', but, if 5 have already passed, one is and another must come, how would the world recognize that 'head' if it were already one? past', unless it was 'contemporary'?

When then does the 'big city' fall? He does it progressively, I estimate that over just a couple of years (not even close to decades): "The seventh angel poured out his bowl into the air; And a loud voice came out of the temple of heaven, from the throne, saying, It is done. Then there were lightnings and voices and thunder, and a great shaking of the earth, an earthquake so great, such as had never occurred since men have been on the earth. And the great city was divided into three parts, and the cities of the nations fell; and great Babylon came in remembrance before God, to give him the cup of the wine of the fierceness of his wrath." (Rev. 16:17-19) This end is described with that great earthquake and the hail from heaven, which are the end of the judgment on this hidden power that "has corrupted the earth with her fornication," and is guilty in addition to the death of God's 'servants' (Rev. 19:1-2)

The end of Democracy

The laws in that country are increasingly reinforced to ensure that the police apparatus has absolute power in the streets, as has happened since 2020 in almost the rest of the nations of the world. Consequently, to knock down the economy and then avoid civil uprising, they have removed weapons and bullets from the National Guard Armories, militarized police posts, changed the type of police weapons to military rifles, they have bought 4 million hollow point bullets (for assault weapons) and another 2.8 million were already on the way by 2013 (http://www.forbes.com/sites/ralphbenko/2013/03/11/1-6-billion -rounds-of-ammo-for-homeland-security-its-time-for-a-national-conversation/#4c098bee5e01 [7]), they have armored and reinforced the protection and equipment of police vehicles, they have given greater powers to the police force (http://www.usatoday.com/story/news/world/2017/01/25/trump-plans-ramp-up-deportations/97052306/ [8]or http://www.washingtontimes.com/news/2016/nov /22/pentagon-personal-guns-firearms-allowed-on-base/ [9]) to act as "judges and executioners", they have enabled detention centers that were created in the FEMA REX-84 program and other facilities throughout the territory of USA, I have even in Alaska (where one of the worst concentration camps the country has) and Canada.

The story of immigration consists of reducing the defense capacity of the people, getting rid of the belligerent components that could represent a greater civil offensive. The government knows

7. http://www.forbes.com/sites/ralphbenko/2013/03/11/1-6-billion-rounds-of-ammo-for-homeland-security-its-time-for-a-national-conversation/#a5c02393e59c943d6a75a9241140faca34c098bee5e01

8. http://www.usatoday.com/story/news/world/2017/01/25/trump-plans-ramp-up-deportations/97052306/

9. http://www.washingtontimes.com/news/2016/nov/22/pentagon-personal-guns-firearms-allowed-on-base/

that Hispanics and blacks are the poorest societies and that they traffic the most in weapons and drugs, and they control entire neighborhoods in a large number of cities, especially in metropolises. These gangs would be a great opposition to the curfew and the state of exception, which is why strategies such as fear of viruses have helped reduce this danger of civil uprising. That's why they deport Hispanics and imprison blacks. Once this threat is reduced, according to leaked information from senior officials, there are more than 10,000 UN troops carrying out maneuvers inside the US for a long time, to enter house by house and take weapons from citizens (https : //dailyreckoning.com/when-they-come-for-your-guns-you-will-turn-them-over/ [10]). The NSA and the CIA have provided the officers of these groups with databases of all Americans who have a history of opposition to the system, retention of weapons, survivalist interests, activism, radicalism, etc., so that they will be the first to be detained once the mass deportation ends. These people will be treated as "highly dangerous," even if they have no criminal record.

Legally now it would still be premeditated to prosecute the entire nation if there was a popular uprising, and it could not be controlled. However, what Trump does is create hostilities and incitement against all groups that are not passive. That means that the NSA, the FBI (which was the one who actually created Facebook to register databases: https://www.theguardian.com/world/2010/mar/16/fbi-facebook-crime-study [11], http ://venturebeat.com/2014/05/15/how-the-nsa-fbi-made-facebook-the-perfect-mass-surveillance-tool/ [12], http://venturebeat.com/2014/05/15/ how-the-nsa-fbi-made-facebook-the-perfect-mass-surveillance-tool/ [13], https://socioecohistory.wordpress.com/2016/09/29/how-the-nsa-

10. https://dailyreckoning.com/when-they-come-for-your-guns-you-will-turn-them-over/

11. https://www.theguardian.com/world/2010/mar/16/fbi-facebook-crime-study

12. http://venturebeat.com/2014/05/15/how-the-nsa-fbi-made-facebook-the-perfect-mass-surveillance-tool/

fbi-made-facebook -the-perfect-mass-surveillance-tool/ [14]) and the CIA already know the groups of people - who will oppose what is happening throughout - across the US, and they just want to add to those who have not yet decided. For many years the US has been calm and with few protests and in minorities, but with large demonstrations (which are discussed and organized digitally, through gmail, facebook, twitter, whats app, blogs, websites, etc.) they already know of those who are the option to the government and reject the legitimacy of the governmental state and its decisions. These people are listed as "terrorists", even though they really are not, and will be prosecuted as if they were terrorists.

The more uproar Trump causes, the more people will rebel and the more reasons they will give to strengthen the Police State to contain the marches and protests (https://en.wikipedia.org/wiki/Federal_law_enforcement_in_the_United_States [15]), and pass laws in Congress to prohibit the demonstrations and mass gatherings of people (thus they would undermine the start of any revolution). And Trump doesn't need to say anything. The American people throughout 2021 have already made it clear that they do not agree with the measures that are being taken in the so-called pandemic. Some of these statements have even encouraged the use of force and weapons if necessary, and things do not change. Although, to carry out such an action, too many pieces located in their respective places and a cunningly prepared strategic plan are necessary, but take away the people's freedoms and they will create a tinderbox. Furthermore, touch their finances, and you will have awakened a roaring lion.

---

13. http://venturebeat.com/2014/05/15/how-the-nsa-fbi-made-facebook-the-perfect-mass-surveillance-tool/

14. https://socioecohistory.wordpress.com/2016/09/29/how-the-nsa-fbi-made-facebook-the-perfect-mass-surveillance-tool/

15. https://en.wikipedia.org/wiki/Federal_law_enforcement_in_the_United_States

The people believe that they elect their leaders, but those leaders were chosen by the elite 6 months, 2 years or sometimes even much longer before the presidential candidates even began, especially in countries like the US. The apostle Paul warned about the " "birth pangs" (the way Jesus describes the prelude to his coming, and which is also the way Orthodox Jews call the events prior to the appearance of the Messiah) that represent the 'Great Tribulation' with which the birth begins. Apocalypse that would have several keys (these are complemented by other prophecies, and they are: the return of the Jews to the land of Israel, the high increase in technology, science and general knowledge, apostasy and a false peace and brief security): «For you know perfectly well that the day of the Lord will come like a thief in the night; for when they say, Peace and security, then sudden destruction will come upon them, as pain upon a pregnant woman, and they will not escape. (1 Thes. 5:2-3, RVA 60).

VIII.
WHAT DOES DONALD TRUMP PLAY?

Trump clearly played one public face and another to attack the Deep State. You just have to observe how this man attacks all social groups, whether doctors (https://intereconomia.com/tendencias/salud/trump-ordena-al-fbi-que-intervenga-al-cdc-por-el-encubrimiento -de-vacunas-contra-el-autismo-20170130-0933/ [1]), environmentalists (http://internacional.elpais.com/internacional/2017/01/25/actualidad/1485372859_073422.html [2]), Muslims (http:// www.abc.es/internacional/abci-democratas-reclaman-trump-revoque-orden-migratoria-201701310225_noticia.html [3]) – which would only justify violent actions in response -, the anti-Zionists – such as the UN – (http://www.eluniversal.com.mx/articulo/mundo/2017/01/28/netanyhau-respalda-muro-de-trump-es-una-gran-idea-afirmam [4]or http://internacional.elpais.com/internacional/ 2017/01/25/actualidad/1485372859_073422.html [5]or

1. https://intereconomia.com/tendencias/salud/trump-ordena-al-fbi-que-intervenga-al-cdc-por-el-encubrimiento-de-vacunas-contra-el-autismo-20170130-0933/
2. http://internacional.elpais.com/internacional/2017/01/25/actualidad/1485372859_073422.html
3. http://www.abc.es/internacional/abci-democratas-reclaman-trump-revoque-orden-migratoria-201701310225_noticia.html
4. http://www.eluniversal.com.mx/articulo/mundo/2017/01/28/netanyhau-respalda-muro-de-trump-es-una-gran-idea-afirmam

https://actualidad.rt.com/actualidad/229285-eeuu-propuesta-ley-onu [6]), neighbors (https://actualidad.rt.com/actualidad/229626 - trump-decreto-reconstruir-fuerzas-armadas-eeuu [7]or http://www.elmundo.es/internacional/2017/01/25/ 58884bd122601d473d8b45bf.html [8]), independentists (https://actualidad.rt.com/actualidad/ 229632-eeuu-california-indepencia-separarse-votacion [9]or http://www.merca20.com/ california-le-advierte-a-trump-defendera-a-los-mexicanos/ [10]), speaks Spanish (http://www .bolsamania.com/noticias/ internacional/donald-trump-cierra-la-version-en-espanol-de-la-web-de-la-casa-blanca—2470684.html [11])

Now, what role does this tycoon play in this whole story? Was Trump's objective to inflame the population, instigate and pressure them to rebel, to protest, to rise up against ? By doing this, do the president, the Senate, and the police take enforcement measures to "protect" the federal state and the resources and structure of the nation? (https://actualidad.rt.com/actualidad/229298-republicanos-ocho-estados-eeuu-consideran-aumentar-castigos-protestas [12]). Do they keep "peace" by increasing the police state and citizen control laws? Thus, together with apparent peaceful relations

---

5. http://internacional.elpais.com/internacional/2017/01/25/actualidad/1485372859_073422.html
6. https://actualidad.rt.com/actualidad/229285-eeuu-propuesta-ley-onu
7. https://actualidad.rt.com/actualidad/229626-trump-decreto-reconstruir-fuerzas-armadas-eeuu
8. http://www.elmundo.es/internacional/2017/01/25/58884bd122601d473d8b45bf.html
9. https://actualidad.rt.com/actualidad/229632-eeuu-california-indepencia-separarse-votacion
10. http://www.merca20.com/california-le-advierte-a-trump-defendera-a-los-mexicanos/
11. http://www.bolsamania.com/noticias/internacional/donald-trump-cierra-la-version-en-espanol-de-la-web-de-la-casa-blanca--2470684.html
12. https://actualidad.rt.com/actualidad/229298-republicanos-ocho-estados-eeuu-consideran-aumentar-castigos-protestas

with Russia that reduce the risk of war between these two superpowers, the heavy hand to definitively eliminate the threat of terrorism? (http://www.lavanguardia.com/politica/20170120/413536517405/trump-promete-erradicar-el-terrorismo-islamico-de-la-faz-de-la-tierra.html [13]), and the apparent abandonment of Israel regarding the UN that was seen before Obama left the White House? (http://www.enlacejudio.com/2017/01/23/la-onu-declara-la-guerra-a-la-civilizacion-judeocristiana/ [14]or http://www.eldiario.es/sociedad/Abas- Trump-embassy-USA-Jerusalen_0_601590051.html [15])... things are presented as a scenario of supposed security.

But deporting immigrants and making all that fascist propaganda was not what it seemed: Trump wanted to stop the wave of child trafficking from Mexico to the US for elite pedophile networks. Apart from that, they expel from the country and imprison all highly dangerous individuals for the system, since they know that there will be an increasingly worse revolution that will lead to a civil war, and that had been warned by the Pentagon itself in mid-2014 (https ://www.theguardian.com/environment/earth-insight/2014/jun/12/pentagon-mass-civil-breakdown [16]). When the elite learned of Trump's true intentions, they began to close their doors, attack him, discredit him, and turn the press against him.

The prison and immigration control program had actually already been officially established by Ronald Reagan in 1984, it was

---

13. http://www.lavanguardia.com/politica/20170120/413536517405/trump-promete-erradicar-el-terrorismo-islamico-de-la-faz-de-la-tierra.html

14. http://www.enlacejudio.com/2017/01/23/la-onu-declara-la-guerra-a-la-civilizacion-judeocristiana/

15. http://www.eldiario.es/sociedad/Abas-Trump-embajada-EEUU-Jerusalen_0_601590051.html

16. https://www.theguardian.com/environment/earth-insight/2014/jun/12/pentagon-mass-civil-breakdown

reactivated by Donald Trump (it is called '1033 Program' (https://en.wikipedia.org/wiki/1033_program [17]), part of the 'FEMA REX-84' device that establishes 800 prison camps in the US, including Alaska and centers in Mexico, Canada and other centers in other parts of the world where the US Military-Industrial Complex has bases (http: //www.hispantv.com/noticias/ee-uu-/331346/trump-carceles-prisiones-secretas-cia-torturas [18]), and which began to be legislated by FDR in Executive Order 9066 of February 19, 1942 (The first camps were for Japanese, and existed before the Nazi camps: https://es.wikipedia.org/wiki/Campos_de_concentración_para_japoneses_en_los_Estados_Unidos [19])).

Hispanics and blacks are the majority in the US, and sadly the elite has managed to keep these families in a general state of poverty, low resources and education, so that the majority of organized gangs, smugglers and criminals are from these communities . It's more than racism. When the new American civil war begins, the neighborhoods controlled by arms and drug traffickers will be the main points in the cities where shootings will break out (in fact, many of the school shootings, for many experts, are the work of the government itself to feed fear and insecurity). This is part of the reduction in force capacity of civilian retaliation. Police force is increasing in the US. Freedom from the use of force is increasing for the police apparatus.

Regulations that stipulate an understandable limit to the meaning of "terrorism" have been and are being expanded, including activists, war veterans, conspiracy theorists, Muslims, blacks,

---

17. https://en.wikipedia.org/wiki/1033_program

18. http://www.hispantv.com/noticias/ee-uu-/331346/trump-carceles-prisiones-secretas-cia-torturas

19. https://es.wikipedia.org/wiki/Campos_de_concentración_para_japoneses_en_los_Estados_Unidos

Hispanics, Christians, survivalists, weapon bearers, and anyone who says anything publicly or online against the government (https://www.theguardian.com/commentisfree/2014/aug/30/ terrorist-watch-list-rules-innocent-people [20]or https://theintercept .com/2014/07/23/blacklisted/ [21]). That's really what happens. And given the moment – soon – it will no longer be undocumented immigrants, but all people with alleged criminal records, arrested on the sidewalk and in their homes, UN soldiers in charge of this forcibly entering (http : //internacional.elpais.com/internacional/ 2017/01/25/actualidad/1485372859_073422.html [22]).

Some think that Donald Trump was elected by the elite at least 3 years earlier to complete this self-destruction plan of the so-called "great whore" or "great Babylon" (USA), but that would contradict the version of the plan. by Hilary Clinton. I have already commented many times, practically everything is ready, and the master move is to bring down the US economy, to make the US dollar die definitively, and it does not matter that Trump had excellent intentions and tried to save the economy of the United States of America. Many in high places have been aware that they had to assume that yes or yes this would lead to a civil war in which the elite is not willing to see the same thing happen as in the Civil War. Therefore they decided that there would be no other option than to "sacrifice the queen" to win the game. This nation is pro-freedom and pro-rights and has many opponents of the Deep State. The people know a lot about the New World Order and oppose it, and although Obama tried to take away the people's weapons to achieve this successful transition, that Orion project did not work.

---

20. https://www.theguardian.com/commentisfree/2014/aug/30/terrorist-watch-list-rules-innocent-people

21. https://theintercept.com/2014/07/23/blacklisted/

22. http://internacional.elpais.com/internacional/2017/01/25/actualidad/1485372859_073422.html

Americans, thanks to the Second Amendment of their Constitution, have the right to bear arms and shoot anyone who enters their home (burglary). There are too many war veterans organizations, organized gangs, mafias, neighborhoods under non-governmental control... this would make it very difficult to impose martial law (which is the main objective to destroy the US while its army is sent abroad to fight with NATO against Russia: https://actualidad.rt.com/actualidad/229185-ejercito-britanico-temer-rusia-destruir [23]). For this to be successful, it must remove the opposition and ensure that people and governments are completely loyal to its purpose, whether in the direction of Immigration (http://www.abc.es/internacional/abci-democratas-reclaman-trump- revoque-orden-migratoria-201701310225_noticia.html [24]), the Prosecutor's Office (http://www.abc.es/internacional/abci-trump-fulmina-fiscal-general-funciones-ordeno-no-defender-veto-migratorio-201701310336_noticia. html [25]), showbiz (http://canal44.com/donald-trump-madonna-lo-amenaza-y-servicio-secreto-la-investigara/ [26]), the Media (http://internacional.elpais.com /internacional/2017/01/25/ actualidad/1485372859_073422.html [27]), or even the UN (http://www.elperiodico.com/es/noticias/internacional/nikk-haley-embajadora-trump-onu-debuta-con -tono-menazante-5770025 [28]) and, on the contrary, make sure who is entirely on your side, such as

---

23. https://actualidad.rt.com/actualidad/229185-ejercito-britanico-temer-rusia-destruir

24. http://www.abc.es/internacional/abci-democratas-reclaman-trump-revoque-orden-migratoria-201701310225_noticia.html

25. http://www.abc.es/internacional/abci-trump-fulmina-fiscal-general-funciones-ordeno-no-defender-veto-migratorio-201701310336_noticia.html

26. http://canal44.com/donald-trump-madonna-lo-amenaza-y-servicio-secreto-la-investigara/

27. http://internacional.elpais.com/internacional/2017/01/25/actualidad/1485372859_073422.html

Israel and England (https://actualidad.rt.com/actualidad/229626-trump-decreto-reconstruir-fuerzas-armadas -eeuu [29]or https://actualidad.rt.com/actualidad/229185-ejercito-britanico-temer-rusia-destruir [30]).

The First Horse

<<And now you know what holds him back, so that in due time he may be revealed.>> (2 Thessalonians 2:6, KJV 60) When saying 'manifest' or 'reveal', note that the Greek word reads 'Apocalipsthinai'. We can also structure this phrase as, "the Apocalypse will come when we are incapacitated," because those of us who are part of the resistance will end up having our hands tied when it comes to living in cities as well as when it comes to continuing to prophesy. The concept of Revelation does not mean "end of the world" or "destruction," but rather revelation. And because this has taken on another way of being understood, apocalypse comes to denote an ambivalent identification: a great tribulation and destruction, and something that is manifested. That is why this passage contains a behind-the-scenes code, which refers to the fact that when said person who is now restraining the rule of the Beast is removed, the hour of iniquity, the empire of the Beast, will begin to "manifest." Beast. The same is if he said that the "apocalypse" will begin when the one who opposes the manifestation of the Antichrist is no longer there. There are many of us, and some of the resistance are in politics, they support the US Constitution, which is the last bastion left standing before the planetary dictatorship.

The book of Revelation is the most famous when it comes to prophecies about the end of this age and the beginning of the next,

---

28. http://www.elperiodico.com/es/noticias/internacional/nikk-haley-embajadora-trump-onu-debuta-con-tono-amenazante-5770025

29. https://actualidad.rt.com/actualidad/229626-trump-decreto-reconstruir-fuerzas-armadas-eeuu

30. https://actualidad.rt.com/actualidad/229185-ejercito-britanico-temer-rusia-destruir

a time of peace, harmony, union, prosperity, abundance, longevity and happiness. This transition of events has been seen in many eras, but we will agree that only small and isolated details fit into the context. The order of events in the chronology of that mysterious book of the Bible is not usually understood, but after more than a decade of study I can explain it to you like this: 1° chapter 6; 2° the beginning of whose end is described in chapter 17; 3° chapters 8, 12 and 18; 4th chapter 7; 5° chapters 9, 11, 13 and 14; 6th chapter 16; 7° chapters 19, 20, 21 and 22, consecutively. This first part, which corresponds to the descriptions of chapter 6, speaks of 7 seals, and it is my interpretation that what is concluded in chapter 17 are events that have to do with the beginning of what is described in chapter 6. I would say that it is the trigger , and it is a series of events that extend throughout that time that is mentioned in the seals, ending up collapsing just before the system/government of the Beast does. Points 3 to 7 do not concern this book, being a topic that, as I have already said, has been addressed by this researcher in three previous works.

To continue, I also want to clarify a common error in theological and eschatological jargon, regarding the definitions of these events to happen. What is described in the first section of events is often called 'The Seven Seals', 'The Great Tribulation' or 'The Birth Pangs'; What concerns the second point is the 'Fall of Babylon the Great'; The third is often called 'The Wrath of God', 'The Wrath of the Lamb' or 'The Seven Trumpets', and includes the famous 'Rapture of the Chosen'; The fourth is the immediately subsequent state of those Chosen Ones, who are taken away for 3 and a half years, as is also mentioned in chapter 12; the fifth is called 'The Reign of the Beast', 'The Fall of Satan to Earth', 'The Return of the Two Olive Trees' or 'The Three and a Half Years'; the sixth is known as 'The Consummation of Wrath'; the latter is called 'The Messianic Millennium', 'The Return of Christ', 'The Millennial Kingdom' or

'The Second Coming'. Although these are only designations, mostly of a religious nature, they serve to place these elements in their appropriate section. There is another reference used in Christian eschatology, which is, 'Abomination of Desolation'. It is not accepted by everyone, but it is accepted by some, and it is actually a conceptual and structural confusion of certain past events: the Judeo-Roman wars.

The beginning of the great tribulation begins with a "white horse", in Greek 'Ippos Leukos', and in Hebrew 'Sus Laban'. The horse is a symbol of power, strength, vigor, good health, authority, leadership and military victory. White is a symbol of purity, conscience, peace and morality. Chapter 6 describes 4 horses, then the persecution of the Chosen and then the "signs from heaven" that precede the famous "Rapture" and the "Fire from Heaven", which marks the end of the Great Tribulation and the beginning of the " Wrath of God", as it is known in the popular slang of Christian theology and eschatology. The four horses are white, red, black and yellow, in this order. Much was noted about the last three, and in considerable detail, but the target has been the subject of great analysis, speculation and conjecture. There are various word games with these concepts. For example, the name Jesus is associated with the French sound 'Je Suis' (I am) or the Hebrew 'Iéh Sus' (I will be a horse). Another interesting sound is associated with the Greek 'Zeus' (giver of life) with the Hebrew Sus. But among these curiosities is that the Greek numbering of Ippos Leukós adds up to 777, a characteristic of Christianity to refer to the number "of good", in contrast to the misinterpretation of the meaning of '666'. The 777 is found in the Torah in other words such as 'Zerach' (your seed, your seed), which appears in 19 cases, starting with Barashit (Genesis) 3:15, when it speaks of "the woman" and " the snake". This word is used to refer to offspring, although seed and semen are the same thing in the ancient meaning. Another word that adds up to 777 is Ezraj (your help, your help), which appears in Dbarim (Deuteronomy) 33:29.

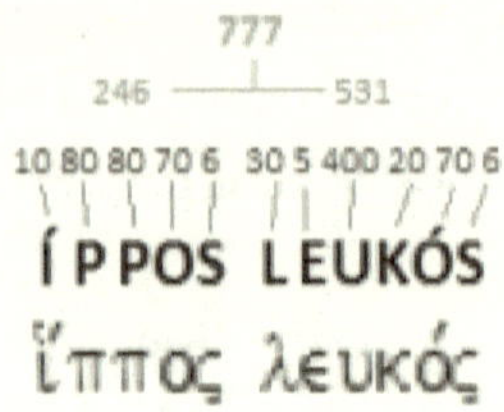

ACCORDING TO CHAPTER 6 of Revelation, verse 2, the one who rides said horse has a Toxon, or bow – it is assumed that it is the type that is for shooting arrows -, and he wears a 'stefanos', which translates as "crown." It must be considered that, just as in Spanish, the word bow is used both for the instrument used to launch arrows, and for the prismatic curvature called rainbow. Although both bow and crown are symbols of reign and power, if we apply them to a current cultural meaning we can find a hypothetical relationship with the LGBT symbol (the rainbow) and the covid (corona [virus]). The description is not emphatic regarding the details of the wearer, so I do not see the possibility of even speculating that whoever enters before the Red Horse takes the scene within the context of the events of the LGBT movement worldwide, and the coronavirus, is unreasonable.. In fact, unlike other cases, here neither the characteristics of the materials nor their color are determined, as in other cases, where it is specified that they are gold or gilded, for example.

This may sound far-fetched and forced, but knowing how Kabalah can decipher profound messages encrypted in passages and concepts of Scripture, this is not entirely incoherent. Ergo, if we look at the characteristics of the individual who is mounted on said horse, it is said of him: <<kai exilthen nikon, kai ina nikísi>>, which has been translated as, <<he came out winning and to win >>. But what does it mean that "he comes out victorious" and "to conquer," if that is a redundancy? He may have won and will win again. Another alternative translation is "he emerged victorious, and to conquer." But what did he emerge victorious from? And over who or what will he win? If this is prior to the Red Horse that brings what is understood as World War III, who is this individual that drags the prelude to the Great Tribulation? If we say that he has emerged victorious or triumphant, and that he is going to win in a broad sense of the term, such as, over a great enemy, a power, or over the world, we must return to the principles of Kabalah, where the names of people are related to their dharma (life purpose) or shem (destiny).

καὶ εἶδον, καὶ ἰδοὺ ἵππος λευκός, καὶ ὁ καθήμενος ἐπ᾽ αὐτὸν ἔχων τόξον καὶ ἐδόθη αὐτῷ στέφανος καὶ ἐξῆλθεν νικῶν καὶ ἵνα νικήσῃ. — BGT Revelation 6:2

Καὶ ἰδού, ἵππος λευκός, καὶ ὁ καθήμενος ἐπ᾽ αὐτὸν ἔχων τόξον· καὶ ἐδόθη αὐτῷ στέφανος, καὶ ἐξῆλθεν νικῶν, καὶ ἵνα νικήσῃ. — BYZ Revelation 6:2

kai exilthen nikon, kai ina nikísi

et vidi et ecce equus albus et qui sedebat super illum habebat arcum et data est ei corona et exivit vincens ut vinceret — VUL Revelation 6:2

Y miré, y he aquí un caballo blanco; y el que lo montaba tenía un arco; y le fue dada una corona, y salió venciendo, y para vencer. — R60 Revelation 6:2

Let everyone judge if this is mere coincidence, if I have forced it or if it is consistent: world ruler is the meaning of the name 'Donald'; Actually, 'Trump' is the meaning of the surname 'Trump'. It is an alternative translation of "ruler of the world who emerges triumphant." But triumphant over what, if war precedes it? Using the kabalistic notarikon system, I found in the phrase from the Greek text of Revelation 6:2, <<kai **e** xilthen **n** ikon, **k** ai **i** na **n** ikísi>>, the variable acronym structuring of the Koine words 'kinísis' and 'kineo', in the form 'kinen', supported by the animism of the temura system. Kinísis means to move, stir or agitate, while Kineo means commotion, sedition or tumult. Both assessments correspond to the context prophesied for the Great Tribulation. On a geological level, earthquakes, and on a social level, protests, demonstrations, civil war, sedition and the beginning of commotions. Some conspiracy theorists would say that the name of the Sumerian god 'Enki' (meaning heaven-earth) is also encoded in these initials.

The idea that Donald Trump is an Abraham Lincoln or a Martin Luther King of our time should not surprise us. The surprise would be to trust them or idealize them, because they are merely human beings, and like each and every one of us, they play their role in history and the historical moment that was given to us. They also have their defects and their virtues. And to add to this theory that I propose, that Donald Trump may be the rider of the White Horse of the Apocalypse, I looked up the last name 'Trump' in the B Code - or secret code of the Bible - in the Torah (Pentateuch) section. , and where it has appeared to me 4 times. This occurrence of the US president's last name is found backwards on 3 of those 4 occasions, and I found it in a search of 1 to 50 equidistant letters.

The first is found in the book of Exodus, chapter 37:9, where Mashah (Moses) writes: <<And the cherubim spread their wings above, covering the mercy seat with their wings; and their faces facing each other looked toward the mercy seat.>> (King Valera translation of the year 1960). The name runs through the entire chapter 9 with 19 letters of distance between letters of the Trump surname. The letter Tet (T) crosses the word Shitim, plural of Shitah (acacia) in verse 10, while the Resih (R) crosses the title 'Kerubim', plural of Kerub, which is who the passage speaks of. For its part, the Mem (M) goes through the reference 'Ba.knafihem', which means, "on its wings." And finally, the letter Pe (P) again crosses the word 'Knapim', or Canafim, in modern Hebrew, which means "wings."

According to the cabalistic interpretation, this "coincidence" could only be attributed to a prophetic premeditation that alludes to this individual as someone "protector" sent by the god of the

Hebrews. By the way, another word that is intertwined here is Kimah (Pleiades), closely linked to angels. Again, let us assume that all this is a mere invention. I go to the second correspondence of the surname Trump that appears again from back to front in the Torah, appearing, 8 letters away, in Leviticus 13:45, where RVA translates, <<And the leper in whom there is a wound will wear torn clothes and his head uncovered, and cloaked he will proclaim: Unclean! Unclean!>> Just as in Shemot (Exodus) 37 he spoke of the kerub protecting the Mercy Seat, here in Va.Ikrá (Leviticus) he speaks of "leprosy" (Tzarúa, which in our case is an analogy of disease). Now, what is 'cloaked'? In Hebrew it says Sapam. Embozar comes from the same cognate as the word 'muzzle'. It is covering the lower part of the face, specifically the mouth area, with a type of garment or fabric. In that word the letter 'P' for Trump appears across the text. Exactly, it is unequivocally a reference to masks or plugs. He is talking about leprosy as a simile of the coronavirus, and so much so that the word Nagip (virus) also appears in the same verse. This is because in the Hebrew language Nagah means not only a sore, but also a blow, mark, disease or virus.

But before continuing with this point I want to make a parenthesis. The Hebrew word Nagah (NGH) I assume derives from the same cognate that gives rise to Nagas in Sanskrit, the name of some anthropomorphic reptilian beings of the Vedanta culture. This is precisely where the Hebrew word 'Najash' (copper snake) comes from, referred to in many biblical passages, such as Barashit (Genesis), in the metaphor-myth of "original sin". What do I intend with this association? Link the idea that comes to my head. When you have been in a field of study for many years, you end up having an intuitive erudition about that field. Therefore, a word in your language or culture may seem like a simple and naive word, but to me it is not. Nagah-Nagap-Najash, the three definitions start from the letter 'N' (Semitic Nun), which in this case designates something that comes from above, falls or rushes. The mythology of the Nephilim, or "fallen angels," is a classic in Abrahamic theology. As you can see, it begins with the letter Nun. But this does not designate a descent like someone who comes down a flight of stairs to give you a chocolate, but rather something that in a moral sense is thrown from a higher position to a lower one, or someone who intervenes abruptly and unjustifiably from a place of superiority and makes use of his supremacy. to subdue those who are in that other seat of inferior conditions.

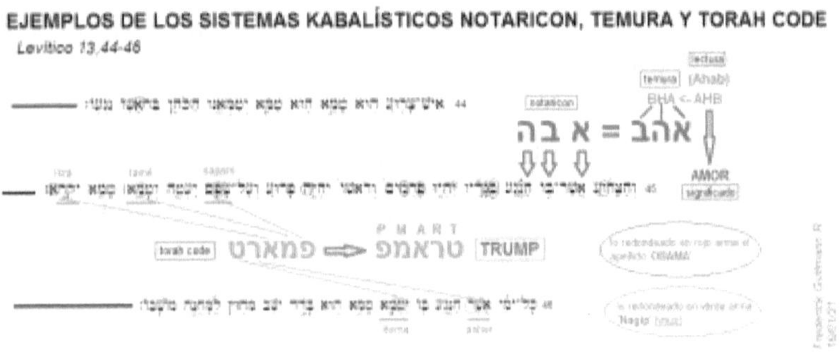

SO I WAS SAYING THAT the surname Trump appears in Va.Ikra 13.45, and that the letters that make up it intersect with certain definitions. Now, the word Tema (not clean), has the 'T', for Trump, as well as it is crossed with the 'M'. That is, crossed twice, which, in Kabbalistic analysis, is considered a reaffirmation of the concept, as when in Shemot we had seen a moment ago that the same surname had two letters that crossed Kanaf (wing) and Kanafim (wings). Does this suggest that Trump is impure or unfit? What it suggests is based on the context of the topic: an infectious agent or disease. Placing it in its corresponding space-time, the location of the concept 'TRUMP' in the biblical codes places it in a circumstance of a virus, of a victory and an advance towards victory, and divine protection. So Trump is going to defeat evil in the world? As seen with the following horse of the Apocalypse, this is not the case.

Rather, what seems to be deduced is that he will come out promptly winning the war that they have waged against him, and he will go out to fight against those who came against him, those whom he has previously been confronting and those who have wanted to destroy and ruin him, and remove him from his position. half. This is not a story about the victory of a war, but the victory of a battle. The next battle would then be fought in the international military arena, and from then on things are no longer clear in Trump's favor. This may not shed much light on this Kabbalistic "research", but reviewing Va. Ikra (Leviticus) 13,45 with a notaricon there are some words that I will leave here so that the reader can see if, like me, he finds analogies, Or yes, on the contrary, he sees this as mere chance. Notaricon is the use of the initial letters (acronyms) or the last letters (bacronyms) of the letters of a phrase. They are combined with the temura (anagram) method to create new words encoded there.

In acronyms the words are found here: Ab (father, offspring), Ahab (love), Abib (from his father), Boá (arrive, come, enter), Shup (hurt, crush), Ishú (saves), Pi (his mouth), Shiv (the lamb), and in the Aramaic language Ab is appreciated as 'fruit'. As I had said, the letter 'Pe' (P), for Trump, was in the definition Sapam, from the old Shpem, or Shepem, which is a mustache, muzzle or mask that covers the lower part of the face. It is precisely the initial of Sapam (the letter Shin), from which two acronyms are made: Ishú (his salvation) and Sheiv (his lamb, the lamb). In fact, of all the above, only these two words appear in the text extension from which the designation of said president is located. These types of words, as well as who wears the crown, who wears white, who is anointed, etc., are designations only granted to people chosen by the deity, and who hold an important consecration for a transcendental mission.

But the surname Trump is not simply in verse 45, it runs through it and covers a large part of verse 46: << *As long as the plague is in him, he will be unclean* ; [he will be unclean, and will dwell alone; outside the camp will be his abode.]>> I remind the reader that the use of the term Nagah is not simply "sore", but any symptom or association of epidemic, disease or virus. Where you read in verse 46 "that the", is from the Hebrew term Asher, where whose 'Reish' (R) intersects with that of Trump. Likewise, 'unclean', which is actually 'Itema' in Hebrew, refers to "becoming unclean", unfit, dirty, inadequate. There are two postulates that I see here: on the one hand, a public fame that designates such a person in a derogatory way, ridiculing him as an individual and defaming him. On the other hand, the context of the circumstances, where it speaks of "for that time" those who see themselves within the concept of illness will be designated as "sick."

In other words, he says 'Kol-iamei' (every day), in reference to the entire period of time in which the disease is promoted and/or for the time of his presidency. For that period, Trump will be criticized, and for that period, he will continue to categorize people as sick with the virus. This, in my opinion, coincides with the passage of the apostle Paul of Tarsus, saying "until he himself is taken away in due time." But I will talk about this later.

Be careful, I am not a "Trumpist", I have no political interests, I have not even voted once in my life. This analysis is merely neutral. For its part, with bacronyms, in verse 45 I find definitions such as: Ar (adversary), Ir (awake), Aver (blind, blind, blind the eyes, blindness; awakening; chaff; skin, leather), Alah (climb), Milah (word, speech), Al (up; yoke), Alam (boys; hide), La (throat), Mahal (adulterate [a substance]), Amal (he who suffers, he who toils; misery) , Hem (them), Lemah (for what?). However, of all these definitions of verse 45, the ones that intersect with the letters 'M' and 'P' that end Trump, are relative to manipulation, toil, misery, the individual who is suffering, the one who is speaking, that of 'why' reasoning and that of young people and hiding. A former CIA agent said in an interview at the beginning of January 2021 that Trump "does not want to be president," and that what he does is more of a duty that he has set out to do, a more "spiritual" mission, thus that, "why... why lend yourself to being humiliated and ridiculed, or push this whole global movement against the Deep State?" That is the answer.

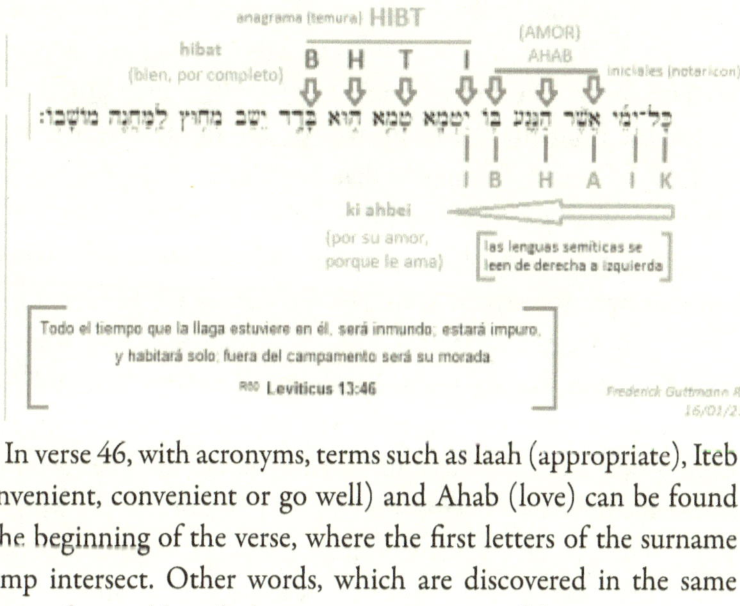

In verse 46, with acronyms, terms such as Iaah (appropriate), Iteb (convenient, convenient or go well) and Ahab (love) can be found at the beginning of the verse, where the first letters of the surname Trump intersect. Other words, which are discovered in the same section of verse 46, with the accompanying use of the anagrammatic system, are: Ií (island) and Abah (reed; consent). And in the second section of the verse there are other words, namely: Behat (alabaster), Hibat (good, completely) or Iba (sister-in-law). But I must emphasize that there is greater relevance in an acronym to which the temura has not been applied, and in that sense, the part where the verse begins also has the article 'Ki' (because, due to), and in Ahab it is There is also the letter Yud, as reinforcement. In other words, it literally reads: 'KI AHBI' (<u>because I love him</u>). With the bacronym method the definitions that can be discovered are, firstly, and now carefully, based on the letters T and R: Raa (ugly, bad; friend; scream; thought), Rai (grass), Raiv (in conflict (as a root of 'Raiván')), Ria (your friend). In the second section of the verse, definitions such as: Daab (languish), Ed (steam), Batz (mud), Batzad (swamp), Badá (invent) and Abad (lose, perish, die, disappear) already appear. This puzzle has a lot to draw from, but if we apply it to the context of said president, shouting is something he is known for, he lives in conflict, he is not an enemy, he is the right person for the job he is doing and he has chosen this work of one's own free will.

But there is even more, the text says, <<As long as the sore remains in him, he will be unclean; He will be unclean , and **will live alone** ; **outside the camp will be his abode** .>> It is known that since Donald Trump saw that the White House was not a safe place for him, he decided to carry out his operations from his own residence. In May, a blackout at the White House left that place without light for several hours. Never seen in US history. Internal cameras other than external ones, microphones. Trump chose a non-American security team: Israeli. It is clear that Trump has not trusted his people for a long time. The MassMedia came against him, even people from his party and friends turned their backs on him. He seemed to have the cross on him, bad luck or half the world not liking him. The fact is that this may be revealed in the coded words of this final part of the verse of Va.Ikra 13,46. On the other hand, the Hebrew text uses the word 'Isheb' (to sit), in the sense of settling or establishing, and the concept of chair (Kiseh) is the same as throne, and is still used today to identify the position of the president: seat.

Conducting another, much larger study using the Torah Code, I found another appearance of Trump in the Torah. On three occasions the name is read from back to front, and in the other case there are 37 letters separating it. I call this case "Hitler antagonism." Adolf Hitler raised the Third Reich, and wrote a first work titled 'Mein Kampf' (My Struggle) in 1925. The work reflects Hitler's "love" towards "his people" and accepts the Protocols of the Elders of Zion (a plot Jewish world), emphasizing the threat of said regime to dominate the world. He also emphasized the freedom of his territory. If we make an analogy, this is similar to the words and policies of Donald Trump: he loves his homeland, wants to make America free again, and opposes the global plot of the Zionist Deep State. If we translate the German concept 'Mein Kampf' into Hebrew, as a name, it gives us 'Naptalim' (Naphtali). It is on the descendants of the Israelite patriarch Naphtali that the appearance of the surname Trump turns once again in the Torah: <<These are the families of Naphtali by their families; and 45,400 of them were counted.

These are those who were numbered of the children of Israel, 601,730. And the LORD spoke to Moses, saying, To these the land will be divided as an inheritance, according to the number of names. To the more you will give a greater inheritance, and to the few a lesser inheritance; and to each one will be given his inheritance according to what he has counted.>> (Numbers 26:50-54, KJV 60) In these 4 verses, apart from mentioning Naphtali, he gives us two numerical patterns, one of Naphtali's family (who has his own fight), and another of the "children of Israel", who will "divide" the land as an inheritance, according to their "age". You must understand that when reading the Bible, you should not take things literally in the geographical, temporal, literary, scientific or nomenclature sphere. It is about the background of the message from those who sent these books to be written. We talk about CODING, and that is what we should care about.

Thus, when we read that it speaks of such "sons of Israel," the code refers to the Elect, to all those who have reached the Mysteries of Light and are going towards transcendence, on whose path are those who profess the "faith." " in Jesus of Nazareth (that is why we speak of the priority of the "elders", or of greater psyche-experience, and of inheriting the earth, that is, the Future Kingdom). Who was Naphtali? It was one of the 12 tribes of Israel. Of these 12, at least 10 were distributed throughout the world, it is said, after having been captured and taken captive by the Assyrian empire, establishing them in Nineveh in 722 BC. C. It is, however, the code of Naphtali here, a reference to a Hebrew ancestry, which designates, in the context, a connection with the principles of the god of the Israelites and his commandments. So this group of devout or faithful people belong to a larger global group, and the numbering given designates the 3 subjects of the passage: Naptali, his children and the entire people of Israel (those of the Covenant).

We have 2 numerical sequences: 45400 and 601730. For the first count, the text in Hebrew is divided like this: 5-40-1-4-100. The 5 and 40 make up the 45, and you can add the 1: 46; the 4 and the 100 multiply the 400. We can see here either a 45-401 or a 46-400, or simply eliminate the additional Elef/Alef (1000/1). One of the exercises to do here is to see that 45 (man's number, that is, from the Hebrew Adam) responds to the letters Mem (40) and He (5). The 400, for its part, corresponds to the letter Tau (T). Taking the subsequent letters of these 3 values, we get: H (5), M (40), A (1), T (400). These 4 letters form 'Ha.Met' (the dead one). Mot was the form that later became alternative and then fixed for Mevet (death), but in principle it was the proper name of the Semitic-Canaanite god of death. Who is dead or will be dead? The code is talking about the "sons of Naphtali", whose analogy here would be the American people.

Let's compare this with one of the prophecies that speaks of the USA (whose hidden code in the Bible is 'BBL' (Babel), transliterated into Greek as 'Babylonos', or Babylon): <<wherefore in a single day his plagues will come; death, crying and hunger, and it will be burned with fire; because the Lord God is powerful, who judges her.>> (Rev. 18:8, KJV 60). I continue. Just as the number 45 refers to humanity, to the human being, 400 refers to the end of a period of time, a complete cycle. This was called Baktun by the Mayans, but in the work Oahspe (1882) it receives the name of Dan, which is also the name of one of the 12 tribes of Israel, and the only one that does not appear in the millennial Abrahamic worldview described in the book called Revelation. The number 400 has resulted from adding the phrase from Barashit (Genesis) 49,10, which says, "until Shiloh comes", that is, the Peaceful Envoy, the Messiah. Curiously, the name Shiloh – which alternately appears in the Hebrew text along with Shiloah – accompanies the name Trump in this same passage from Ma.Midbar (Numbers) 26,50, with 7 letters of separation.

Have you stopped to think that during Donald Trump's first term there was the only known occasion in decades where the US Military-Industrial Complex was neither invading nor attacking any foreign nation? There was no more war in Syria, there was not even talk of terrorist attacks again. Still, if my assumption is correct, and Trump identifies the White Horse of Apocalypse, that apparent peace will be followed by a terrible war the likes of which there has never been on our planet. The number 400 also comes from the Hebrew word Katzir ([the] harvest), which is frequently used to refer to the end-world cleansing of the planet through war: <<And another angel came out of the temple, crying with a loud voice to him who was standing. sitting on the cloud: Put in your sickle and reap; because the time to reap has come, for the harvest of the earth is ripe.>> (Rev. 14:15, KJV 60)

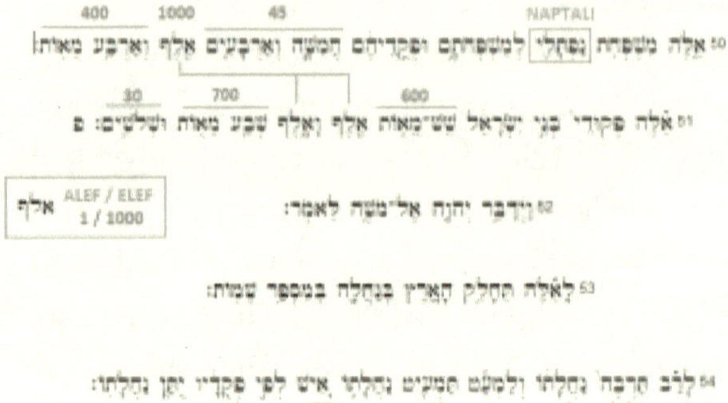

Números 26,50-54

I will take another biblical reference to compare this one, such as the one where Yeshua (Jesus) makes a descriptive allusion regarding the end of this era (which translators call 'century') in which we find ourselves: <<The enemy who sowed it is the Devil; The harvest is the end of the century; and the reapers are the angels.>> (Matt. 13:39, RVA 60). What was sown was the tares of the parable that he told them. As if that were not enough, 400 is also the count resulting from the first portion of a chapter of the book of the prophet Daniel, which says: <<But the prince of the kingdom of Persia opposed me for twenty-one days...>> (Dan. 10 :13, RVA 60). The Persians are the current Iranians, or ancient Iranians. We know that there is tension with the Iranian government, threats from both sides between Iran and Israel, and Iran and the United States of America. The proto-Hebrew prophet Enoch knew this by revelation thousands of years ago: <<In those days the malachim* will return and rush towards the east, on the children of the Parthians and Medes and will shake the kings, and a spirit unrest will invade them and overthrow them from their thrones (chairs), so that they will flee like lions from their dens and like hungry wolves from their pack.>> (1st Enoch 56,5) Malachim is what they translate as "angels." The Parthian Empire, also known as the Arsacid Empire, was one of the main

Iranian political and cultural powers of ancient Iran. All these references cannot be a coincidence.

Since January 3, 2020, when a drone reportedly assassinated Iranian General Qasem Soleimani, tensions between the US and Iran have increased. Although Donald Trump claimed responsibility for the attack, leaked information from the Israeli secret service defined the attack as an Israeli operation. Trump would have claimed responsibility for the attack order so as not to damage the strategy of the Peace Treaty that would be signed later in September between the State of Israel - by decision of Prime Minister Benjamin Netanyahu - and the Arab Emirates and Bahrain. Already at the time, prophecies attributed to Sara Hoffman in 1979 described a nuclear attack by Iran against Israel from a secret position in Libya. Well, Persia (Iran) appears here again. The passage from Ba.Midbar (Numbers) 26 had given us another coded computation, remember? 601,730. As in the previous case, we disassemble the code by sections, according to the reference of the original Hebrew text: 6-100-1-1-7-100-30. I put together the sequence as 600-1-700-30, as 601-730 and as 600-731. If you're wondering why I don't use the figure "thousand," it's because in the original language thousand and one have the same root, they just change their location in a numerical description. However, pattern 601-731 can also be considered. Here is Iran once again, and once again from the prophesied book of Daniel: <<and I remained there with the kings of Persia.>> (Dan 10:13, KJV 60). This passage totals 731, and is the third part of the structure of the same verse of the same chapter mentioned above.

This type of statements could explain the prophecies of the Swiss Billy Meier, such as the so-called number 120, where he stated – in the 80s – that <<it will be the time when human beings are afraid of the future >>, adding, < <since the world, political, military and nature situation will be very precarious >>, and adds, <<because **the leaders of the US and Israel will threaten war and destruction**

, as will the terrorists. revolutionaries everywhere>>, and ends by saying, <<that the human being has exploited, violated and ruined nature in such a terrible way that it will be counterattacked with powerful earthquakes and tidal waves, with enormous floods and storms , typical of the most remote times of the Earth>>. Meier had already made a similar prediction before that, stating: <<menacing thunder will explode over the Earth and there will be thousands of deaths when powerful criminals from the US government unleash wars around the world>> This is notable if we see how The Bushes launched a campaign of conquests in the Middle East, motivated by the Deep State.

But Meier adds something else: <<when the violent leaders of Israel also spread terror, crime, death and ruin just like the Palestinians themselves...>> (prophecy 84) This could be something future, or not, since Certainly the corrupt powers of the Israeli government have moved the Mossad to participate, along with the CIA and MI6, in the training of revolutionary leaders, to encourage wars in the Middle East. I prefer to think that prophecy 84 has already been fulfilled, but prophecy 120 is about to be fulfilled sometime between 2021 and 2025.

I have already explained previously in 'Remote Viewing' that the Red Horse refers to the Third World War - or Nuclear War - and what for me is the unequivocal proof of this is that in Hebrew 'Sus Adom' (Red Horse) , adds 731, and is exactly the same figure as the Hebrew definition 'petzatzah atomit' (**atomic bomb**). Regarding the other numbers, 730 is the sum of Caporet (cover, mercy seat), which is what covers or protects something that is sacred. The 700th solo is armed with the curious word Shet (buttock, foundation; referring to 'drink', or 'six', in the Aramaic language). 701 adds Rosh (head), symbol of a leader, and Shaat (rise; swelling; desolation; majesty, eminence). The 732 adds up to the Hebrew letters of 'Seder Olamei Chadash', or 'New World Order'. The 600 is the sum of the

Greek phrase from Revelation 13:16, <<that a mark be put on their right hand>> (NKJV 60), which I must remember – as I already explained in works such as Remote Viewing II, Recognizing the Time of the End or Armageddon E-5 – which is a **'subcutaneous incision' or 'puncture'** , not a "mark" , as it can be expressed in its various meanings in the Spanish language. That is why many anti-vaccine Christians relate "vaccines" to the so-called Mark of the Beast, or as a prelude to it.

Now I will place greater emphasis on another Kabbalistic method, that of numbers. In Hebrew gematria Trump is 330, and in Greek it is 741, while Donald Trump is 425 in Hebrew and 1592 in Greek. The correspondences between numbers, with other words, and especially with passages or contexts lead to the clarification of greater values. The same is true for close numbers, and this is where things become "peculiar". The number 425 appears in the book of the prophet Daniel when prophesying about who would later be known as Iehoshua ha.Notzri, that is, Jesus of Nazareth. There they define him as 'Mashiach Nagid', which adds up to 425, and is just above Mashiach ben Dauid (Messiah son of David, 424). Another detail with the number 425 is that it appears in the Torah several times, such as with the words Naaseh (make), Haiit (be), Takah (crush), Shelem (peace sacrifice, peace), Ve.Shpatij (and judge)., and variables of these definitions.

But in addition to this, the resulting calculation of the Greek value of Trump (741) corresponds with the sum of the Hebrew values of 'Ieshua ha.Notzi' (Jesus of Nazareth), and with the phrase from the book of the prophet Malachi (1,6), <<the son honors the father>>. But if this is not curious in itself, let us take the number 741 and see what association it has with words from the Torah: Lebanhem (make them white, make them white), Amen (so be it, I believe it), Meaminim (believers), Ve.Naartiah (the maidens), Tzaanam (his sheep), Ve.Tarainah (and grazed), Meán (hardened, refuse), Ve.Ikehan (and exercise priesthood), Ve.Naskahem (and his libations) or Lekaraatei (proclaim). I have not leaked any words that did not interest me, so it is clear that 741 has a component of consecration to a mission related to the deity. Oh, and by the way, in Hebrew the name Donald is 95, same as the definition Garanit (nuclear).

There is another aspect to consider here. The number 6 is observed recurrently in many parts of the book of Revelation. In Kabalah the number of man is 6, as well as additionally in the Hebrew aspect 18 and 45 - or in Greek 46 -. Trump is the 45th president of the US, yes, the 45th, just like the verse I mentioned from the book of Leviticus 13. If we look in Hebrew, the term horse is 'Sus', which numerically is 60-6- 60. The 4 horses of the Apocalypse are written in the Hebrew language with 6 letters: SUS LBN, SUS ADM, SUS SH.JR, SUS IRK Apocalypse is divided into 3 groups of 7 events, but the seventh incorporates the following 6 and 7. That is, It has 7 seals where in reality the 7th has the trumpets, where the 7th has the 7 bowls. In addition to this, the "apocalyptic" story of this book does not begin until chapter '6', and it is in verse 6 of said chapter where this mystery seems to begin to be clarified: <<I heard a voice from the middle of the four living creatures, which said: 2 pounds of wheat for a denarius, and 6 pounds of barley for a denarius; but do not harm the oil or the wine.>> (RVA 60). If we look further, chapter 13:18 tells us that the numbering that identifies the Thirion system (of the Beast) is the calculation of the Greek letters Ji, Xi and Stigma, which correspond to 600, 60 and 6, apart from also with 24, 15 and 6. As we see, both calculations take us to 6 and its variables, as well as 45. In the Hebrew language the calculation is different from the Greek, and although the numbering is taken from the letters Tau, Reish, Samech and Vav to result in the infamous 666, the sum of the letters gives 63, the same as 'Israel' or 'Bilderberg' .

I could go on and on. Where I want to go is that there is a close relationship between the concepts of what the apocalyptic context is and the number 6 connecting the "computes" and "codes", war, man and the government of Thirion . Also, the fact that according to the prophet Edgar Cayce, the 44th president of the US was supposed to be the last, but it was not the case, but could be the 45th, representing humanity, or the destiny of humanity. Although I have already addressed all of this in detail in previous works (especially 'Remote Vision'), the important thing to emphasize here is that the link between the event of the White Horse and the following three horses is subject to a plan of global control through biometric recognition, population identification and registration technology and population reduction, and the transition to achieve that underlies a collapse of markets, shortages of food supplies and a world war. It is the sequence that always follows a resounding fall in the economy and that accompanies or precedes a great world war. Whenever an elitist system wishes to redesign the global social model, they introduce a conflagration that would restore the markets and the financial system to prepare the guidelines for a new false democracy.

Before continuing, I want to leave you here some other curiosities that I would not like to be left out.

1. You will have seen that the name Obama was in verse 44 of Leviticus 13. The president who preceded Trump.
2. Another detail, I mentioned that the word acacia was intertwined with the name Trump, and the acacia is a symbol of immortality and hope.
3. The name Trump is where the Anglo-Saxon term 'Trumpet' is derived from , meaning "trunk". If anything has spread in biblical eschatology, it is the archetype of the trumpet, a Shofar (ram's horn) sound or thunderous sound that

announces what is coming.

4. Adolf Hitler's first book, My Struggle , was written in 1925 , and we are not far from 100 years since then.
5. Another detail, which I haven't put because it was too big to fit on the chart, is that Leviticus 13 has other words later on that are contextual: **Gog, USA, Riots, Shaking, Babylon, Deportation, Rome** .

All these words are related and are found in verses 49, 51, 54-56 and 59, and continue in chapter 14, where, from verse 7 to 12 there are more words that revolve around the theme: tower, ram (Aries), the Beast, and once again, TRUMP. The Lev connection. 13.45 to 14.7 starts with Trump and ends with Trump. Leviticus 14:11 has the name Trump with only 2 letters of separation: <<[And the man who [*is*]] to be cleansed/purified will be presented to the priest who cleanses/purifies him and with those [*things*] before/ before the face [of IHVH...]>> What I underline are the already translated definitions where Trump appears, and which in Hebrew is transliterated as "Ha.Mi **t** ahi **r** ve. **O** ta **m** La. " **P** nei." But if that doesn't catch your attention, there's something that will. I have taken the bacronyms (final letters of the words) of this verse looking for a hidden meaning and the following has been put together: NRT (illuminate, be a lamp , shine on), H.SH.RIM (the goats , the dragons, the lords , demons), JLD (existing , living, of the world). A breadth of this analysis, going back to verse 10 reveals the letters TR (explore, turn , bull), DN (judgment, cycle), HGN (of the garden). This can be translated as "dazzling the demons of the world, their turn to judge."

By early March 2021 – as I write this – Trump supporters hope he will once and for all take out the military and continue the fight against the Deep State. Trump was able to impose martial law (https://cnnespanol.cnn.com/2020/12/21/trump-menciona-la-ley-marcial-y-alarma-a-trabajos-de-la-casa-blanca/ [31]) , or take advantage of the Insurrection Law (https://www.nytimes.com/es/2021/01/11/espanol/estados-unidos/ley-de-insurreccion-usa.html [32]), knowing that there really was electoral fraud (https://tierrapura.org/2021/01/09/italia-habria-usado-guerra-cibernetica-tipo-militar-para-desviar-votos-de-trump-a-biden/ [33]), however, he and His family ended up encouraging their compatriots to "wait." Proponents of the 'Q' movement have waited and waited since the presidential election took place in November 2020. They expected something to happen on Inauguration Day (January 20, 2021), and sure, it did, but not exactly what they had in mind. At least 6 hours before the event, and in a different place than it should have been, Joe Biden's inauguration oath was taken. A complete unconstitutional setup. The National Guard remained in Washington, ostensibly for the protection of the state. The FBI would have warned the Capitol that a coup d'état was going to take place. Biden didn't even take AirForce One, and instead, Trump happily left and set up his "new office" at his place of residence (https://www.msn.com/es-us/noticias/otras/trump-abre -his-office-of-the-former-president-in-florida/ar-BB1d6V97 [34]).

---

31. https://cnnespanol.cnn.com/2020/12/21/trump-menciona-la-ley-marcial-y-alarma-a-empleados-de-la-casa-blanca/

32. https://www.nytimes.com/es/2021/01/11/espanol/estados-unidos/ley-de-insurreccion-usa.html

33. https://tierrapura.org/2021/01/09/italia-habria-usado-guerra-cibernetica-tipo-militar-para-desviar-votos-de-trump-a-biden/

34. https://www.msn.com/es-us/noticias/otras/trump-abre-su-oficina-del-expresidente-en-florida/ar-BB1d6V97

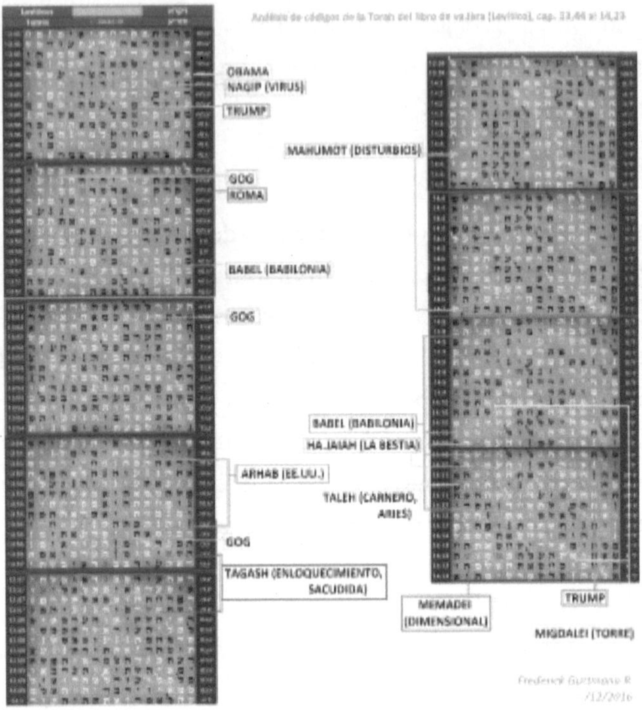

Strangely, it seemed that Biden was not really in the White House, but in a building that is a replica, designed for other purposes, among which is the filming of Hollywood movies, when they film on the White House. Meanwhile, the real White House was with the lights off and the lock on the bars on. All kinds of Biden presentations were seen on recording stages, not in official buildings. Well, you can investigate all this yourself. What I want to get at is that, if my theory is correct, Trump's victory at the end of 2016 symbolized that White Horse, and his "conquest" were the many victories he had over the Deep State in his 4 years in office. If so, how much time is supposed to elapse between the White Horse and the Red Horse (nuclear war)? With Joe Biden – or his clone (because today's Biden bears no resemblance to the one from years ago) – everything returned to the point where Barack Obama left things.

If so, the Christians who prayed for a president they liked saw their prayers manifested, but what then? What is relevant, asking for a Christian president to do what Christians long for, or "fulfill the will of God"? destiny is marked, and praying for a pregnant woman so that the contractions don't hurt or the baby doesn't come out is a bit absurd, right? Where is the vision of Christians? Do they want God to adapt to them, or do they want to accept the designs that have been set to bring about the true "kingdom of God"? There are two things I want to add to this chapter of the book before moving on to the next section. I haven't addressed the question of the Q move, and I'd like to give you space to lay out the part that's been pushed with all of this. Finally I will add the descriptions of the so-called 'Enoch Prophecies', which are not from the Enoch compendium, but from the Swiss prophet Billy Meier (famous for reporting his contacts with the Plejaren aliens). But what is the "Q movement"? If you heard names or words like Anonymous, Panama Papers, WikiLeaks, Edward Snowden, Julian Assange, PizzaGate or Jeffrey Epstein, then I won't need to give you details.

However, if you didn't hear about these disclosure scandals, 'Q' will probably be something new to you as well. 'QAnon', or 'Q', is a movement that claims to support Donald Trump in his fight against the Deep State. According to QAnon, <<there are progressive Hollywood actors, Democratic Party politicians and high-ranking officials who participate in an international network of child sex trafficking and carry out pedophile acts;and that Trump is investigating and persecuting them to prevent a alleged coup d'état orchestrated by Barack Obama, Hillary Clinton and George Soros.>> (Wikipedia) The English version of Wikipedia adds that those involved are "cabalist pedophiles" and the "secret cabal that worships Satan." QAnon supporters are very large in number in the US, and have spread since 2020 to huge masses in England, France, and especially Germany and Japan.

The Capitalist system no longer resists

According to QAnon <<the Corona Virus Pandemic was a final act intended to delay the release of the GCR/RV after Nancy Pelosi's (House Speaker) stunts, Mueller's bogus investigation into Russian relations, and attempted Impeachment have failed and failed to stop Trump and his Agenda for GESARA.>> And <<This is why Trump said on Monday, April 6, 2020 during a press conference that: "This is a military operation." The same was confirmed by Vice President Pence and Second Assistant Admiral Brett Giroir. On Saturday, March 21 [2020], the president said: "We will win and there will be many celebrations when we win. And we will win with as few lives lost as possible. He is a difficult enemy. He is a tough killer, much bigger, much crueler than ever." Since late March, Trump has begun alluding to a war against the Deep State, "the creators of the virus.">> They maintain that <<The Democrats The Deep State deliberately released the virus in the upcoming election year to force the US economy into a recession under President Trump's watch. Blocking citizens would also be their excuse to introduce digital mail-in voting in the upcoming November elections. Such a vote would allow him to falsify millions of votes using illegal immigrants and the identities of the dead.>>

<<Everything was going well for them until the best virologist on the planet, Dr. Raoult, under the protection of Putin, announced to the world, on Saturday, March 28, his magic potion to kill the Corona Virus, based on the medicine "chloroquine." ". Which was already being used by the Chinese with spectacular results to treat patients who improved by adding a pulmonary antibacterial called "azithromycin", saving each of their first 1000 cases (except one).>> And they also claim <<Putin, with its rescue activity, in the last week of March it sent 15 military planes full of doctors and supplies directly to northern Italy (after the Czech Republic blocked a rescue plane from China). European countries fear that China or Russia

will find the truth in the Lombardy Region, where people are not dying from the Corona Virus, but probably from a deadly hybrid cocktail of two previous vaccines injected into the population with separate vaccination campaigns for meningitis and The flu, which combined with the radiation taken by 5G, causes the appearance of lethal viruses. Know that EMF weapons used for population mind control include 5G, Bluetooth, cell phone radiation, WiFi. Please visit the article published on this site published by CNN in 1985 regarding EMF weapons used for mind control (https://eraoflight.com/2020/04/12/cnn-in-1985-emf-weapons-being- used-for-mind-control-emfs-include-5g-bluetooth-cell-phone-radiation-wifi/ [35]). On February 19, 2020, President Trump created a space force to combat these weaponized technologies (https://www.whitehouse.gov/briefings-statements/president-trump-establishing-americas-space-force/ [36]). Not far away in Germany, Dr. Wolfgand Wodarg internationally praised the fact that the engineering panic was totally unnecessary, since this virus is no different from the others that affect us every year.>>

The amount of information that has been leaked by the Q movement is very extensive, especially thanks to the help of intelligence personnel, many of whom first passed through WikiLeaks. They were the first to report that <<Dr. Fauci was hired by the Center for Disease Control, owned by Bill Gates, which intends to make billions with vaccines for Covid 19 thanks to the patent he obtained ago. years under the Obama administration.>> They made it known that <<According to sources, Anthony Fauci also participated in the creation of the virus: http://www.paulstramer.net/2020/04/welcome-to-Boer-guerra-

---

35. https://eraoflight.com/2020/04/12/cnn-in-1985-emf-weapons-being-used-for-mind-control-emfs-include-5g-bluetooth-cell-phone-radiation-wifi/

36. https://www.whitehouse.gov/briefings-statements/president-trump-establishing-americas-space-force/

antony-Fauci-and.html [37]. This allowed Bill Gates, Anthony Fauci, Tedros Adhanom, George Soros, Jared Kushner, Jiang Zemin and others to continue their 18-month global vaccination and lockdown plans. Bill Gates has always been the mastermind behind this and has always tried to introduce microchips to the population: https://21stcenturywire.com/2019/12/23/bill-gates-sviluppa-new-id-tattoo-to- check- [38]for vaccines. All of the people mentioned above have a strong financial interest in spreading the virus and developing a vaccine: https://www.armstrongeconomics.com/world-news/corruption/did-bill-gates-buy-the-cdc [39]. However, there is strong opposition to his plans and Robert Kennedy Jr., a member of the white nobility Kennedy bloodline, was indirectly threatened by the murder of two of his relatives found dead and murdered to make him stop his anti-vaccine work. : https://www.rumormillnews.com/cgi-bin/forum.cgi?read=143670 [40].>>

<<Instead, Robert F. Kennedy Jr. is exposing and continuing his fight against Bill Gates. https://childrenshealthdefense.org/news/government-corruption/gates-globalist-vaccine-agenda-a-win-win-for-pharma-and-mandatory-vaccination/ [41]. The Trump administration has opposed Bill Gates' vaccine tracking system from the beginning on the grounds of "personal freedom" limitations. Know that if you wish, you can join the White House petition, which has gone viral for the elimination of these criminal acts.

---

37. http://www.paulstramer.net/2020/04/welcome-to-Boer-guerra-antony-Fauci-and.html

38. https://21stcenturywire.com/2019/12/23/bill-gates-sviluppa-new-id-tattoo-to-check-

39. https://www.armstrongeconomics.com/world-news/corruption/did-bill-gates-buy-the-cdc

40. https://www.rumormillnews.com/cgi-bin/forum.cgi?read=143670

41. https://childrenshealthdefense.org/news/government-corruption/gates-globalist-vaccine-agenda-a-win-win-for-pharma-and-mandatory-vaccination/

https://petitions.whitehouse.gov/petition/we-call-investigations-bill-melinda-gates-foundation-medical-malpractice-crimes-against-humanity [42]. Vaccines, for Bill Gates, are a façade of strategic philanthropy that fuels his many vaccine-related activities (including Microsoft's ambition to control a global vaccine identification company) to implement dictatorial control over global health policy: the diamond council of corporate neo-imperialism. Gates' obsession with vaccines seems to feed on his messianic belief that he is ordered to save the world with technology (replacing humans with humanoid robots) and for this reason he has the divine right to experience the lives of humans considered "underage." age ". Already pledging to eradicate polio with $1.2 billion, Gates took control of India's National Advisory Board (NAB) and mandated 50 polio vaccinations for all children by age 5. Indian doctors now blame Gates' campaign for a devastating epidemic of polio vaccine strains that paralyzed 496,000 children between 2000 and 2017.>>

<<In 2017, the Indian government cracked down on Gates' vaccine regime and evicted Gates and his cronies from the NAB so polio paralysis rates fell precipitously. In 2017, the World Health Organization had to reluctantly admit that the global polio explosion is predominantly a variety of vaccines, meaning it comes from the Gates vaccine program. The most terrifying epidemics in the Congo, the Philippines and Afghanistan are linked to Gates' vaccines. By 2018, ¾ of the world's polio cases came from the Gates vaccines. In 2014, the Gates Foundation funded experimental testing of the HPV (papillomavirus) vaccine, developed by GSK and Merck, on 23,000 girls in remote Indian provinces. About 1,200 suffered serious side effects, including autoimmune and fertility disorders. Seven died. Indian government investigations have accused Gates-funded researchers of committing widespread ethical

---

42. https://petitions.whitehouse.gov/petition/we-call-investigations-bill-melinda-gates-foundation-medical-malpractice-crimes-against-humanity

violations: pushing vulnerable village girls into the process, oppressing parents, falsifying consent forms and refusing medical treatment for injured girls. The case is now in the United States Supreme Court. In 2010, the Gates Foundation funded an experimental GSK malaria vaccine, killing 151 African children and causing serious adverse effects such as paralysis, convulsions, and convulsions with febrile states in 1,048 of 5,049 children. During the Gates 2002 Men Afri Vac campaign in sub-Saharan Africa, Gates agents forcibly vaccinated thousands of African children against meningitis. Between 50 and 500 children developed paralysis. South African newspapers complained that "we are guinea pigs for drug manufacturers." Nelson Mandela's former economist Professor Patrick Bond describes Gates' philanthropic practices as "ruthless" and "immoral". Bill and Melinda Gates have already been accused of paralyzing 490,000 African children with their vaccines.>>

<<In 2010, Gates pledged $10 billion to the WHO promising to reduce the population, in part, through new vaccines. A month later, Gates told Ted Talk that the new vaccines "could reduce the population." In 2014, the Kenya Catholic Doctors Association accused the WHO of chemically sterilizing millions of unwilling Kenyan women with a bogus "tetanus" vaccination campaign. Independent laboratories have found the sterility formula in each vaccine tested. After denying the allegations, the WHO finally admitted that it has been developing infertility vaccines for more than a decade. Similar accusations came from Tanzania, Nicaragua, Mexico and the Philippines. A 2017 study (Morgensen et 2017) showed that the famous WHO DTP is killing more Africans than the disease it claims to prevent. Vaccinated girls suffered mortality rates 10 times higher than unvaccinated boys. Gates and the WHO have refused to reveal the lethal vaccine that the WHO imposes on millions of African children each year. Global public health advocates around the world accuse Gates of diverting the WHO

Agenda from projects proven to contain infectious diseases; clean water, hygiene, food and economic development. They say he diverted agency resources to serve his fetishistic criminal system and that, according to him, good health only comes from a syringe ("murderer"). In addition to using his philanthropy to control the WHO, UNICEF, GAVI and PATH, Gates funds private pharmaceutical companies that produce vaccines and a vast network of pharmaceutical industry front groups that spread misleading propaganda, develop fraudulent studies, conduct and psychological surveillance against vaccine hesitancy and Gates' use of power and money to silence dissent and force compliance.>>

<<According to sources, the actual creation of the virus involved teams supervised by Bill Gates. Frank Plummer, a former Canadian biolab director who was directly involved in the creation of the virus, was a victim of the MK-Ultra-controlled Cabal, who was developing the virus against his will, and was killed by the Cabal before he could speak much (https://www.sciencemag.org/news/2019/07/mystery-surrounds-ouster-chinese-researchers-canadian-laboratory [43]; https://phiquyenchinh.org/2020/02/23/tb-in-hiv- cov-shut-down-the-brain-plus-the-korean-cult-role-in-wuhan-pt-10/[44] https://phiquyenchinh.org/2020/02/20/hiv-laced-covid-19-targets-human testicles-its-tb-strand-blocks-the-mune-system/ [45]) Trump has always declared himself against Bill Gates' agenda and a digital tracking system that could inform authorities about the history of all these things. vaccines of an individual. For this reason, for weeks Trump has promoted his daily briefings in the press

43. https://www.sciencemag.org/news/2019/07/mystery-surrounds-ouster-chinese-researchers-canadian-laboratory

44. https://phiquyenchinh.org/2020/02/23/tb-in-hiv-cov-cierra-abajo-el-cerebro-más-el-culto-coreano-role-in-wuhan-pt-10/

45. https://phiquyenchinh.org/2020/02/20/hiv-laced-covid-19-targets-human-testicles-its-tb-strand-blocks-the-mune-system/

declaring that it was useless to wait for a vaccine if there was already a cure for the Corona Virus. Just this week, he withdrew all money from the World Health Organization for a collusion between the Bill Gates Foundation and the Clinton Foundation, China and the Soros Foundation. They were using their collaboration with the United Nations "Peace Force" (which has nothing to do with peace) to cross borders under this pandemic of fear. He continued to follow the tank barrier on the southern border against the so-called "peacekeeping force" of the United Nations and then blocked everything by "playing", including the MS13 infantrymen.>>

<<Know that the Khazarian mafia does not want to give up without a fight. The White Dragon Society sent the following message last week: "We have ruled this planet for thousands of years and we will destroy it rather than abandon it.">> They add that <<the epidemic in China can be traced back to the Wuxi pharmaceutical company in Wuhan, China. But guess who owns Wuxi? The Soros Foundation. If you scroll through the list of companies it owns in the SEC database below, you will find the name "Wuxi Pharmatech Cayman Inc." The spread of infection in the United States is also predominant in areas where the headquarters of the US Wuxi laboratory are located in Texas, Maryland, New Jersey, California, Minnesota, etc. See in the archives: https://www.sec.gov/Archives/edgar/data/1029160/000101143811000207/form_13f-soros.txt [46]. Chinese scientist named Li Chen defected to the United States and brought with him a disk of China's most dangerous new biological weapon, called "Stuff Wuhan-400" because it was developed in its RDNA laboratories outside the city of Wuhan. The biological weapon has four hundredths of vital strains of artificial microorganisms created

46. https://www.sec.gov/Archives/edgar/data/1029160/000101143811000207/form_13f-soros.txt

at that research center. Wuhan-400 is therefore a perfect weapon. It affects only humans and is therefore called Zombie virus.>>

Their strategy evidently sells a screen of fallacies and deception and distraction, behind which there is a virus, which has not yet been truly dispersed, but will be when the resistance to mandatory vaccination ends up taking the streets of the main cities of the world. world. <<The Soros Foundation supports the Rothschild family and other Khazarian mafia families, many of whom are hiding in Switzerland, New Zealand and the British Virgin Islands. Cabalist archivist and Rockefeller "bagman" Henry Kissinger said: "The institutions of many countries will feel bankrupt... The reality is that the world will never be the same after the Corona Virus... its spread is exponential: American cases are doubling every fifth day. At the time of writing, there is no cure. Medical supplies are not enough to cope with the rising wave of cases. Intensive care units are on the brink and beyond being overwhelmed. The The crisis effort, however extensive and necessary, should not preclude the urgent task of launching a parallel enterprise to transition to the post-Corona Virus order for a collaborative global vision of the Marshall Yaws Virus and the Manhattan Project. "The Corona Virus is, in its speed and global scale, unlike anything known in history. Failure could set the world on fire" (https://www.wsj.com/articles/the-coronavirus-pandemic-will-forever-alter-the-world-order-11585953005 [47]).>>

<<The Corona Virus originated in the city of Wuhan in China and has now reached all corners of the world. But this virus did not reach Beijing, the capital of China and the economic capital of Shanghai near Wuhan, why? Because Beijing is the city where all the leaders of China live, the military leaders, those who wield the power of China, those who still work for the Deep State. The Chinese were informed that the Coronavirus had been found at

---

47. https://www.wsj.com/articles/the-coronavirus-pandemic-will-forever-alter-the-world-order-11585953005

their facility at "666 Gaoxin Road" (number related to the Devil), in Wuhan, China (https://www.wuxiapptec.com/about/location [48]). Deep down, these people from the "Deep State" are people without morals and ethics. These people lie and deceive and prefer intimidation to negotiation and fair payment for our products. Their method of operation is to sue us to destroy you financially and emotionally. Trials are very expensive and these Deep State people control most of the big law firms. These Deep State people are well funded and bad for your bone marrow. They also want to control and destroy us because they do not use sneaky and legal means. However, Trump and the Alliance have used this "pumping" pandemic against the Deep State to cover the launch of the GCR/RV and Pentagon inspectors are carefully monitoring the $2 trillion aid that will be released to the market for the Corona Virus in to avoid further criminal actions.>>

<<The old Fiat financial system run by Cabal is now imploding also thanks to the latest heavy money printing which will lead to a huge hyperinflation due to the mold of too much paper money, causing the ultimate collapse of the system. Basically, unlimited fiat currency is printed in debt to overload the system so everything can be locked into the Federal Reserve, which will then be reset to zero during the global debt jubilee. On Friday, March 27, 2020, the addition of the Federal Reserve to the Treasury was implemented, one of the most surprising news of the century. Trump therefore took control of the Federal Reserve, which is now led by two Treasury representatives. After three years in power, Trump finally fulfilled his election promise to remove private banks from US public affairs, ending a century of exploitation of American and world citizens. He appointed the famous investment group Blackrock to implement the purchase of major companies dedicated to the real economy, which results in the fact that he is nationalizing

48. https://www.wuxiapptec.com/about/location

the blockages of the real economy, while avoiding market collapse by involving important private investors in the market. 'agreement. The Fed also began purchasing mortgage packages from Fannie Mae and Freddie to try to support the lending market from crashing. The Federal Reserve Bank, Keizer Report, Max and Stacy, are now also buying junk bonds to save private equity funds and hedge funds that, once again, have made a lot of bad bets.>>

<<The US Treasury Department will now determine which markets/segments need capital (could be equities, munis, specific sectors, even corporate debt - there appears to be no restrictions). It is the Treasury Department that now tells the Fed how much money to print. All the Fed does is print money. There is no longer any authoritative decision-making or control process. A third party (Blackrock) carries out the operations dictated by the Treasury Department. This takes everything out of the Fed's hands except money printing. In recent weeks, the Federal Reserve has repeatedly and unexpectedly reduced the cost of money, also presenting big news on the Quantitative Easing (QE) front. The goal was to stop the economic shock caused by the pandemic, which, however, we know is no longer possible. The Fed has also announced that it intends to offer dollars to the other central banks that depend on it by launching a new temporary lending system that, for the first time in history, will allow foreign central banks to convert their holdings into dollars (through exchange lines). government bonds. The new program will not only target foreign central banks, but will also extend to international financial institutions with New York Fed accounts (https://www.federalreserve.gov/newsevents/pressreleases/monetary20200319b.htm) [49].> >

<<In fact, this is a new repurchase agreement structure from FIMA. In essence, this allows any Central Bank, including emerging markets, to exchange its US Treasury holdings for USD, which can

---

49. https://www.federalreserve.gov/newsevents/pressreleases/monetary20200319b.htm)

then be made available to local financial institutions to deal with the liquidity crisis. To put it bluntly, this buyback facility is like a swap line. The last possible move of the Federal Reserve was to support the global financial markets by offering money to the other central banks to maintain their criminal fiat system, which in fact has already collapsed. The Bank of Canada, the Bank of England, the European Central Bank, the Swiss National Bank and nine other countries have already had access to the Fed's swap lines with Australia, Brazil, South Korea, Mexico, Singapore and Sweden, all in capable of extracting up to $60 billion and $30 billion available for Denmark, Norway and New Zealand. Despite all the Fed actions implemented so far, the USD continues to rise relative to emerging market prices, this is because the current crisis differs from the 2008 GFC and requires direct end-user policies that They go beyond the banking sector. These companies, especially those involved in global supply chains, constantly need working capital, primarily dollars. Preserving the flow of payments along these chains is essential if you want to avoid a further economic crisis. That is why we are moving rapidly towards the "End Game" where, in effect, the Fed, even supporting the global financial system, will collapse in on itself.>>

<<If the Fed did not support the market now, there would be a partial collapse of the Eurodollar, which however is already foreseeable because the Fed has no interest in saving all foreign companies. And most developing countries still do not have enough dollars to cope with periods of euro-dollar liquidity stress. The only exception is Saudi Arabia, whose currency is pegged to the USD, although Taiwan and Russia keep the USD close to what would be needed in an emergency. In short, the magnitude of demand for USD outside the United States is clear, and so far the Fed is responding by issuing new currency. It continued to expand its balance sheet to provide liquidity to the markets at a rate never seen

in the past. We've basically seen almost five years of QE1-3 in five weeks! However, it will never be enough, because one thing is now clear: that global trade in goods and services will be affected by this crisis and that American imports will collapse. This will threaten one of the main liquidity channels of the USD in the Eurodollar system and will accelerate its fall because if there was already a fiscal deficit of $ 1 trillion before COVID-19, now with this pandemic the liquidity deficit of the USD has been extended around $3.2 billion. As we have recently argued, this is a peak level we had during World War II. So now we are no longer conspiring by announcing the collapse of the system and the eurozone for years, but the situation is clear to everyone who realizes that we are facing a system that has already collapsed for some time.> >

<<The "Atlantis report" was anticipated on April 9, 2020 and it was announced that the market had gone wrong with the Fed's purchasing actions. Normalization is long gone and will never return. That's why everyone now knows that this paradigm is dead. The FED after 107 years of domination (starting in 1913, the year of its constitution) has ceased its work of enslaving people. With this, neoliberal or neo-Keynesian economics also ceases. This is the end of consumer economic theory because the debt-laden fiat currency standard has failed. The renaissance of the United States and the entire world began with the recovery of control of the money supply, the financial system and the currency that has now been removed from the globalist bankers (who dominate the market with their international private companies) and returned it to the Treasury , under the government of the "Republic", which will soon be fully restored. The U.S. Treasury now has secured assets and interests in federal debt of about $22 trillion and the Federal Reserve will owe all of that $22 trillion.>>

<<Basically, the Federal Reserve will buy over 2 trillion of US debt per month to get the US out of debt by the election date

(November) 2020. After that the Fed could declare bankruptcy and disappear, along with your privately held IRS which will also lead to the elimination of income taxes. No more credit from bankers due to the criminal debt-based monetary system. This will be replaced by a currency revalued by gold and the new quantum financial system. Remember that Trump and the Alliance have told us that gold will shrink the Fed. The transition may take a few months, but currently the Fed has been reduced to a mere debt-bound private bank that for a time will simply process transactions like a trading company. Wall Street brokerage with small transaction fees. Meanwhile, the US Treasury will hold the collateral for that debt, no longer the Fed, and this makes the debt an asset right now. In essence, the Treasury is using the Fed's instruments against them. Thank God, the process has been reversed. We must remember that Lincoln persecuted the Central Bank (Fed) with the issuance of the greenback. JFK launched EO11110 taking a swipe at the Fed and Reagan took a bullet after deviating from Fed policy. But now the time has come to do justice to these great men who came before us and who worked for the people. Because power, step by step, will be restored to the people. The recovery of control of the Federal Reserve system is part of the "Global Financial Reset" (what is striking is not the "Global Currency Reset" linked to the currencies that will be announced after the restructuring of the system, but its precursor).>>

<<The Treasury announced that the release of funds for all levels scheduled for next week was how the "Stimulus Bill," the government-approved $2 trillion stimulus package for American families, would have helped the people and the economy. In fact, the funds released under the Stimulus Act arrived on Wednesday, April 15 immediately after Easter. The law became the largest economic stimulus bill in modern history, more than double compared to the stimulus bill passed during the 2009 financial crisis. The US government is distributing so-called "helicopter money" through

direct payments. in cash to individuals and families. The centerpiece of this plan is a direct payment of $1,200 for those earning up to $75,000 a year. For higher earnings, payment amounts will be phased out, generally ending at the $99,000 income level. Families will also receive $500 per child. The first stimulus funds are intended for individuals and small businesses. Another round will be out soon. The stimulus funding is essentially the precursor to a universal basic income for everyone that will never fall below $1,200 per adult. Stimulus checks are issued by the United States Treasury and sent by the Internal Revenue Service (IRS) to all American citizens. The IRS said Saturday that the first stimulus checks were deposited into taxpayers' bank accounts.>>

<<Mnuchin (US Treasury Secretary) and Trump have said that direct electronic payments and checks are in progress. There were 80 million payments destined to reach recipients' bank accounts by mid-week. Stimulus funds provide other facilities, namely: (1) a temporary suspension of any student loans held by the federal government. This means no payments required or interest accrued until the end of September 2020; (2) the possibility of forbearance on mortgage payments of up to six months for borrowers with loans guaranteed by the Confederation; (3) an expansion of unemployment benefits, including a four-month increase in benefits. These plans include independent workers, gig economy workers and experienced employees. The other countries of the world will soon follow by issuing emergency funds and then at full capacity for the livelihood of the people to achieve universal income for all. Italy, like other countries, will be supported monetarily in this activity by the United States, which approved the granting of funds last Saturday to help the allied country in great difficulty.>>

<<The mass arrests around the world of the Deep State are happening right now behind the scenes without Martial Law being made public, although Medical Martial Law has been activated in

several countries around the world that have declared a State of National Emergency. With the declaration of a state of medical emergency, President Trump was able to freeze the financial accounts of anyone involved in human trafficking, child pornography, child trafficking for pedophilia, or human sacrifice. And this includes politicians and state actors, current or former government officials, or a person acting on behalf of such an official. Recall that on December 21, 2017, Trump issued an executive order that allowed him to block the properties of people around the world involved in serious human rights violations or corruption. The Order affects anyone found guilty of human rights violations and corruption, not only in the United States but also around the world. Therefore, it affects everyone, including foreign governments and their officials as well, by providing blocking and confiscation. It is with this act that President Trump was able to initiate arrests of criminals around the world (https://www.whitehouse.gov/presidential-actions/executive-order-blocking-property-persons-involved-serious-human-rights- abuse-corruption/ [50]). President Trump, the Department of Defense, the Alliance, and decision-makers believe there have been enough global Deep State arrests and containment under the Alliance's military and operations in Europe, the United States, and China, what would not happen. Martial law must be declared publicly. However, Trump attracted a million reservations and recent retired military.>>

<<A war has been waged against Mexican drug cartels, 5G networks (which have been disabled) and FEMA, which has been placed under military control. Some targets are very violent and are expected to react, so for the safety of the people for a short period, Trump has acquiesced to the criminal governments that imposed incarceration on us. In 90 days, they plan to arrest about 160,000

---

50. https://www.whitehouse.gov/presidential-actions/executive-order-blocking-property-persons-involved-serious-human-rights-abuse-corruption/

people, including members of Media Mainstream and Barry Soetoro. Now they are beginning to take down Antifa, MS-13, the mafia, drug gangs and other mercenaries hired by Soros and used by the Democrats and the Deep State. The Deep State, although it launched the Corona Virus, is losing the war. His 16-year plan to destroy America, started by Obama and intended to be continued by Hilary Clinton, who had planned to destroy America's infrastructure, has failed. His plan specifically included reducing the US military and depleting its resources, actively funding Iran and North Korea with nuclear weapons. The goal was to start a third nuclear world war that would cause death and destruction on a global scale. World War III would have been a "fake war" sponsored by government-controlled Mainstream Media.>>

<<The Plan also stipulated that the global elites of Rothchild, Wall Street bankers, Obama and Hillary Clinton had to collapse the American economy to buy back pennies on the dollar, so that the world would remain under the control of the industrial complex deep state globalist. Under these terms of the Deep State, the American middle class would have been completely destroyed and the American population (like the population of the rest of the world later) would have been reduced to a state of slavery, hunger, death and disease. The United States did not have to have borders, the Constitution had to be revised to eliminate the Bill of Rights and all fundamental freedoms and the population would have been disarmed by eliminating the second amendment related to the right to bear arms. After the brutal assassination of President Kennedy, the deep state became the predominant power structure over all governments. Because the moneychangers discovered long ago that control over a fraudulent money supply not only gave them control over the town's assets, but also, in a very real way, control over the town's government, they learned to make money by on the backs of people who increasingly extend their control by applying the

sequence of easy money cycles followed by successive restrictions to spring their trap.>>

<<In a monetary system where money is "created" from nothing in debt, there will never be harmony. If we go to a bank and borrow $250,000 for a new house, the bank does nothing more than record on the ledger to create the $250,000 from scratch and simply by virtue of the fact that we signed our name on a piece. of paper that promises to pay that sum of money, the bank receives as collateral for its false loan, our real asset, our house, which they will then confiscate the moment we fall into their trap during the restrictive cycles. So, the functions of the World Bank or the IMF, aimed at solving economic chaos by restoring order and lending money created from nothing, serve exclusively to solve the problems created by the New World Order that tries to create a world, without national borders, under a single management system, with a single planned global economy, to restore stability, deceptively promised "for the good of all" and to last forever, while the process has brought down 90% of the world's population . However, there is no need to worry, because the sovereign people will now have the power to restore their national government, reclaim their political status from their birthright, and restore their jurisdiction over the land. Our countries, without their own legal personality, are still functioning and can be restored to their original legal status by demanding the return of all stolen identities and property owed by nations and people.>>

<<There are currently more than 170,000 sealed charges filed in federal courts across the United States (most involving accusations of pedophilia), while mass arrests of global elites continue that should end in arrests of political elites. autumn. In January 2016, the morning President Trump took office, he visited CIA headquarters to declare war on human trafficking. Since then, more than 170,000 sealed charges have been filed in federal courts across the country,

most involving charges of pedophilia. Two weeks after taking office, the latter announced the formation of a Pentagon "pedophilia task force" at a press conference that Mainstream Media had not covered. See link: extension-chrome: https://media.defense.gov/2017/Nov/15/2001843802/-1/-1/1/
DODIG-2018-018_CHILD_SEXUAL_ABUSE_V2_508_R_REDACT
[51]. The Task Force. has been involved in child rescue operations since 2017 while also targeting drug trafficking, children in South America, Mexico and the Caribbean. Those arrested will be deported to GITMO, the prison camp in Guantánamo, Cuba. The main obstacles to arresting and convicting these criminals have always been the judges because many of them are corrupt and in the judicial system. That is why GESARA requests a return to a rule of law before the Supreme Court that returns to judging according to the law and not according to an "attempt" to follow other laws.>>

<<Last week a large tunnel was discovered that connects Mexico with the United States. We are now focusing on operations in the Caribbean, where we also reach elite homes in these locations, such as Epstein Island, Richard Branson, Nexus Sex Cult, Haiti Children and the Clinton Foundation. Bill Gates was arrested for his crimes of child abuse and involvement with Epstein following his resignation as CEO of Microsoft. One of his impersonators is used for sporadic public appearances (https://www.nytimes.com/201910/12/business/jeffrey-epstein-bill-gates.html [52]). Bill Gates always had a strong connection with Jeffrey Epstein: https://www.dailymail.co.uk/news/article-7350469/Bill-Gates-havolato-Jeffrey-Epstein-Loliota-Express-2013-anni-pedofilo-carcere -stay [53]. Here Bill Gates praises pedophile Jeffrey Epstein: https://www.mysterious-times.com/2020/04/16b-

51. https://media.defense.gov/2017/Nov/15/2001843802/-1/-1/1/DODIG-2018-018_CHILD_SEXUAL_ABUSE_V2_508_R_REDACTED.PDF

52. https://www.nytimes.com/201910/12/business/jeffrey-epstein-bill-gates.html

gates—pedófilos-Jeffrey-Epsteinslodato-vita-tipo-di-intriganti/ [54]. National Guard and Special Operation military troops are now rescuing children and victims of tunnel trafficking in some of the largest cities in the United States. Child trafficking, sex slaves, riots and cannibalism is the largest industry on the planet and President Trump and his heroic team are stopping it. On April 1, 2020 there was a public announcement of a massive assault under General Milley, Chairman of the Pentagon, who sent his troops to save children and arrest Deep State traffickers, therefore it is no coincidence that the President Trump, as commander in chief, deliberately funded the Pentagon with the largest funds in history. Because, the Pentagon agreed to carry out military arrests of state traitors, under the direction of Trump, who is now secretly protected.>>

<<The Illuminati uses pedophilia to blackmail and control its puppet members. Meanwhile, corruption and sexual abuse are rife and no one mentions the involvement of the Jesuits and Freemasonry. The legal system and the police are knowledgeable and complicit in the subversion of civilization. Hollywood studios are soaked in the blood of innocent children. Drinking blood for babies is so popular in Hollywood that it basically functions as a currency in its own right. "Project Paperclip", "Project Mockingbird", "MKULTRA" are part of human experiments conducted by Nazi scientists and the CIA. See the CIA Mind Control Experiments document: https://www.politico.eu/article/the-secret-history-of-fort-Detrick-the-CIAS-base-of-controllomental-experiment [55].

---

53. https://www.dailymail.co.uk/news/article-7350469/Bill-Gates-havolato-Jeffrey-Epstein-Loliota-Express-2013-anni-pedofilo-carcere-stay

54. https://www.mysterious-times.com/2020/04/16b-gates--pedófilos-Jeffrey-Epsteinslodato-vita-tipo-di-intriganti/

55. https://www.politico.eu/article/the-secret-history-of-fort-Detrick-the-CIAS-base-of-controllomental-experiment

"Out of the Shadows" is a documentary/video released by "Q" (Alliance of Light) among the most sought after we have seen in recent years about how Mainstream and Hollywood Media manipulate and control the masses using Control propaganda CIA Mental. We recommend that you watch it at the following link: https://www.youtube.com/watch?v=MY8Nfzcn1qQ [56]. The CIA is the first to transmit information to Hollywood, which then controls the population with its television and film programming. They make any type of propaganda they want about the population. In every Disney movie they kill a father figure. Hidden themes presented to vulnerable children aged six and under. Hollywood elites are enemies of humanity because they continually act against morals and laws by breaking every taboo of God known to man, including the mental sanctity of children.>>

<< [In] Hollywood unfortunately pedophilia was institutionalized. These pseudostars collect the blood of children and eat their flesh, believing that this gives them life force. If children suffer from physical and mental pain before dying, they believe that this gives them extra life force. These people do not have loving strength and propensity for life. They are happy to cause pain, trauma, stress, abuse and suffering because through the traumatized blood of children they derive a substance they call "Adrenochrome", which would be precisely their life force. However, these satanic atrocities can no longer be tolerated and that is why now many politicians, CEOs, actors, musicians, etc. They are being arrested all over the world. Many elites in Washington DC, Hollywood, Wall Street, Silicon Valley and others have been arrested or detained under house arrest. The house arrests that the Alliance is carrying out behind the scenes are not publicly displayed at this time for security reasons. Some celebrities made public appeals to raise funds, however, their clothes looked cheap, their "decoration"

---

56. https://www.youtube.com/watch?v=MY8Nfzcn1qQ

disappointing, and their appearance unkempt without makeup. If you notice, they look tattered, unshaven, and forced to take unwanted readings. In short, they do not seem to talk under normal circumstances about their condition, so they may be in some way under house arrest.>>

<<The latest celebrity to apparently fall for Corona Virus was CNN anchor Chris Cuomo, President Trump's open enemy. Cuomo is the brother of New York Governor Andrew Cuomo. Oprah Winfrey herself was arrested for sex trafficking related to Harvey Weinstein and Bill Clinton (https://youtu.be/AZ5QohE3nPc [57]). Tom Hanks has also been arrested and is set to be executed. Rita Wilson and Canadian Prime Minister Trudeau have been arrested and are in quarantine in prison. Ellen DeGeneres has been, or will soon be, arrested, along with many, many, many others. They all claimed to have been affected by the Corona Virus. Instead, they are likely to have withdrawn from Adrenochrome, the substance released into the blood by the adrenal glands of traumatized children, which seems to say that it is horrible and causes death for those who took it for a while and cannot come back. to take it. Weinstein is believed to have already died from the Adrenochrome withdrawal crisis. The next celebrity arrests will be Celine Dion, Madonna, Charles Barkley and Kevin Spacey. Some high-ranking religious leaders will be arrested or forced to resign and some will suddenly fall ill. The Vatican will be first and the Pope will be removed in 2020. The production of adrenochrome extracted from humans will be revealed and Hollywood and the Vatican will be exposed as directly responsible for this. Know that most arrests take place at home and with subsequent releases to verify even after the situation. All major arrests will be described in the media as accidental or conspiracy theories. All those arrested will be given "the death of Rommel", meaning they will have the option to choose

---

57. https://youtu.be/AZ5QohE3nPc

between their death being presented to the public as a suicide or accidental death in exchange for guarantees that their reputation will remain intact or, alternatively, they can choose to face a criminal trial that would cause public misfortunes.>>

<<On Easter Sunday [2020], Pope Francis said that the debt burden of the poorest countries should have been forgiven (in essence, he called for a "Debt Jubilee"). The global "Jubilee" is looming around the world, while the G20 has finalized the debt reduction program for the poorest countries. The G20 group approved a critical "action plan" to freeze debt service payments for the poorest countries to avoid a crisis in emerging markets. The new aid program ended on April 15 during a video conference of G20 finance ministers and central bank governors. The IMF has canceled all debt incurred by many countries, particularly when addressing countries with medium-low debt. Your debt will be forgiven in the 76 central banks of the world. The original 27 countries in the worst financial shape will be welcomed first. Then 111 countries would receive debt relief. Eventually, all countries would receive debt relief (https://www.imf2020.org [58]). The intention is to mitigate disruption to the supply chain of essential raw materials. The IMF originated in 1913 as a central clearinghouse for all international goods and was formed with the explicit purpose of speeding up trade between nations. The announcement was made after the video conference meeting on April 15: caribbeanbusinessreport.com. Last week, Sarah-Jayne Clifton, director of the British Jubilee Debt Campaign, called for a global debt jubilee to prevent some of the world's poorest countries from collapsing into chaos amid the COVID-19 crisis. .>>

<<Daniel Lacalle, CEO of fund manager Tressis Gestión, recently said: "QE will not solve this problem. Trade lines will not solve this problem. A debt jubilee will fix this plus trillions upon trillions of write-downs and defaults." Previously, Trump had hinted

---

58. https://www.imf2020.org

that a NESARA "Freedom from Debt" ad was coming this week: https://www.youtube.com/watch?V= yW4NmsQ21Gw [59]As of March 31, 2020, Mortgage Forgiveness Forgiveness applies to approximately 23,000 mortgages, however, the debt forgiveness program will continue and be completed by the end of April 2020. Meanwhile, Easter Sunday , the "Saint Germain World Trust" has launched prosperity funds for an upcoming "gold standard" and "Reset" announcement that will take place after newspaper reports about the fiat currency implosion and the jubilee of the debt. On Saturday, April 11, 2020, President Trump made a first disaster declaration for all 50 states, which was actually the "veiled" admission of the existence of martial law. https://www.msn.com /en-us/news/politics/coronavirus-trump-has-declared-major-disaster-in-all-50-states-at-once-first-time-in-history/ >> Here is an excerpt of the [60]words from a QAnon report from 2020. In chapter 2.3 of my documentary 'The End of the Century' (https://youtube.com/ playlist?list=PLdE1yrli2g3JLzr9O95HF4RuSEfCwmBWc [61]) you can get an idea of how control programs work mental within Hollywood.

59. https://www.youtube.com/watch?V=yW4NmsQ21Gw

60. https://www.msn.com/en-us/news/politics/coronavirus-trump-has-declared-major-disaster-in-all-50-states-at-once-first-time-in-history/

61. https://youtube.com/playlist?list=PLdE1yrli2g3JLzr9O95HF4RuSEfCwmBWc

IX.

THE CONTACT AND THE PROPHECIES OF HENOC

Lastly, here, but not least, some information given by 'Quetzal', an informant who gave Contact 215 of Billy Meier's ufological group on Saturday, February 28, 1987. Remember that the prophecies vary depending on the decisions that each and every one of those involved, in our case, on our planet takes. Some things change, others don't, it depends on how predictable the planetary consciousness is, and tends to always evoke in the same direction if the mind does not change. A prophecy is not something that an arbitrary god decides because he feels like it, but information given by those who know the variables of the future, predict behavior and/ or those who already know what is going to happen due to their technology. It is like saying, " *according to my calculations, if you continue on the right lane at 120 km/h, without stopping, and another vehicle intercepts you at kilometer 3 at 85 km/h downhill, depending on the angle at which that is coming, that has no vision of you, nor can you see it through some trees, the probability of impact between the two is 96%* ." That's a prophecy.

But if the destiny is that there is a change of consciousness and the world is purified, there will be variables. Among them that those who are in the Light are saved. Adjusting this variable creates new lines of probability and possibility, adjusts the time or hour of impact, the consequences of the crash, the victims, etc. The more time left to occur, multiple variables may intervene, since there are also multiple actors involved. Your decisions accelerate or delay that result.

Quetzal: Before giving you a clear account of the Henoch prophecies, I would like to point out that the prophecies are always changing and can be changed for the better if man makes positive changes in his thoughts, feelings and actions, leading to the best. And positively progressive. Prophecies always rest on specific causes; these also result in certain effects, so these effects can be changed at any time if only the preceding causes are changed in form. Therefore, negative or evil prophecies may not have to be fulfilled if the above causes are intentionally changed so that positivity and good develop instead of negativity and evil. However, this does not apply to predictions, as they are based on events that cannot be changed, are inevitable, and will surely and definitely occur in the future.

Predictions are based on a preview and therefore a direct vision of the future, and have nothing to do with prophecy or the calculation of probability. So, when I make you aware of a part of the prophecies of Enoch for the third millennium, it does not mean that they have to be fulfilled, because the prerequisite for fulfillment in each case would be that the already existing causes continue to exist as well as continue to exist. To be created in the future so that the fulfillment of the prophecies is fulfilled. Thus, whenever human beings on Earth become reasonable, there is a possibility that through a reasonable change in thinking as well as a reasonable development in feeling and an equally reasonable way of acting, everything will change for the better and positive., so the prophecies do not have to be fulfilled. However, if this transformation does not occur, a very evil, perverse and negative time is approaching for the Earth and its entire population in the next new millennium.

Billy Meier: Since the Second World War, the thoughts, feelings and actions of human beings on Earth have changed a lot towards the positive and the good, but everything achieved is not enough in my opinion, since the great achievement has not yet been achieved. transformation towards the best, neither by the powerful of this world nor by all humanity on Earth itself. In the past years, you have made many predictions and probability calculations, as well as mentioned prophetic facts about the economic, military and political situation of the Earth, so I was asked to disseminate this information, which in fact I did. I did. Governments and newspapers, radio stations and television stations and many private people around the world were informed by me. But all the effort achieved nothing, and the same will probably happen in the future, when he receives his permission in the time to come to spread the prophecies of Enoch for the third millennium. However, I feel that Henoch's message for the future needs to be made known and distributed, because somehow it can still bear fruit.

Quetzal: Apparently, you never lose hope. His optimism is honorable and deserves to be heard by human beings, but the way things have developed throughout this century, there is not much hope that human beings on Earth will come to their senses and listen to his words. This will be the case only when the prophecies turn out to be true or, worse, have already been fulfilled. Probably only then will the time come when the smears against him regarding his contacts with us will cease, although for a long time to come they will continue to be hotly disputed by his enemies, as well as by know-it-alls and pathological critics who dismiss them as scams, lie and fraud. The full truth about our contacts with you will be demonstrated in the distant future, and then humanity will accept our help that we offer through you, even as it mistakenly assumes that we come from the seven star system known to humans on Earth as the Pleiades. [The Plejaren claim to live in the Plejares, an altered space-time configuration about 80 light years beyond the Pleiades. MH]

Billy: Semjase and Ptaah already explained it to me. But tell us now what the new millennium will bring to human beings on Earth and to planet Earth according to the prophecies of Henoch.

Quetzal: I will in a moment, but before I begin I would like to explain that I am not authorized to give an exact indication of the years officially. If the human being on Earth continues to live in the same way as he has until now, forming his thoughts and feelings in the same way, indulging in the same actions as until now, then the words of Henoch's prophecies may not be true. more clear. The moment in which these prophecies will begin to be fulfilled will be when a Pope stops residing in Rome. Then, all of Europe will be the victim of a terrible punishment from the powers of evil. The Christian religion will collapse and churches and monasteries will end up in ruins and ashes. Monstrous forces will be created by science and will be released by military forces and armies as well as terrorists, causing great destruction. Millions and even billions of people will be killed by acts of terrorism, by wars and civil wars; and finally, in some parts of the world, one in three human beings, and in other places, one in four human beings, will lose their lives. The nations of the East will rise against the nations of the West, the West against the East. Many deaths will be inflicted on people by fighter planes and bombers, and bombs and rockets will destroy and annihilate ever larger towns and cities.

People will be completely powerless against all of this and will live through 888 days of Hell on Earth, suffering from famine and plagues that will claim more lives than the war itself. The weather will be severe like never before on Earth. Ultimately, nothing can be bought or sold anymore. All provisions will be rationed; and if a human being steals even a little piece of bread, he will have to pay for it with his life. Many waters will be mixed with human blood and turn red, as once in the past the Nile in Egypt turned red with blood. And it will be that the fanatics of Islam will rise up against the countries of Europe and everyone will tremble and tremble. Everything in the West will be destroyed; England will be conquered and thrown to the lowest level of misery. And the fanatics and warriors of Islam will retain their power for a long time. However, not only Europe will be affected, but ultimately every country and people on Earth, as the great horror will expand into a war that will encompass the entire world.

After the turn of the millennium, the papacy will exist only for a short period. Pope John Paul II is the third from the last in this position. After him, only one additional pontificate will follow. Then follows a Pontifex Maximus who will be known as Petrus Romanus. Under his religious government, the end of the Catholic Church will come, a total collapse will become inevitable. That will be the beginning of the worst catastrophe that human beings and the Earth have ever suffered. Many clerics, priests, bishops, cardinals and many other Catholics will be killed and their blood will flow in abundance. But also the reformed version of Christianity will be as infinitely small as Catholicism. Due to the fault of the scientists, the power hungry and their military, their warriors and terrorists will seize enormous power, and the power will be seized also by laser weapons of many types, but also by atomic, chemical and biological weapons. Also with regard to genetic technology, there will be enormous misuse, because it will be exploited without restrictions for war purposes, and not least due to the cloning of human beings for war purposes, since this was practiced in ancient times with the descendants of Enoch in the regions of Sirius.

However, these will not be all the horrors; since in addition to genetic technology and chemical weapons, much worse, more dangerous and deadlier weapons of mass destruction will be produced and used. Irresponsible politicians will unscrupulously wield their power, assisted by scientists and obedient military forces who serve them, who together hold a deadly scepter and create clone-like beings who will be raised in a complete lack of consciousness and will be scientifically manipulated to become killing machines. . Division by division and devoid of any feeling, they will destroy, murder and annihilate everything. The United States will confront the Eastern countries ahead of all other financial states and will simultaneously have to defend itself against the intruders from the East. In total, America will play the most decisive role, when under the pretext of fighting for peace and fighting terrorism it invades many countries on Earth, bombs and destroys everything and brings thousands of deaths to the populations. US military policy will also know no limits, nor will its economic and political institutions, which will focus on building and operating a global police force, as has long been the case [sic]. But that will not be enough and, under the guise of a so-called peaceful globalization, American policy will aim to gain absolute control of the world when it comes to supremacy in the economy.

And this will point towards the possibility that a Third World War could develop out of it, if human beings as a whole do not finally reflect on reason, become reasonable and take necessary measures against the crazy machinations of their governments and powers. military, as well as its secret services, and put an end to the power of the irresponsible who have abandoned their responsibility in all areas. If this does not happen, many small and large nations will lose their independence and their cultural identity and will be overthrown, because the United States will gain predominance over them and with evil force will subject them to its domination. At first, many countries will howl with the wolves of the United States, partly due to fear of American aggression and sanctions, as will be the case for many, many irresponsible [those] in Switzerland and Germany, but also in other countries. In part, others will join because they will somehow be forced to do so or will be misled by irresponsible promoters of American propaganda.

Eventually, many Asian, African, and European states will rise up against American hegemony, once they recognize that the United States of America only takes advantage of them for the purposes of war, conquest, and exploitation. In this way, many countries will become puppet states of [North] America before reason and realization arise in responsible governments and much of the population, resulting in a turning away from the United States. However , the great war will hardly be avoidable because human beings on Earth will probably not accept the directions towards the best, thus towards true love, true freedom and real peace, striving instead only for wealth, pleasure and wealth and for every way of life. Material values and unrestricted power. So...

If World War III really occurs, as calculations and observations seem to indicate is likely now and also for decades to come, then, as now, the civilian population will mostly have to bear the brunt of enormous suffering in tremendous numbers in all this catastrophe and, last but not least, the fault of irresponsible scientists who, through cloning, will create human machines for military purposes, devoid of consciousness and feelings, and will create immensely deadly and annihilating computer-like weapons. At the same time, the danger could become reality that the human combat machines, the military clones, will gain their independence and under their own direction will bring death, devastation, destruction and annihilation to the humans of Earth and the planet. The entire planet will become a scene of incomparable suffering, which had never existed on Earth until that moment. The cruel events will last about 888 days and will cause the collapse of civilization. However, the terrible scenario will continue and epidemics and various diseases, as well as enormous famine, will spread among the people, while the world's economy will totally collapse and there will be no possibility of producing any good. All food and medicine will be rationed.

The madness of war will spread not only on earth, but the disaster will equally spread to the oceans, the atmosphere and even outer space. But there will also be settlements under the ocean that will develop in the future and will be attacked and destroyed, claiming the lives of many thousands of people. However, a certain maelstrom of destruction will also originate from underwater facilities; because in the cities at the bottom of the ocean, groups of underwater pirates will form and burst upward from the depths of the ocean and will be involved in destructive combat actions with naval units on the surface. And at this moment, the possibility of extraterrestrial forces intervening against the Western industrialized countries could become a reality, because they will be responsible for the extreme and enormous disaster of the bad times to come. These extraterrestrial forces will abandon their anonymity and secret status and help those who are being terrorized by Western countries acting irresponsibly, should this possibility become a reality. Furthermore, apocalyptic natural catastrophes will occur that will make all of Europe tremble and tremble; but Europe will continue to exist, even after having suffered enormous destruction.

Far away in the West, it will be different; The United States of America will be a country of total destruction. The cause of this will be multiple. With its global conflicts that are continually instigated by it and will continue in the future, the United States is creating enormous hatred against it, all over the world, in many countries. As a result, the United States will experience enormous catastrophes that will reach proportions barely imaginable to the people of Earth. The destruction of the WTC, that is, the World Trade Center, by terrorists will be only the beginning. However, all apocalyptic events will not only occur due to the use of incredibly lethal and destructive weapons, such as chemical, laser and others, and by cloned killing machines; but in addition to this, the Earth and nature, deeply mistreated by the irresponsible human beings of the Earth, will rise up and cause destruction and bring death to the Earth. Enormous firestorms and gigantic hurricanes will ravage the United States and bring devastation, destruction and annihilation, as this from time immemorial has never happened before [sic].

Not only the United States, but also all other Western industrial countries that still live at the beginning of the new millennium in the delusion that they could dominate and govern underdeveloped nations, that is, the Third World countries, will not only soon lose influence over them but They must defend themselves against them. According to Henoch's prophecies, the truth about industrialized countries is that they only appear to be true civilizations, but in reality they are not; because more and more, at the end of the 20th century and the beginning of the third millennium, they will ignore all true love, true freedom and true wisdom, as well as true peace together with all the values of humanity and all the values of men and women. the true being of the woman. But not even all the terrible events will stop the United States from continuing its actions against all countries. Even when the North American continent is hit by the most terrible catastrophe ever recorded, evil military powers will wreak havoc with cyber, nuclear, biological and chemical weapons, so cyber weapons will also become independent and cannot be controlled. already by human beings. Overall, this is the most important part of the Enoch prophecies.

Billy: There's more; At least that's what you told me.

Quetzal: You are tireless; so I will point out some more important facts of the prophecies. From now on, new epidemics have spread among the people of Earth; However, as Henoch prophesied, a good number of epidemics will follow. Not only AIDS will occur throughout the world in the 1990s, but also epidemics such as the so-called "mad cow disease", i.e. BSE, from which different strains of Creutzfeldt-Jakob syndrome will develop, that will last well into the new millennium. Furthermore, an epidemic known as Ebola will cause many deaths, as well as other unknown epidemics and diseases that will emerge sporadically in epidemic proportions and will be new to humans, causing great concern.

However, politics will cause most of the evil. France and Spain engage each other in armed conflicts, even before World War III breaks out. However, France will not only become involved in armed conflicts with Spain, as major unrest will arise within it leading to uprisings and civil wars, as [will be] the case in Russia and Sweden. Especially in France and Sweden, the machinations and dictatorial regulations of the European Union will cause many riots and many uprisings; but also crimes committed by gangs and elements of organized crime in these countries will cause inevitable civil wars. In addition, significant tensions will arise between native citizens and immigrants from foreign countries, who as a rule also observe religious beliefs different from those of the native population. And in the end, this will lead to serious conflicts. Hatred against strangers, foreigners and people of different religious beliefs will be the order of the day, as will the rise of neo-Nazism, terrorism and right-wing extremism. Civil war-like conditions will occur in England, Wales and Northern Ireland and will claim many lives.

The Soviet Union will dissolve within this decade or, at the latest, at the beginning of the next. The decisive man for this action will be Mikhail Gorbachev. But this will not lead to rest, because the new Russia will continue its long-standing conflict with China over Inner Mongolia, with the result that Russia will lose a part of this territory to China. And China becomes dangerous, especially for India, since at this time too China has uneasy relations with it. China will attack India; and if biological weapons are used, around 30 million human beings will be killed in and around New Delhi area alone. However, this will not be the end yet, because the effect of the biological bombs and missiles, etc., used cannot be controlled at that time, and terrible epidemics unknown until that time will emerge and spread rapidly to many areas. Pakistan will also be fooled into instigating a war against India, which will be especially dangerous given that both countries are developing atomic weapons.

However, Russia will not rest and will attack Scandinavia, and in doing so will involve all of Europe. And months before that, a terrible tornado will have hit northern Europe, causing great devastation and destruction. It should still be said that the Russian attack will occur during the summer, in fact, starting from Arhangelsk. Denmark will not be dragged into the war, due to the insignificance of this country. However, Russia will not be satisfied with this war action, since its will to expand will be voracious. And consequently Russia will launch a military attack against Iran and Turkey and will conquer these two countries in bloody battles, causing enormous destruction. Also included in the Russian expansionist mentality will be the drive to gain control of the Middle East oil deposits, as well as to gain control of the southeastern region of Europe. Therefore, he will also invade the Balkans and conquer these countries in huge battles, causing ruthless and devastating destruction with many deaths. This will be at a time when tremendous natural disasters will affect Italy and its population, causing serious difficulties. But this will also be at the time when Vesuvius could become active again and could wreak enormous havoc. At the same time, a war will shake Italy and claim many human lives, as well as causing great destruction.

The destruction of war will descend upon the northern countries as strong military forces will invade from the east and loot and kill, as well as use bombs and missiles, such as falling hail, and hitherto unknown weapons of laser-controlled types. and computers that will destroy and annihilate everything, so the first target will be Hungary and then follow Austria and northern Italy. Switzerland will also be severely affected, but it will not be the real target; This will be France and Spain. However, the main objective of the aggressors will be to put all of Europe under their military control, and for this purpose France will be selected as their headquarters. France will not only be invaded by aggressors from outside, but will also be conquered from within as a result of collaborative and other forces. This can be imagined how the many foreigners of a different religion living in France at that time, and specifically Islam, would be this force working from within. Once France has fallen, a war will take place to conquer Spain and England. Subsequently, an alliance will be formed with the forces of the aggressors, which will invade Scandinavia.

For all these military operations based in France, weapons of mass destruction stored in France's arsenals will be used and will cause evil devastation, destruction and annihilation. The aggressors from the East will force the French Army to unite its military forces and lead a war of conquest against the countries of northern Europe, invading and conquering Sweden and Norway. Later, these northern countries will be annexed by Russia. Military forces will also attack Finland, resulting in many being killed and enormous destruction caused. At the same time, as a civil war rages in Germany, a hugely bloody revolution will break out in England that will claim more lives than the civil war will claim in Germany. And because England and Ireland have been at war for a long time, because of the IRA and the police and military forces of England, the result will be (because this feud will continue until that time) that this revolution will spread throughout Ireland, especially affecting to Northern Ireland. Many lives will be lost during a civil war in Wales, where differences will arise between the various parties before the Third World War. Welsh and English forces will clash especially near Cymru, claiming many lives and causing great destruction.

But death, destruction and annihilation will not only wreak havoc in Europe but also in America, where much suffering will have to be endured and there will be many deaths, as well as destruction and annihilation. The United States and Russia will have at their disposal the most terrible weapons of mass destruction, a fact that is already the case to some extent today, and they will clash with violent force against each other in that moment of conflict, so that Canada will also be dragged in this conflict. The source of this conflict will be the Russian attack on the American state of Alaska and against Canada. This conflict will result in mass killings of human beings, as well as devastating destruction, annihilation and epidemics, etc., which humanity on Earth will never have seen and experienced until that time. Not only will nuclear, biological, and chemical weapons be used en masse, but also highly lethal computer-controlled weapons systems that are only in the early stages of development today, or will be invented and built during the third millennium.

As already mentioned, enormous natural catastrophes and rolling walls of fire and violent hurricanes will devastate the entire United States, while, in addition, all the terrible effects of war will bring thousands of deaths, destruction and annihilation. America's largest cities will be absolutely destroyed and firestorms will cause great disasters and misery. Severe earthquakes and volcanic eruptions will also belong to that time, and these will cause much suffering and misery and death in addition to enormous destruction and devastation, as all of nature and the planet itself will rise up against the madness of human beings on Earth. However, tornadoes, earthquakes and volcanic eruptions will not only wreak havoc in America, but also in Europe and the rest of the world.

These activities have already started today, also during the last decades, with the exception that they will become more and more devastating in the future. And man on Earth is mostly guilty today, since also in the future it is man who will destroy the entire environment: all nature, the atmosphere, water and all the resources of the planet. And through this, a change in weight occurs within the Earth, caused for example by the creation of giant lakes through the construction of dams and the creation of hollow caverns due to the exploitation of oil and gas, etc. And therefore unnatural movements are created within the Earth, which also cause unnatural tectonic effects and cause earthquakes and volcanic eruptions, which also in turn cause enormous climate changes, resulting in horrendous tornadoes of devastating proportions that will ultimately release their destructive energies. in the entire world. All of this will lead to increasingly horrible floods and unusually massive snowfall that will advance to the southern countries and eventually even to the equatorial regions, because through the madness of human beings the Earth has begun to inadvertently [bizarrely] rotate as a consequence. of atomic effects. Explosions within and on the surface of the Earth. And this will be the reason why the planet will slowly but surely enter an extraordinary rotating orbit around the Sun, while the first phase is already happening, causing a change in the climate, leading to a new ice age..

However, the misery on Earth will continue, as two terrible civil wars will break out in America, with one following the other. Then the United States of America will break up and deadly hostility will prevail between it, which will then lead to the division into five different territories; and sectarian fanatics cannot be prevented from playing a dictatorial role. Anarchy will be the world condition that will prevail and torment human beings for a long period of time, since human beings will also be tormented by multiple epidemics and diseases, many of them new and unknown to human beings and therefore incurable. Due to this fact, the bodies of many human beings will slowly and miserably decompose, while excruciating pain, blindness, and terrible breathing problems leading to suffocation will also occur.

The consciousness of many human beings will deteriorate and they will succumb to mental weakness and madness. And all these horrible events will be attributable to biological and chemical weapons, which are the cause of deaths that are not quick, but horrible and slow; and this will also occur due to the use of beam and frequency weapons that are already being developed today. Finally, Henoch's words can be specifically mentioned, which include that Earth's humanity, in pursuit of technology for mass destruction and greed for power, hatred, revenge and riches, will ignore all values of Creation and will trample all the values of love, wisdom, freedom and peace, as the ancestors of the Henoch line have done before, to plunge the world into misery, death, destruction and annihilation, and into the gravest catastrophes that never experienced by humanity on Earth. [End of story]. *Note: when the dialogue says, "America", we must consider that there is the idiom of saying 'America' in English to refer to the USA, which is logically a contextual error, but is still used.

X.

COVID AND ARTIFICIAL INTELLIGENCE

For most people, the word 'COVID' is the name of a disease, and that is what politicians, supranational organizations and news outlets have made them believe since the end of 2019, because they all respond to the WHO, which in turn responds. to the elitists Bill Gates and the Rockefellers. The truth is that the definition 'COVID-19' has existed for years. The idea of a supposed pandemic to take away humanity's rights and freedoms within other types of globalist agendas was already completely designed in 2009. COVID19 is actually a program that belongs to the 2030 Agenda, where the Agenda is directly included. ID2020. However, it is the acronym for 'Digital Identification of Vaccination Certificate by Artificial Intelligence'.

- The letter 'C' stands for 'Certificate' (certificate), and its hidden code corresponds to the carbon symbol, related to biological and aerobic organisms.

- The letter 'O' is from the English 'of', but it can also be used as 'on', since the certificate is intended to be implemented as a wearable device (portable, implantable in the body), being in turn the atomic symbol for oxygen . Both carbon and oxygen are the basis of the structure and life of breathing beings.

- The letter 'V' is from the English 'Vaccine' (vaccine), in the sense of the application of an injection with a certain content, not strictly a vaccine as such (since the so-called "covid vaccine" is not really a vaccine per HE).

- The letter 'I' is from the English 'Identification', which can even be seen as 'ID'.

- The letter 'D' is for 'Digital'.

- The number 19 is not only the year the project was launched but also an alphanumeric code: 1 is 'A', and 9 is 'I', in English order. In this way it creates 'AI', acronym for Artificial Intelligence.

• [*Both CO (carbon monoxide) and CO2 (carbon dioxide) are combinations of carbon and oxygen. A human body is primarily carbon (C), and lives by oxygen (O). We breathe oxygen and release when we exhale that oxygen now loaded with cellular waste, which the trees and micro plankton will absorb, taking the carbon and again discarding oxygen for our breathing. That is the cycle of life. Ironically, we can stop eating for weeks, stop drinking liquids for days, we can stop sunbathing for years, but we cannot stop breathing for more than several minutes. If our breathing is affected – for example, by breathing poorly or without enough oxygen – our system is damaged, starting with our brain. For this reason, it is essential within the COVID Agenda that humanity wears a mask on the face that covers the nose and mouth with the excuse of supposed particles that only an irresponsible person would throw in another person's face with a sneeze (instead of covering the face). face, like we all do*)].

The so-called coronavirus pandemic was planned as far back as 2009, which appears in elite protocols and memoranda. Its objective was to implement a digital personal identification certificate at a global level, which would ultimately be controlled and centralized by artificial intelligence. But what does a vaccine, or pseudo-vaccine, have to do with it? Well, the point is not simply that everyone has a numerical "health" record in digital format, but that it allows artificial intelligence to control the person. How do you control a carbon and oxygen organism? Their oxygen is now controlled, since they previously privatized the Sun, water, food, land, electricity, time, etc. We talk about absolute control over humanity. The mask that they persuade everyone to wear not only takes away 20% of the oxygen necessary for the proper functioning of the body and its immune system, but is also an indoctrinated symbol of subconscious submission and consensual censorship.

So how do they control us as living beings, as carbon beings? Becoming something other than what we are. By damaging brain functions for so many months with a muzzle on, contaminating the air with toxins, contaminating water with fluoride, contaminating food, the only thing left to do is contaminate the Sun and our DNA. [By the way, Bill Gates is already trying to do the Sun thing (he intends to block the Sun)]. Regarding our DNA, it is not so easy, this requires injecting a wide series of things. The human body is a perfect design, and it knows how to defend itself very well. Consequently, for a computer with artificial intelligence to be able to control us, our body would need to have a high amount of electrically conductive and wave-receiving material. Since it is not feasible for us to be connected to a database by a cable, the logical thing is to do it wirelessly, and the way in which Wireless systems work is by transmission of short and long distance waves, a receiver and a transmitter.

The satellites for this have already been placed in orbit by the thousands since the 1980s, and especially since 2019 with NASA's SpaceX project. Regarding antennas that do this work, it is already achieved with 4G systems, and especially with 5G technology (imagine what they will achieve with military technology: 6G). But we return to the fact that although our biological body responds to waves, they can only impact us - from a warfare point of view - with microwave propagation. In cases they can induce words, sensations, emotions, pain, fatigue and other elements with a specific wave level fired from an antenna (something that has been done since the Cold

War). However, greater precision is needed, in light of the interests of the ID2020 Agenda, which is part of the 2030 Agenda.

The implementation of metals has been carried out since the 70s through unnecessary vaccination campaigns. Injections are promoted instead of instilling in society the habit of taking sunlight, fresh air, bathing in the sea, doing physical activity and eating in an alkaline way to enhance health, because the so-called vaccines are the way in which the DNA incorporating particles from organs of other animals and aborted fetuses, and heavy metals, such as thimerosal (mercury), aluminum and even chelates such as copper. Now, there are materials that are more conductive than copper, such as graphene (200 times more conductive), which is the essential component of the COVID pseudo-vaccines in graphene oxide format. Thus they can transmit clear and concise signals to the mind from satellites and antennas. But that's not the point.

• [*If we take the letters of COVID with the atomic values from the Table of Elements, 'C' is carbon, 'O' is oxygen, 'V' is vanadium, 'I' is iodine, and 'D' is deuterium, one of the two stable isotopes of hydrogen. Graphene is a component derived from carbon, in union with oxygen and hydrogen, and from there comes the graphene oxide that is in the COVID pseudo-vaccines, which are also magnetic* .

Apart from damaging our biological organism with unnecessary and toxic vaccines, they also alter our DNA with messenger RNA, and also sterilize us with the supposed protein encoding Spike, which is actually a neutralizer of Synsitin (responsible for male and female sexual reproduction).. This is to reduce the world population. Progressively they will have an army of zombies and robots. But they are accompanied by another even more macabre factor. The so-called vaccines contain luciferase, which is part of various nano devices that are being put into the body of those who are placed on their shoulders to be injected with an experimental product. These are nano crystals, which are better than microchips for storing information. And what do they get out of that? They alone, not much. A system full of graphene and luciferase can be controlled remotely from a central station, and even permanently direct the person's behavior, know what they think and introduce everything desired into their mind. But to make this 100% effective, a microchip would be missing that centralizes the system and acts as a connection, for example, by radio frequency.

We reach the end of this article. The paper COVID certificate is the first part. They will put it as a card and later digitize it with biometric recognition systems. However, the obligation will be total despite the marches, protests and civil war that this will cause worldwide. When the obligation is combined with the financial crisis, the use of a quantum dot tattoo on the back of the right hand, or an implantable RFID device, will be imposed, where only those who possess the certificate, its registration by name or its numbering will be able to receive aid from the State. That's because there will be no money. However, if you do not have the chip, its digital certificate or its number, you will be outside the system and will not be able to buy anything nor will they be able to pay you.

This system has long been known among the elite as the '666' target, or '600-60-6'. It is the registration system of human control by numbering and under control of artificial intelligence. If you look at the letters COVID you can see that the 'C' is 100 in Roman numerals, the 'D' is 500, which adds up to 600. If you take the 'V' and the 'I' you have the 6. Meanwhile, in the Pythagorean and Coptic alphabet 'O' is 60 (in addition to the fact that in the Hebrew and Egyptian languages the graphic form or pictogram 'O' also represents the figure 60). However, if you count the number of this Beast (the emerging Global Super State) you find the code that represents it, that infamous 666 that has nothing to do with religious myths.

Note 1 : You can see that apart from the letters 'CO' based on the biological body, the letters 'VI' exist as the name of a new charging system for mobile devices. Keep in mind that progressively all electrical elements become synchronized. You can use your smartphone with your Smart watch, your Smart TV, your computer via Bluetooth or Wireless, and some are already starting to use RFID chips (radio frequency identification). In fact, people not injected with placebo or saline solution for the SARS-CoV-2 coronavirus are already traceable and synchronizable by Wireless (check it out yourself with someone tapped using your phone's Bluetooth system).

Note 2 : The acronym 'OV' corresponds to a maneuver, resource and management control system of the US Department of Defense, called 'Operation View', within the DoDAF framework. This system actually seeks complete synchronicity of all systems.

Note 3 : Another fact that you should know is that the elite have a preference for ancient languages, especially of Sumerian origin, where the Semitic ones come from, and even Sanskrit sounds. Therefore, you can find hidden messages with Hebrew, Egyptian or ancient Greek, among others. In the case of the Fertile Crescent languages, they are read from right to left, and in their case, COVID, written in Latin characters, would be read as 'DIBOK' or 'DYBUC'. In Jewish folklore, a dibok is demonic possession, the taking over of the body by an alien dark entity that subjugates it.

Note 4 : If COVID is read in a Semitic way (DIBOK) there are other hidden elements with its letters, as happens if you investigate 666. It corresponds to the same thing, directly associated with technologies and transhumanism. Anagrammatic examples are: 'DI', acronym for 'digital'; 'DC', direct current (pulse conductivity, if associated with the functionality of an implanted microchip); 'OC', is boss in English; 'IV' is a device for administering fluid intravenously.

The virus that breaks the network

Let's look at children's programming, which is for the most vulnerable. For example, to look at one of countless cases, I will tell you about my daughter and I's favorite animated film, 'Wreck It Ralph', from Disney, from 2012. Since the end of 2020, I had been finding a lot kinship between Anthony Fauci and the character there called 'Fix It Felix', who embodies the figure of the avatar who fixes the Wreck It Ralph game. It is negative primacy. People don't recognize it directly but their subconscious does, and they see someone coming to solve a problem and their mind tells them "yes, he fixes it", because there was a prior conditioning preparation through an image. That's called Stealth Programming. Another curious detail is that 'Félix Junior's job is to prevent the spread of a virus that Ralph unleashed because "he didn't want to be the bad guy anymore", he was tired of the monotony, of not knowing the world, of his life being robotic, predictable and limited to a small space, and, above all, being the one on the receiving end of constant humiliation. You want to be a winner and be recognized, so you look for a medal that honors you. In an accident in another game, a virus escapes and infiltrates Sugar Rush and threatens to destroy the entire game room. The person who helps Felix Junior is a secret operations "military" and his future wife. To accept this soldier's intervention favorably, they make her very attractive and in high definition, even with her dictatorial temperament. It is interesting that despite the chaos, there is no general board of directors to take action on the matter, but rather Felix and his "friend" (Sergeant Tamora Jean Calhoun, from the game Hero's Duty) take the job. of saviors for themselves.

The analogy here with the 'coronaplan' is evident: it is not the government that is actually in charge, but the medical and military cartel, led by the WHO (similar to the later footage 'The Emoji Movie' (2017), where the focus are "computer failures" (avatars that act differently from the standards, like you and me), the digital age, viruses, corporate imperialism and the police dictatorship in technocratic service). Now let's see, Vanellope, the girl in the game in danger, was a victim of mental programming, which in the game they define as "erasing her parent program", so that she does not know who she is, and they treat her as "a bug" that must be removed. Everyone in that game is a victim of brainwashing by their ruler, and lives in a world of "fantasy" and "candy", and is distracted by car racing - like television, sports, movies - until The problem is now unstoppable. They do not remember who they are nor do they know that they are being manipulated. In fact, they attack Vanellope and don't let her win the game to prevent the system from being "reset." The 'Reset' of the game is key to saving the machine room (of video games), which is an analogy of our world. What they introduce here is a key element that aims to say that the virus crisis can only be resolved with a complete "reset" of the entire system. And since Vanellope can't start the "gold medal," we have to assume that it's all about the economy. Everyone must pay, but she puts up the "gold" medal, a financial symbol by nature.

Curiously, through the film 'Zootopia', Disney presented another preview in 2016 about a "serum" (virus) that is injected into the "potential enemies" of society in SmartCities, making them "dangerous." Now, in Wreck It Ralph, both Vanellope and Ralph suffer from contempt and criticism and are intended to be eliminated by whoever controls the game. Turbo, who causes problems in one game (country, system) infiltrates "another" – like Bill Gates – corrupting the data of all the avatars – as a good computer and Trojan connoisseur knows -, and making himself the "king". " (King Candy, or King Candy). Only the "bitter candy" – the resigned one – knows about the conspiracy and reveals the truth to Ralph through threats. They all use such beautiful names, to be accepted by the subconscious, even though the conscious area sees them as bad. Another aspect of the mental program here is that all people must accept their roles and limit themselves to "not leaving their corresponding games" (as is the case with 'Emoji, The Movie', where being "different" implies tacit elimination).

The key phrase here is said by Sonic in an advertisement: "remember, don't leave your game, because if you die outside your game, you don't regenerate, goodbye." Here we see the newscasts represented in the famous figure of Sonic, and what Arcade lover would not pay attention to Sonic. Of course, the news is always presented as "now, all the information", "in seconds, you will have all the events that happen", etc., implying to the subconscious that you will know the outside world and the truth of what is happening around you. through the "truth" that they present to you, and as they present it to you.

Let's also see how Sonic introduces the idea that if you leave your game (your house), you will die. The idea of the game is that "you can die inside it", because you regenerate, but if you die outside, you don't regenerate. I could venture to interpret that this may even be a hint at globalist ideas of introducing transhumanism and certain drugs in the future, which will prevent people from getting old or sick (compare Rev. 9:6), but of course, those that have left at the end of the "planetary purification of the species". On the other hand, they indoctrinate you, "live your life at home, because you are safe there, no matter what happens, but not outside." Here is the letter that Disney had incorporated into this film 8 years earlier. We also see how bullying is essential against detractors and those who do not allow themselves to be brainwashed, even undermining their creativity and free thinking, as I already said they did with Ralph and Vanellope. But going back to the "reset", as I said, Ralph takes a gold medal (symbol of wealth, prosperity, economy) from the game Hero's Duty, and takes it to Sugar Rush where Vanellope enters it into the race.

The medal decomposes and becomes "data", whose value is translated into the registration to compete (in the future, a mere cryptocurrency, without which you will not be able to "run", or have a place in society). Here I interpret that they clearly suggest a change from physical to virtual currency, without which "you can't run", and running is, in Sugar Rush, the only purpose. Only if you run can you be chosen again, and if you win you are among those who can enjoy the benefits of the game's avatars. This is an analogy to the chip that would replace cash, and without which you will be nobody in the system, which will become a complete digital network.

Something a little more cryptic in this whole story is the fact that all the inhabitants of Sugar Rush, except for sour candy (King Candy's spokesperson), the king and the police, are children, "candy children" (clearly a reference to pedophilia, childhood vulnerability). Avatars serve the interests of the humans playing in the Arcade Machine Room, just as the masters of the world use our race, or the Reptilians and Orians use everyone else under them. These types of subliminal sexual messages are found in many places, especially in advertisements, and Disney has already had complaints in the past, and has had to pay millionaire fines in courts of law for the evidence against it that shows the merciless bombing of subliminal messages and sexual sigils in his films, especially in 'The Little Mermaid', 'The Lion King' and 'Pocahontas'.

These types of concepts are not seen with the naked eye and are often hidden behind representations only understood among adepts, among those under Monarch mental control, or those who understand picaresque ideas. That is the case of a scene where Ralph leaves the PacMan game eating some cherries and when he sees orphan avatars (without a game) he gives them to them, already bitten. As reflected in the PizzaGate scandal, these ideas have a greater meaning behind them, but it doesn't take a genius to argue that two cherries are commonly used in SexShops as a cultural representation of testicles. We see the same example with a bitten apple, like the slogan of the Apple company, which is used to refer to "original sin", which are also sexual ideas and erotic or passionate temptation (adultery, fornication, prostitution, etc.). I only add that no one is demonizing sex itself, at all, but the perversion and degradation of values.

In 2018, Disney released the second part of Wreck It Ralph, called 'Ralph Breaks the Internet'. As if by chance, the film came out exactly one year before the decision of the US elections between Trump and Madame Clinton. The plot revolves around how Vanellope gets bored of the game and Ralph creates a new driving track. The player "breaks the steering wheel" while "fighting against the driver's rebellion" and now they must find a handlebar on Ebay to replace it, or it will be out of play. The message here evokes how there is a clash between the resistance and the elite, which forces a reset (if the helm is not replaced, the game will be withdrawn). Ralph and Vanellope oppose the elite and this poses a threat to the safety and subsistence of the Arcade game.

The director of the room (Mr. Litwack) installs the internet (the digital world, the Internet of Things) and these two rebels escape to find how to fix the problem, find a "cure." Meanwhile, Fauci and the police state... sorry, I meant, Fix It Felix and Sergeant Calhoun, are in charge of "taking care" of all the "candy game children", now "homeless". From that point everything revolves around "raising the most money" to "defray the costs" of the steering wheel. Translated into our language, pull all the strings and make use of all "digital" means to "pay" for the "solution", which here essentially translates into the problem of unpayable global debt. The digital idea of the internet world suggests how society is embarking towards a completely virtual reality and entertainment.

Vanellope meets the fatherless feminists: the Disney princesses. They understand each other perfectly, independent of men, without parental relationship, without children, without family, without husband, in their own bubble and lacking general culture. They all coincide in an external beauty and an internal intellectual emptiness, not having grown up with a father figure, since this is an important strategy of Walt Disney to introduce into the minds of children, and part of the feminist agenda of the Rockefeller Foundation. Vanellope then meets another girl, a daring racer, played by Israeli actress Gal Gadot, and wants to stay in her high-resolution, multi-hazard car racing game, but Ralph gets jealous and puts a virus in that game. Yes, we are represented by the spoilsport Ralf, who does not want this new improved digital world. This is where it gets interesting. Once again a virus threatens security, but this time it is no longer local but global.

Once again the solution is a reset, now on a global and total scale. If we compare it with the covid agenda, first there was a quarantine of decapitalization to begin to destabilize the planet, and then comes a real virus, both biological and cybernetic, to restart the planetary structure, first financial, and then global and contextual. The virus actually spreads through **people's "insecurities," that is, their fears** . And here is the ace of this deck: the real virus that attacks the world is fear, and thanks to this fear it spreads and achieves the goals of the creator of the "worm". Feminist independence wins (the anti-family and exclusive philosophy of the value of man), and the network is saved. What does it mean in Illuminati language? Reduction of world population, with viruses, sterilization and eugenics. Once again, society can continue in its virtual world and the masters can direct their avatars, but now in a "renewed" system.

If there is one way the elite can use to tell you whatever they want and you won't realize it, it is through cartoons, and now with animation. And if you realize it, what are you going to say? Will you tell your friends that you see the intentions of the Illuminati because of "a cartoon"? It doesn't sound very credible. That's what it's about. Disney princesses, for example, are represented in practically all the films, and they are always instilling the same idea: worship of the monarchy. It is the "princess" who presents the kind and acceptable face of some type of royalty or caste. This is a success in England, where the royal house is almost a showbiz icon, more famous and admired than film or music stars. Thus they become untouchable, and their image remains well seen. How is it that in the 21st century we continue to feed parasites? What purpose do monarchies have? But there they are, seen as an idol to love, care for and respect.

It is so easy to introduce these ideas to children that there have been debates for years about the use of subliminal messages in young people, because it is known how susceptible and vulnerable they are to them. Advertisements are a clear example, and anyone who is a parent knows it well: their child comes after watching a spot and tells them they want that toy they just presented . Now imagine a Disney Channel putting girls daily in the trend of the Barbie series, and boys addicted to their hobbies, in a bubble and without interest in the outside world or culture (knowledge). Children are the objective of the elite in a crazy way, and that is why it is so common in Disney films to see orphans or children without one or both of their parents (based on the emotional imprint of the uprooting of one of them). In 2016, DreamWorks released the film 'Trolls', which is about some horrible, big people who want to "eat" the "little ones", those divine little heavens of love and colors. But I will not focus this book on the dark strategy of pedophilia, I only intend to give you an idea of what is not seen with the naked eye. Let's continue.

XI.

GATES AND SOROS: THE TWO HORNS OF THE BEAST

The gist of most of the things you read in this book have been covered in my previous works, such as 'Armageddon, Close Encounters of the Fifth Kind', 'Recognizing the End Time', 'Apocalypse, Remote Viewing I, The Great Tribulation', 'Apocalypse, Remote Viewing II, The End of the Century' and 'COVID, The Greatest Conspiracy in History', but I wanted to address more specific issues here that relate to the situation in the United States, because Since 1870 it has been a great power and has been used as a platform for international control. It is precisely for this reason that it is determined that it must collapse, and with it the social, political, economic, financial, industrial and constitutional system as we have known it in the last two centuries. In light of these changes we have revelations from various sources of a prophetic nature, announcing this paradigm shift and what it will mean for the entire planet. Once the US falls, the last hope for freedom for this time will disappear.

Just as in the visions of the prophet Daniel, the book of Revelation speaks of several Beasts, one of them coming into action as a creature with two horns. I have been venturing for several years to say that one of them is the Microsoft magnate, Bill Gates, and since the beginning of the plan-demic I have considered that the other horn is another magnate, George Soros, both heavyweights in international finance, and both Americans. Soros pushes the Kalergi Agenda and Agenda 201, while Gates pushes the ID2020 Agenda, the COVID Agenda, among many others. Together with Gates and Soros, the Rockefellers are operating, and this mafia, this triad, the one that most strongly pushes the Agenda of the Antichrist, the Agenda of the Illuminati New World Order.

For more than a decade I have been talking about who the Rockefellers really are, and in my first works I make clear the monopoly they have had in the banking, financial, oil, political, geopolitical, institutional, academic, educational and pharmaceutical systems. Soros and Gates are his partners and public tools on the media and international stage. Soros was expelled from Austria in 2020 following warnings from President Alexander Van der Bellen himself, because his attempt to destabilize the country was evident. Not so with Spain, where it was known before the 2020 presidential elections that the current government leader, Pedro Sánchez, received help to come to power from Soros, and that the mission to fulfill was to destabilize Spain. The CNI itself (Spanish National Intelligence Center) already considered Soros a threat to the security and stability of the nation, according to a 2019 report.

George Soros pursues the elitist interests of the Illuminati by wanting to disarm Europe. There is innumerable evidence that points to the tricks of this magnate to Islamize Europe and destabilize it, eliminating the values of the regions of the European Community and pushing social unrest among the population against African and Middle Eastern immigrants who are welcomed daily in large number to various countries in the region. This destabilization is seen first in labor areas, it is observed in insecurity, in that while Europeans are seeing a difficult economic situation, their governments offer economic and housing aid to immigrants, above their own people. Unrest is created between Europeans and Muslims, and idealists (Shiites) attack the integrity of Europe and its citizens without much to lose.

Bill Gates plays another role, equally or more sinister, and monopolizes more sectors. When the so-called 'Spanish Flu' took place, Mr. Frederick L. Gates – grandfather of Bill Gates – was involved with the Rockefellers' experimental meningitis vaccine, the main cause of the so-called pandemic at that time. As I explain in my previous work, the Spanish Flu was actually the result of a cocktail of vaccines given to American soldiers at the end of World War I. The Rockefellers were aware from the first decade of the 1900s that oil could have an infinite number of uses, and one of them was its "medical" application, which led to the creation of the pharmaceutical system and the persecution and suppression of traditional medicine, that is, That is, natural medicine.

The ties between the Rockefellers and the Gates are incredibly close. They are precisely the main financiers of the so-called World Health Organization, or WHO. Indeed, as they are the ones who pay more than 73% of their activities and funds, they have the leading voice in their guidelines. The Rockefellers are to the US what their Rothschild colleagues are to Europe. Both are two of the groups that make up the Illuminati (the 13 families that dominate this planet). Although in the Illuminati there are families that only seem to look after their own interests, such as the Kennedys, they do not share the philosophies of global control, as far as the Rockefellers and Rothschilds are concerned, they are obstinate by Luciferian ideals. The Rothschilds have held SARS-CoV-2 patents since 2015, and are linked to the Windsors (the British royal house) since ancestry dating back to Prince William IX. It is therefore important to know that there is apparent evidence of the link between the Windsor monarchy and the financing of biological weapons laboratories, such as the one in Wuhan. Precisely the advisor to the president of the United States, Anthony Fauci, and Mr. Gates, have been financing this type of laboratories, notably in Wuhan, China.

Bill Gates and George Soros bought the "COVID test" company Mologic in July 2021, and two days later – coincidentally – the FDA (US Food and Drug Administration) revealed in an internal document that the infamous test PCR was carried out without real tests of the Chinese virus, and consequently a new test was going to be implemented from December 2021. And guess who is going to provide it? That's where Mologic comes in. Gates, the founder of the computer company Microsoft, is now interested in vaccines, having said on TED in 2010 that good work with vaccines would enhance the reduction of the world's population. Microsoft patents "COVID vaccines," and Bill Gates is a shareholder in Pfizer-Biontech. That same Gates created an international corporate movement at the end of 2020 to attack all social networks whenever people speak against vaccines.

Their lobby reaches Silicone Valley, where programmers design algorithms with artificial intelligence that ban you if you say something against a vaccine. But they call this hacking "independent fact checkers", those so-called 'FastCheck' that ensure the security of the official version of the medicine. They participate together with Google in this global campaign. Since Google owns YouTube, it is not surprising that they also punish you on YouTube and delete your account if you tell the truth about vaccines, or promote natural or holistic medicine, since Google invests in AstraZeneca/Oxford shares . Here you have their mafia, because Facebook is part of this plot, and therefore they punish you for the same reasons, and since Facebook owns Instagram, they will also ban you for what you publish on any of these networks, no matter how much official evidence and true contributions.

The issue of pseudo-vaccines is not just a matter of the pharmaceutical network. DARPA, which is the advanced weapons study department of the DoD (US Department of State), is one of the main parties involved in the introduction of elements that contain these such COVID vaccines. What is the logic here? The advanced weapons study area messed with a supposed antidote for a mere virus? Recently, information has been leaked claiming that Bill Gates bought the US CDC, or Center for Disease Control, as well as the UK Health and Medical Products Regulatory Agency. Ironically, the CDC is itself a vaccine-creating institution, which holds at least 20 patents on them.

It is interesting to see the connection, because Gates has been promoting the ID2020 Agenda for years, for the implementation of wareable chips (RFID devices implantable under the skin) and quantum dot tattoos, for personal identification and monetary transactions. That would explain the interests and links with the US Department of Defense. An RFID device is a radio frequency identification system, which emits waves like Wi-Fi, and can receive and emit signals to the outside. Some naive person believes that Bill Gates is a philanthropist, but one would have to be an idiot not to connect the dots and see that first of all we are talking about a corporate lobby, of vested interests that are, at most, sinister.

XII.
THE END THAT NEVER COMES

It is part of every culture and human thought to believe or hope for an end to each historical cycle. Some often wonder what determines the end of one era and the beginning of another, such as, for example, all the prehistoric periods of the Earth, which are distinguished by certain thousands of years and specific names; Determinant markings, decisive changes, dying and rebirth, a complete or almost total change of an entire system or an ecosystem.

Human beings define the most remote eras or ages as those in which the earth and life were formed, renaming them according to abrupt changes that would have occurred, according to the results of stratigraphic studies and dating and their estimates. At the beginning of the most recent era – known as the Holocene (the last and current epoch of the Quaternary period, which is believed to have begun around 10,000 BC, when the cold episode called 'Recent Dryas', belonging to the last ice age, ended) – sub-periods are categorized, in line with various factors, especially climatic, such as the 'Medieval Warm Period' (900 AD) or the 'Little Ice Age' (1300 AD). We know that also in the sense of universal history it is usually defined in three periods: prehistory (Ancient Age and Middle Ages), 15th-17th century (Modern Age) and 18th-21st century (Contemporary Age).

The most significant changes of these periods have been caused by developments, advances, war conflicts or similar things, little significant compared to the abrupt or dramatic alterations that millennia or millions of years ago changed the geography, the environment, the fauna, the flora or other scenarios of that nature.

Science considers that these cycles are periodic, so they repeat in a sequential and repetitive way, with their own variants. The Olmecs, Mayans, Aztecs, Jopi, Vedas, Egyptians and many more peoples of the past defined history in very specific eras that were marked, whether by patterns of sequential years and/or by "natural" disasters. Both they and many others, whether wise men or scientists, prophets or mathematicians, priests or seers, were convinced that this pattern would continue to exist, at least until the end of an era that - according to their estimates - is the one that concerns us now (although others would come after this, but with different patterns within the same long cycles).

Just as ancient ages passed and new ones arrived, this same parameter would be relative to our present, not according to the hopeless idea that has been around – or is still around – the minds of those little understood in this matter, but only the end of this era. to see a new rebirth - even more glorious than the eras that have preceded us -. According to many of the sources of this type - from ancestral cultures - short periods enter into large periods, and just as we measure these ideas, also for them the largest cycles are the most determining, and the smallest ones only punctual and included within the largest. The primary cycles or patterns were defined in periods ranging from 52 to 60 years, within others of almost 400 years and/or 600 years; older than these were especially those of 2,160 years, then those of 5,200 years, then those of 12,500 years, then those of 26,000 years, then those of 75,000 years, and so on even longer periods, each related to stellar movements.

What implication can the stars – including the Earth – have with significant changes in our world? In a skeptical sense regarding the Higher World, in principle there would not be an objective answer to it, but if one believes that higher spheres of reality govern the lower ones, one begins to understand the relationship of these kingdoms and stars with the "earthly" changes (and we must consider that the photons that travel from the stars are particles of consciousness).

What would be the point of having this knowledge? Although it seems clear that at least since the 70s of the 20th century the calculations or sequences to conclude the age of Pisces and begin that of Aquarius must have been accompanied by global chaos and its prior rebirth, this does not seem to occur yet. If we looked at time through the prism or eyes of "Long Time," or the perspective of the eternity of the universe, this change would have already been seen, perceived as a quick snap of the fingers, or even conceived as something past (since the past, present and future are an illusion of the determining time factor in each sphere within the cosmos, and depends on different variants). That would explain why Jesus of Nazareth, as he left, said, " I am coming soon , " given that by now almost 2,000 years have easily passed. Taking the Baktun cycles (144,000 days), we would speak of the passage of 5 stages since then (even Revelation uses the pattern of "144,000", in sequences of 12,000 x 12 (where 12 also usually represents half of a day and even the months of the year)). A precise period of 5 Baktun – the longest sequence of the Mayan calendar, representing 394.3 years, each – is equivalent to 720,000 days, which is a pattern that also corresponds with sacred geometry and the mathematical mechanics of the universe.

With the 1st Baktun after the birth of Jesus Christ, came the era of early Christianity until the emergence of Catholicism and the misrepresentation of Christianity (circa 5-12 BC to 380-394 AD); With the 2nd Baktun, after this, came the Roman Catholic era, which was stopped by the Islamic era (until 790, more or less); With the 3rd Baktun, Saracen power prevailed, being the "century of the Arabs" that continued with the time of the Crusades (until approximately 1180); With the 4th Baktun came the greatest changes in modern society, since the Middle Ages concluded and the birth of the period of great advances in our known history took place, not without great epidemics and wars in Europe (which is where the changes were most notorious) - until 1,570-1,580, more or less -; Then came the 5th Baktun - as I said, starting from the birth of Jesus Christ -, which was the beginning of Protestantism and the most intense decrease in the religious influence of Rome (a stage that would have lasted until the 70s of the 20th century).

One way or another, these 5 Baktun would be ending sometime between the 70s and early 90s of our time, which coincides with various estimates about the conclusion of the age of Pisces - or age of Christianity (either or wrong, since it would be the period of Christianity in its general context, with its pros and cons) -. Consequently, the expected new era would begin, but in accordance with the warnings so pointed out throughout the centuries and millennia prior to the present, there would be a transition before the full era of human rebirth, characterized by a new fictitious system, a globalized world. based on deception and control of the few over the majority, which would be accompanied by an "apocalypse", an average of 4 to 7 remarkably critical years.

Without this process, similar to a birth, the utopian age that would mark the birth of our planet towards perfection, eternal peace, immortality and the joy and health of all creation could not truly begin. But the idea of the "end of the world" has been discussed for so long, firmly maintained that the end is coming – and the truth is that it is –, but everything seems to remain the same in the eyes of many. It is clear that nothing remains the same, and that significant changes have unfolded in the last 100 years unlike anything seen in our known history. The real problem does not lie in the ability of the interpreters of the prophecies to be correct, but rather in the probability/possibility factor of time/space. This means that although there are cycles that repeat and patterns that also repeat, within what we can call "Destiny", there are probabilistic variants or various possibilities such as equations depending on the extension of time within a space. There are events that can be changed, events with nuances that can be altered, circumstances that can be delayed or values that can be added, due to Free Will, that is, the decisions of the people themselves. However, the point is that things are not even going to happen because it is prophesied; What is prophesied is the mathematics of the variables if everything continues according to that course.

Among the many examples that could be given, and the many complementary ideas that would be addressed, one could conceptualize this argument as the case of many people who are warned that a natural disaster is going to occur: a majority pray and ask for forgiveness for something. that they could have done wrong to trigger this, and the other party quickly leaves the place (even though they did not repent, they believed the announcement). All "Effects" are caused by "Causes", and if the "punishment" that is to come upon someone is remitted by the intervention of many, and the rest also make a radical determination regarding what they have believed will happen, the Destination is "modified" or "altered", depending on the corresponding variants. In other words, the disaster may not occur, it may occur but to a very small extent, or it may be delayed for a long time, even waiting for the next generation (and seeing if the next one also avoids it by acting accordingly).

While the power establishments of today's world become stronger and stronger, at a social level an awakening of conscience is fueled, resulting in a clash of polarities; If in the 70s increasingly convincing glimpses of the end of this era began to be seen, the powers that be had to ensure that the awakening of consciousness that was rising in society diminished, so they introduced new musical trends, festivals, drugs, philosophies and trivial local conflicts (even external wars to send young people to die, or plunge them into fights against their neighbors). However, that did not help, since the people protested wars and injustices, counteracting at that moment the power that could have triggered the end of this period.

If the conclusion of this age is now, and highlighted by a global awakening of consciousness, what causes that awakening and what does it look like? It is and is plausible if one knows how to look and discern, but given the strong opposition of "evil" – so to speak – in this world, the currents of mental manipulation and social and psychological conditioning, degrading fashions and movements, virtual and passionate distractions , fully absorbing occupations, media fears, apathy and faction divisions due to truly ridiculous things - all behind which is the dark power elite -, it is understandable that the "tug of war" keeps us in WAITING longer, hiding the baby from the new world and keeping it in a state of latency. Does this mean that the resistance and opposition movement carried out by activists, conspiracy theorists, deniers and Christians, the work of NGOs, civil protest movements and other uprisings should stop? One of the two currents will end up winning, but given the parameters of possibility/probability of this space and time, it is difficult to know each factor with complete accuracy, except to understand it, roughly speaking, in a general context. Some question if then the anti-system opposition movement will achieve its goal, and abolish tyranny, it would manage to avoid the prophecies about the Apocalypse, but for those who believe in the predictions and in the Words of the messengers of God, what has been warned regarding What is going to happen is going to happen, "yes or yes."

Consequently, if the announced events are to take place anyway, there would then be a Global Government with Global Dictatorship, at least for only a few years, and it will arise in the midst of the "End Times" debacles that will conclude with the total fall of this rising planetary empire and all the structures of life and society that have defined us in our known history. However, at some point the Opposition to the system will be defeated, and will not achieve its goals, being, on the contrary, reduced to independent hidden and dissident groups persecuted by "justice", and their ideals will be fulfilled, not by them, but by the planetary consciousness itself, but years later (at the beginning of the era of glorious light).

In other words, “Destiny” will follow its cycles and carry out its guidelines - above human decisions - since in the long run, Free Will will be conditioned by human determinations born of chaos, hopelessness, anguish and the fear that are promoted by the powers that be and the forces of darkness that are behind them, and the disasters added to a global war and hunger, and their direct and indirect consequences. Therefore, the social unification of values and principles that tries to fight and become strong will be slowed by problems and concerns of force majeure that will disperse the masses, thus weakening their ability to confront elitist power.

Within the parameters of possibility/probability of this space/time, the most “elementary” applicable elements would be: 1) wait for the climatic and geological, as well as social, shocks to begin to launch the apparatus of the New World Order (let's look at the example of the so-called covid pandemic); 2) create scenarios of social unrest and fear - such as terrorism or a health crisis - to reinforce the police structure and citizen control; 3) cause a considerable financial decline; 4) provoke a war between two or more world powers; 5) release deadly or highly virulent pathogens; 6) simply two, three, more or all of the above. According to the various prophecies, especially from the book of the Apocalypse of John, all of these scenarios mentioned are precisely what are going to occur, and will be linked in various ways just before and throughout the time of dominance of the emerging imperialist system, or “the beast” - but it will not be something lasting (even if it were only 2 or

7 years - at most - it will in any case seem eternal if every day is hell for those who do not have their faith placed in God or in Jesus Christ) -.

For followers of predictions about the future, investigating the Apocalypse is one of the cornerstones of interest, par excellence. But to study this book, one must know the context on which it revolves, and that implies delving into Hebrew culture and the sequence of previous announcements whose thread continues and concludes the so-called Apocalypse. The concepts that Hebrew tradition and culture provided about the conclusion of this era and the beginning of the beautiful period of lasting peace are strictly subject to the role of the Messiah expected by the people of Israel. The chronology of events that were to take place began to tick on the prophetic clock potentially with the warnings of the Jew Daniel in Babylon, and for Christians these were complemented by the vision of the apostle John on the island of Patmos. The Jews assumed that the manifestation had to take place within a context of a liberator who saved them from their oppressors, but what the movement that was born with Jesus of Nazareth implied was that the Redemption was something primarily spiritual, and that there would be a series of events that would follow after the fulfillment of the predictions of the Jewish prophet Daniel.

Comparing the announcements of this prophet with history, we already know that it was clear that he warned that the Messiah would appear under the rule of Rome, and that he would be killed just before Judeah was devastated by this empire and the Jews were expatriated. Starting from there, the words of the apostle John in his Revelation entered the scene, but having already passed almost 20 centuries, what should we expect or assume? With other announcements, together with extra content from the Hebrew culture itself – although many of these other predictions are not in the canon called 'bible' – it is understood that the Seals of the Apocalypse play their opening role after the Roman era and in a time of world war and international conflicts possibly fueled by a very serious social crisis. Thanks to the Eschatological Sermon himself, Jesus himself gives the guidelines to know what would be the prelude to this period of time that would end this era and inaugurate the famous era of peace, justice, love, unanimity, longevity, health and blessedness.

It is thanks to these words, and their triangulation with the majority of prophecies related to this matter, that we can understand that the guidelines given to understand this historical phase could not have occurred in all the centuries that have preceded us, and that they clearly belong to this epoch. When talking about international wars and all kinds of world conflicts, Jesus' words enter a context combined with apparent virulent diseases, earthquakes, famine, serious and large protests and globalization. That could be unleashed at any moment, and although it may seem terrible, it is a clear sign that the glorious utopian era is already on the horizon and can almost be felt. Without this hope, knowledge, understanding or belief, going through this historical phase would be hopeless and distressing, and it makes total sense that although these things cannot be changed, they would have been told to us a long time in advance, with the great desire that more and more individuals and unions knew it: " after the storm there always comes calm ," they say, or "nothing lasts forever . "

The topic in question usually produces a lot of fear, anguish and affliction because it is not approached in the correct way, it is not presented in the correct way or its context is not studied in the correct way (as seen in the records of the past when we appreciate that the prophets announced things, and when those who heard them did not like them, they persecuted them and killed them); It is often said that " he who owes nothing, fears nothing " , so just, upright, perfected, honest, virtuous and faithful people to the highest values will not be touched by any of this, their confidence and conviction in destiny will even be reinforced and you will see these events from afar for your own personal experience and maturity.

No one who is on the spiritual path will be ashamed; No one who is on the path of perfection and synchronicity with truth and light will fail to be warned – in one way or another, and in multiple ways – about the things that are going to happen, in advance, with details and support, and every time. even more so before they take place. Thus, they will prepare progressively, taking all appropriate measures. The Father never abandons his children. You don't have to be a scholar to compare geopolitics with prophecies and see that the first phase of the most important events that will begin the Apocalypse is about to happen - good or bad, with approximations here or predictions there -, but fear or be filled with Anxiety should not be the correct reaction of those who live according to spiritual teachings, especially those given by Jesus Christ, since they directly contradict his entire doctrine: there is nothing that can destroy our being, and there is nothing that can shame a child of God. .

Are we in the prelude to the Great Tribulation?

A very typical theme of Christian eschatology is the 'Great Tribulation'. A topic that, although it seems to be clear, over the centuries – especially the last few decades – has created several different theories or doctrines. Initially, it must be clarified that there is some confusion regarding terms when we talk about eschatological matters (relative to the end of these times). Therefore, before addressing this section of the book I must first clarify some terminology for you, whether or not you are familiar with it.

Apostasy . Greek word that means to distance or move away. It was used among early Christians to refer to someone who betrayed the values or principles of their beliefs or culture. In the Latin translations the term Discessionem was used, from which the Spanish "dissension" and "dissent" are derived. There was a prophecy since the time of Enoch that stated that the Antichrist would come with a great apostasy from the values of the people, which the apostle Paul ratified.

Abomination of Desolation, or Desolation . There were two events that took place in Ihudeah. The first was motivated by Antiochus IV Epiphanes, of the Seleucus dynasty, a Greek commander who desecrated the Jewish faith in the years 167/8 BC. C. Something even worse was repeated between the years 66 AD. C. and 135 AD. C., which led to the expulsion of the Jews from their land, but not before their sacred Temple was destroyed for the last time.

Great Tribulation. It refers to a global social situation that arises in the face of the growth of world tyranny, the waves of protests and demonstrations and the economic instability that have increased after the apostasy (LGTBI agendas, pro-abortion agenda, feminist agenda, ecumenical agenda, social hypersexualization, child sexualization agenda, decriminalization of pedophilia, decriminalization of rape, vaccination imposition, transhumanist agenda, agenda of apathy and social distrust, etc.). In its own terms, the Great Tribulation are the years that precede the reign of the Antichrist, the "birth pangs" that weaken humanity to leave them kneeling before the government of the so-called Beast. The phases of this period begin with the systemic collapse of the markets, addressing a Third World War (or red horse), a food crisis (or black horse), a wave of environmental disasters, a genocide agenda with the use of various strategies advances (or brown horse), a Purge, the Blue Beam agenda and the fall of an asteroid into several pieces (or the Trumpets). During this last part, the so-called Rapture of the chosen ones takes place, and soon the reign of the Beast begins, which lasts 3 and a half years.

Very good. Having said this, and now that this question has been clarified, I will develop these matters in a more extensive manner.

The New Testament emphasizes a critical period of great affliction that humanity will experience before the end of this era and the beginning of the messianic time of peace, promised both by the Bible and by other cultures. Although basically in the canon of the Hebrew-Christian Holy Scriptures itself the word 'tribulation' appears about 40 times, there is a context of it that mentions a 'great' tribulation (Isa. 8:22, 33:2; Zeph. 1:17, Rev. 7:14) or time of final tribulation (called 'birth pangs of the Messiah' by rabbinic eschatology), that is, one of greater proportions than any that has been spoken of in history. Although some 23 of these biblical quotes correspond to the New Testament, only 5 of them literally say 'great tribulation', it is understood that only 3 speak of a future event related to the beginning of the Apocalypse, and a few others may have a related component of hidden form.

The First Signs: Apostasy. In that sense, the first clear mention of such an episode is in the synoptic gospel of Matthew (chapter 24:21), where it says: "Then there will be great tribulation, such as has not been since the beginning of the world until now, nor will there be." This surprising statement is taken from Jesus' words regarding the prelude to his return. But how does this event develop and what signs precede it? There are references or guidelines that have been marked from the time of the apostles to the present, giving rise to multiple Hebrew prophecies announced and fulfilled, among which the history of Rome, the advancement of science and technology, globalization, the return of the Jews to Israel, the reestablishment of the State of Israel, the recovery of Jerusalem, the apostasy and the beginning of upheavals (these last two phases are where we are).

Although it could be said that apostasy is not only religious, but also social and moral, the breadth and implications of this must be understood, since they lead to another prophecy that has been fulfilled: "For many will come in my name, saying: I am the Christ;

"Many will deceive." (Matt. 24:5 and Mark 13:6. Reina Valera 1960) And also another that, although it has had many cases seen, must still be manifested accordingly: "Many false prophets will arise and deceive many..." (Matt. 24:11, Reina Valera 1995) This serious phenomenon will be oriented precisely towards Christianity: "For false Christs and false prophets will arise, and will perform great signs and wonders, in such a way that they will deceive, if possible, even the elect." .» (Matt. 24:24, R60)

But as this approaches, there are other events that mark the beginning of said tribulation, but before discussing them it would be important to clarify what the 'Great Tribulation' encompasses. There have been multiple assumptions and religious studies in this regard, and few have accepted the objective part, and not what Christians should believe. That is, believers in the Rapture (a moment in which before the apocalyptic judgment, Christ takes away a group of his chosen servants, understood as those who have deserved it, as an analogy of the exit from Egypt (Neh. 9:27)), they discuss whether this event will be before or after the Great Tribulation. The problem lies especially in theses with nuances and touches that omit the pragmatic part of the development explained, both by Jesus and by the apostle John or the scribes Baruch and Ezra.

The Eschatological Sermon. Although John and Baruch mention the matter in an orderly manner, Jesus is the one who even provides details just prior to it. It all started with a conversation between Jesus and his disciples on the outskirts of Jerusalem. He had announced the future of the city and the Temple - as the prophet Daniel had also warned in Babylon - both when entering the city on its last Passover (Luke 19:44), and when leaving that day still in preparation for the same (Luke 21:6). Most scholars have been confused in this dialogue, as seems to have happened even to those present and to later listeners, who believed that the destruction predicted over Jerusalem was part of the return of Christ. The truth is that what was warned took place about 3 decades after those words, and did not end until late in the 2nd century AD. C. The error of the interpreters stemmed from not understanding the dialogue based on the questions that his disciples asked Jesus: «... when will these things happen? And what sign will there be of your coming and the end of the world? (Matt. 24:3 R95) The dialogue that had begun when leaving Jerusalem in the direction of Mount Zitim (of the 'Olive Trees') had to do with 3 questions, so Jesus responded on 3 different topics: 1. About the destruction of Jerusalem and the temple (which began in 66 AD and ended with the expulsion of the Jews from Judeah in 135 AD), 2. About the sign – or signs – of his coming, and 3. About the end of the century, that is, the conclusion of this age.

Because of the lack of understanding of the future vision of these events, and possibly because of the desire for everything to end now, the evangelists wrote the dialogue without differentiating between the 3 themes, so that the biblical analyst at first glance would not assume that there were 3 different things. Consequently, it would be necessary to extract from the conversation the part that concerns the signs of Christ's return, and these coincide in the stories of the 3 synoptic gospels that deal with the subject: Matthew, Mark and Luke (the latter making a complete and later documented). These, like Revelation chapter 6, explain that the Great Tribulation is immediately preceded by world wars, religious deception, and civil protests and revolts. In its context, it is understood that these events trigger the following escalation of events, which encompass the Great Tribulation: the fall of the great Whore (USA) with nuclear war – and in extension world war now involving all against all (Red Horse or Second Seal) -, the economic and food crisis (Black Horse or Third Seal), and the massive earthquakes and new epidemics and infections (Brown Horse or Fourth Seal).

False Sentences. As we have seen, the first reference to the prelude of "birth pains" apparently speaks of people who claim to be "Christ." It is notable that this has been seen in recent decades - because someone who had done it under the Catholic empire would have gone to the stake or the orca - but being objective, the context seems to speak of something more specific or radical. The Greek passage from Luke that cites this agrees with both Byzantine and Textus Receptus references, saying: "Take heed that you are not deceived, for many will come in my name, saying, 'I am he,' and 'The time is at hand.' " Do not go after them. (Ch. 21:8) If this portends a global phenomenon, it has not yet materialized in that way. The passage suggests that by "coming in the name" of Jesus, those "many" would be from within Christendom. Furthermore, if the disciples and their followers were the founders of Christianity, and were based on faith in Jesus Christ, they would not accept something from outside, but they could be deceived by something from within (as La Salette's vision predicted). This reinforces the idea that apostasy will continue in the Great Tribulation, at least to some degree and with certain masses of predominantly Christian people.

Consequently, they could be Protestant and/or Catholic leaders, or even political, public or famous figures who, either by saying that they come from Christ, or that they are Christians, would persuade Christians either to believe that they are Christ. or that they are emissaries of Christ. Matthew and Mark confirm these words, recording: "Many will come in my name, saying, I am the Christ; "Many will deceive." (Matt. 24:5 and Mark 13:5). But we must clarify something fundamental, the term 'Christ' is not a proper name. If someone says that he comes "in the name of Jesus" or "in the name of Christ," but he is Christ, such a statement does not make sense, because either he is Christ or he comes from Christ. The word 'Christ' is an epithet that comes from the Greek word 'Christos', which means 'anointed one'. In Hebrew tradition, the Anointed One has always been awaited, whose role is to liberate Israel and give it the former glory it had in the time of King Solomon and at the end of the reign of his father, David. In other words, Jesus was warning that many individuals would come toward believers (whether Christians or Jews) making them believe that he – or they – are the "elect" or "liberators" of some type of movement, possibly political-religious.

The false Kingdom Now. Otherwise, the liberators, saviors, chosen ones or messiahs for what? To vindicate the values of Israel. But what sense does that have if Christians know that the promised Redemption for Israel announced long ago by the Hebrew prophets is only fulfilled with the return of Jesus? That is, assuming that Christians really know that or understand it. Just take a look at the popular Christian environment, anywhere in the world, and it is clear that there is a great disconnect between what was taught in early Christianity and what is taught now, and that includes its vision of the events that are to follow. come. Many leaders are saying that Jesus has already come, but he is here in a "spiritual" sense, and others that he is here in a "metaphorical" sense, and others that he is here in a general context but has established a 'Temporal Power'. This doctrine, called 'Dominionism' (or 'the Kingdom Now') is one of the most popular worldwide, especially among followers of false teachings such as the 'prosperity gospel'.

In Dominionism the Apocalypse is suppressed, and it is often said that those that were prophesied are already past events. Consequently, the prophecy of Jesus is speaking of other types of characters who will lead or direct religious masses, making them believe that these figures (themselves) are the ones chosen to bring the biblical promise, even though they will say that we are in the end times. However, those words of "we are in the end times" will be disguised, making it seem that we are at a point in events that does not yet correspond. For this reason, in the same dialogue, Jesus warns: «But when you hear of wars and rumors of wars, do not be troubled, because this must happen; but it is not the end yet. (Mar 13:7 R60) Why does he say this? Because these false monotheistic leaders will say that it is already the end, when it is false, because the end will only be beginning. What do they gain from that? Facilitate the deception of a false rapture before the real one and, above all, dissuade us from the global reality of what is happening on a progressive and chronological level (to really know what is happening, where we are and what we expect), so that These leaders present a new, distorted vision of the apocalypse, where the coming of Jesus is not from heaven, after the Great Tribulation, but before, either in another way or through other individuals (or just one).

What this leads is to think that the mass of Christendom will be manipulated to make mistakes when it comes to seeing what is happening and how Christ should come, and that is so that they too accept the new leaders with their new proposals. For that reason, the Ammonian Gospel describes this as the manifestation of the Antichrist (representing both a person, a group or a movement). It would not be unreasonable to say that there are already signs of this since Donald Trump appeared on the scene saying that he was a Christian, and many have believed him. He even says that he is a friend of Israel and Israel trusts him. It is an awakening that promises a re-union or alliance of 'religion' and 'state', and doing so under the supposed protection of God, as it was in the reigns of David and Solomon.

Beginning of Global Wars. But what other sign would we then see with the beginning of the great Tribulation? Jesus said that this tribulation would be the sum of various events; and the order is almost the same in his words as those of the apostle John in the vision of the Apocalypse and those of Baruch and Ezra in their visions - without going any further -. He says that everything will really begin once we hear about "wars and seditions" (Luke 21:9). We know that there have never been so many wars in the world as since the

UN was established, even though it was supposedly at the expense of the results of the Second World War. Despite everything, we must add that the wars have been isolated, intermittent, momentary (at most a couple of years), but since 9/11 (2001) everything has changed radically. International wars have been unleashed that have not stopped and show no signs of stopping. With the 'Arab Spring' (2011) the problem increased, and now more and more terrorist groups cause conflicts in many countries, especially those of Muslim beliefs, and even perpetuate attacks on European soil.

The thing does not stop there, but it got worse with the war in Syria, where the interests of several countries, some in favor and others against the government of Bashar al-Assad, have been seen supporting both internal and external groups (from Iraq), both from the government and the revolutionaries, and even to Kurdish groups. At first, as in the Afghanistan war against Russia (1978-1992), there was logistical and weapons support from the US to expel the Russians, but since mid-2015 active troops from these countries began to participate (US). USA, Russia, China, Saudi Arabia, Israel, France, England and Turkey), turning the Syrian war into World War III, even though few have dared to call it that. But the problem did not remain in Syria, and even in Iraq, but in Crimea, where problems broke out in mid-2014 on a scale that is still increasing. Tension has never been higher between the US and Russia since the beginning of the Cold War, not even with the 'Cuban Missile Crisis' (1962), leading to a unique deployment in history since WW2 in the countries of the former Soviet Union, and even in others that were the trigger for WW2 itself by Adolf Hitler.

Atlantic Resolve. The situation is so serious that this week alone at least 100 US Army helicopters arrived in camps in Eastern Europe. Sergei Lavrov, Russia's Foreign Minister, and the Center for Arms Control and Non-Proliferation, state that the US has nearly 500 nuclear warheads deployed in the region. Operation Atlantic

Resolve goes beyond securing the border with Russia, but rather intervening in the war in Ukraine, surrounding Belarus (Russia's ally) and preparing for an imminent NATO confrontation with Russia. Thousands of US troops are deployed across Europe, especially from late 2016 until now, with troops in Portugal, Spain, Italy, Germany, Bulgaria, Romania, Slovenia and Croatia. This is without counting on the air force, which is also taking troops and planes to the United Kingdom, the Netherlands, Poland, Bulgaria, Estonia and Lithuania. In addition to this, the US Military-Industrial Complex has also increased its numbers in NATO bases with naval force in the Baltic Sea and the Black Sea, and has also increased its armed force exponentially in Estonia, Lithuania, Latvia, Poland, Czech Republic, Ukraine, Slovakia, Hungary, Germany, Romania, Bulgaria, Italy and Croatia. What is happening? Why such a unique deployment in US history in "peacetime"?

All these reports do not stop coming out, and many times there are more movements and confrontations than one can find out about even if one spends all day gathering news. There are so many "rumors" of wars spreading and others about to break out, whether in this area or with other belligerent groups in other parts of the world, or even in the Pacific (where 60% of the US naval force is being deployed). (and there are already 97,000 American soldiers in Japan alone). What is the US planning? Luke said the Great Tribulation would begin after we heard of "wars and seditions," and Mark (13:7) and Matthew (24:6) said it would be "when you hear of wars and rumors of wars." It is notable that these words are being fulfilled, at least since 2014, both those of Matthew-Mark and those of Luke.

Many have interpreted for quite some time that the Third World War would begin in Israel, but this is a confusion regarding the simultaneous wars of the Kidron Valley and that of Harmageddon, which represent either a Fourth War, immediately following the

Third, which the same final phase of that Third. That's why Jesus told them that it would be "when you hear," not "when you witness." Israel at the beginning will not be participating in this war that is about to move to a nuclear scale between world powers (in fact it has already been made known that Russia, the US and Ukraine have been using weapons of mass destruction and depleted uranium in the conflicts in Ukraine, Iraq and Syria).

The End of Peace. However, if the Antichrist wants to deceive Israel and make it the greatest nation, the others must be reduced, and that explains why an atomic conflagration and an economic collapse put an end to the great powers now predominant. Likewise, with the power now held by European nations, the US, Russia and China, among others, there could not be a unilateral global government. But let's return to Luke's words, since it is significant that he spoke of "seditions", something similar to what Mark describes at the beginning of the Great Tribulation - according to his version of events - defining them as "riots."

Even though everything indicates that the Great Tribulation begins "For nation will rise against nation, and kingdom against kingdom" (Mar 13:8 R60), as John describes (speaking of the horse that will represent the world war, to which "it was given power to take away peace from the earth and cause them to kill one another. And a very great sword was given to him" (Rev. 6:4, R95)), the scenario prior to this, and which seems to accompany and follow to deception in the monotheistic guild, are manifestations everywhere. In the 4th of Ezra we can find similar quotes, which state: "Therefore, when earthquakes, tumult of people, intrigues of nations, vacillation of leaders, confusion of princes appear in the world, then you will know "That is what the Most High spoke of from the days of old, from the beginning." (9:3-4)

We can find that it speaks of a combination of things, or even that they can be seen in isolation, citing earthquakes (like the other prophecies), tumult of people (which is understood as protests, agglomerations, mass demonstrations), intrigues of nations (i.e. , government conspiracies) and confusion of princes (leaders who do not seem to act in an orderly or logical manner, errors and lack of clarity when many people or many things come together). Baruch also warns this, giving another order, and saying that the beginning of these events would be from the "beginning of commotions." [...] murders of the great [...] the fall of many with death [...] the sending of the sword [...] the famine and the withholding of the rain [...] earthquakes and terrors." (2nd Baruch 27:2-7) In all cases, war, famine and earthquakes are accompanied, and the prelude to everything are rumors of wars, increasing sources of armed conflicts and civil revolts, without mentioning the destruction of the great Babel (or 'great Whore', which is the prophetic way of referring to the USA) throughout that beginning of chaos.

Worldwide protests. However, what for some seems to be futuristic, in light of the prophecies and the events coming true, it is evident that this scenario has already begun, and right now we are in the last phase before the beginning of the Great Tribulation. Given that the doctor Lucas was the one who carried out an investigative study to put together all the data at the time, it is understood that his thesis consisted of organizing the sources in the best possible way. That means that his words have begun to be fulfilled, when he said that the signs of Christ's return would begin "when you hear of wars and seditions," adding that "these things must come to pass first" (Luke 21:9).), and then the others will follow, since "the end will not be immediately" in those days (because the tribulation will last, at least, apparently, a couple of years). We must emphasize that the word that was translated as "sedition" is the Greek 'Akatastasía', which, in addition to sedition, addresses other meanings, such as riots, disorders, tumults, revolts and protests. The outbreak of demonstrations, strikes, revolts and concentrations on a global level is unique and unprecedented at the present (not even close to those that occurred due to the Vietnam War and the invasion of Iraq), both due to the political activities of Donald Trump, as well as other independent events, whether in the US or in other countries.

If we look at Mark 13:8, he writes about this as well, stating that "...there will be [...] riots; These are the beginnings of pain." Although some versions omit this word (such as the Spanish Reina Valera translation of 1995), possibly due to changes in later Greek translations - such as 'Nestle-Aland' (1993) or 'Westcott and Hort' (1885) - in the Greek version base (Textus Receptus) and the oldest (the Byzantine), the word 'Tarajaí' appears, which refers to disturbances, commotions, perturbations, agitations, revolutions, confusion, disorder, hubbub, tumults. The current stage is linked to the prophetic fall of the United States of America, which the prophets called 'Babel' (Babylon), which is the trigger for the Great Tribulation, and its beginning phase (Jer. 51, 50: 8-16; Isa. 13, 14:4-7; Rev. 17 and 18, 14:8).

He who perseveres to the end will be saved

It is surprising to see that ancient prophecies announced for so long are being fulfilled in our present. Understanding that things warned of even thousands of years ago are taking place feels like you are suddenly asleep, dreaming an uncomfortable nightmare. It's like being inside a surreal fiction movie. The exact affinity in the words that were said by certain individuals with what is definitely happening takes away all trace of naivety and disbelief about what is to come and its seriousness. Seriousness that leads us to be one of 3 groups that will exist in the coming years: the robots, the resistance or the preparationists.

In a remote text known as the Gospel of Ammonius, the case is stated in which a few days before his crucifixion Jesus of Nazareth was speaking with his followers on Mount Olivet, and on that occasion he predicted to them what the advent of the Antichrist would be like. The keys that he gave them are referred to in many other writings throughout the world - and at different times - that warn us of the signs that we would see to know that that time had already arrived. Nostradamus had predicted that in the future there would be 3 antichrists. Experts have agreed that the first was Napoleon Bonaparte and the second was Adolf Hitler. Although, for many of the first Christians, however, the first was Nero Caesar, but there would be one who would come at the end of the current age of men. A bigger one would be coming, and it would control the entire world. He was spoken of in early Christianity as Belial, in Judaism he is known as Armilius, in Islam as Al-Dajjal, he is the false Maitreya, the Hindu Kalki, the messiah of Freemasonry, the heir to the Arthurian, Davidic throne. and Merovingian of the European monarchies.

I will revolve this exposition around the words of the Jewish prophet Ihoshua, or Jesus of Nazareth, as you surely know him. Ihoshua (or Yeshua) reiterated words from other of his compatriots in a context that for centuries had not been known when it should fit. Certainly, determining something like that over such a long period of time would not be easy. One of the keys were the predictions about the return of the Jews to their land, something that occurred from 1917, with the taking of the "Holy Land" by the British Empire from the hands of the Ottomans, but began to consolidate after the Second World War with the defined Jewish State, in 1947. It had also been announced thousands of years ago that Irushalim (Jerusalem) would return to the hands of the Jews, which occurred after the Israeli victory in the Six Day Wars (1967) and Yom Kippur (1973). This also coincided with the prophecy about the military power that Israel would recover after millennia of not being a war power. Next we come to the words of Ihoshua in the eschatological sermon, when the teacher reiterated what the ancients had said when announcing that Israel would once again be a super power, maintaining that they would first be humiliated, <<until the era of the goim is completed. >> (Ev. Luke 21.24).

By Goim he refers to humanity without connection to the Hebrew people. Israel's influence is increasing, being the largest military power currently and with the best intelligence service in the world. These references already put us in context, but the one that would be pivotal would be the attack on the World Trade Center, when the prophet Isaiah announced in the 6th century BC. C., nothing more and nothing less, than in chapter "9-11" about this event, and the beginning of the war against "terror". This fight against the Invisible Enemy was the beginning of the Coup d'état against humanity by the aristocracy that controls this planet. Ihoshua (Jesus) clearly said that everything would begin with DECEPTION. Humanity knows the world around it through television, and this is precisely the number 1 source of misinformation, mass manipulation and deception used by the planetary aristocracy (which you surely know by the title of 'the Illuminati'). ').

Here the Jewish teacher Ihoshua was very emphatic giving two initial keys that had to coincide simultaneously: 'Polémous' and 'Akatastasías'. Polemos are conflicts, wars, military confrontations. Akatastasias are commotions or upheavals. Other prophets said the same thing, referring to sedition, demonstrations, protests, riots and civil war. The concept of freedom of opinion and worship became popular after the Second World War, and had a great push in the world from then on. Only in the United States did the Vietnam War create a national campaign against the conflict, at the birth of the hippy era. These events were isolated until 2003 when the US Military-Industrial Complex began a new wave of invasions in the Middle East. Then multiple protests worldwide called for peace. Since then, simultaneous global protest movements were unleashed, gaining more and more strength, almost seeming like a common current of thought that crossed borders, barriers, colors, ethnicities, ages, sex and languages.

Although there have been more and more demonstrations of all kinds globally, since 2020 they have come together with the same sentiment in more and more places, in a more massive and constant way, this time in favor of freedom, against the deception, opposing pseudo-vaccines and masks, and rejecting apartheid. At this moment we can say that we are at a very accurate point in that prophecy, but we could not yet affirm that it is the decisive moment of that end of the Era that those people announced, since these events had to be accompanied by "wars", confrontations wars of a global nature simultaneously. Other prophecies defined this as a Third World War. But Ihoshua warns of other things in that context, such as annexes to said events, which could give more information about that conflict period that anticipates us.

Yeshua (Jesus) and the Jewish prophet Yoel (Joel) warned that the Holy Spirit would come upon many at this time to give them courage, knowledge and impetus to warn of the things that are happening and that are going to happen, and this would then be the " new gospel" of this generation: warn what is coming and who is behind all this. This is the Resistance, those who are increasingly persecuted, censored and silenced, and part of those who will be chosen for the new kingdom, known as perfect or saints. Although, one of the keys of the Illuminati is to destroy the opposition, and they will face their karma: <<If anyone takes captivity, he goes into captivity; If anyone kills with the sword, he must be killed with the sword. Here is the patience and faith of the saints.>> (Rev. 13,10). Yeshua referred to them saying, "He who perseveres to the end will be saved" (Mark 13:13), knowing that only Resistance will remain firm despite the attacks, deception, persecution and tribulation: <<With your patience you will win your souls.>> (Luke 21,19).

It is thought that these words were originally written in the Hebrew language, but they appear in Koine Greek, in which the word "captivity" appears as Aijmalosian, relating to confine or confine, take prisoner or arrest. This is a reiteration of the Law of Retaliation, "an eye for an eye, and a tooth for a tooth." Why is this phrase cited in the context of this theme that Ihoshua prophesies, both on Mount Olivet and decades later by a messenger to another of his followers on the island of Patmos? This is to remind those who read that every action has a reaction, and there is nothing that is not left to receive compensation. Therefore, if you kill iron, you must die; What you sow, that you reap. The context of this is due to other prophecies spread through passages of the same nature in the same development of events, which is the fact that the System or State is going to wage war on humanity, and not even those who seek the Truth They will be exempt from falling into its network, being, in fact, its main objective.

This is a way of saying not to worry about being forced to not be able to leave your home, or being imprisoned for opposing the State's directives, because what they do to you will be returned to your executioners. Because of this, those other passages in the same context warn that they must be calm and stick to their principles, beliefs and knowledge: what they have understood (the Truth of the deception that is being perpetuated). But there is more behind this Greek word Aijmalosian, which is the root Aijma, from which it comes. This word means puncture. Whoever forces another to be pricked or pricked will receive the same. Those who now believe that they have benefits from their position will also later fall into the same network, who abuse their position to violate people's freedoms and rights by forcing them to be tapped. The threats of not being able to access benefits, not being able to work, and then not having access to the transaction system (money), to later be locked up, and one day sent to be murdered (when Artificial Intelligence takes power). But let's not anticipate events, because there is a lot to say about it and alternatives exist. That is why Ihoshua repeated and reiterated that we had to endure the pressure that they are giving us due to their coverage of threats and social pressure.

Revelation 13.10 not only mentions the importance of not giving in to pressure, but also know that no one who does wrong will get away with it, because Destiny brings compensation to each person for what they do, and that in addition - and above everything - the escape route will come. DO NOT GIVE UP. The pressure will increase. Both in the synoptic gospels and in Revelation they exhort us to resist and trust, warning that the cornering will become greater and greater, leading to imprisonment and persecution to an ever greater extent. The passage in question says "he who kills with the sword must be killed with the sword." The reason why these definitions "captivity", or confinement, and "death by sword" are in the same verse and in the same context of the theme is due to their intrinsic relationship . Furthermore, the Greek word used in this passage does not refer to when you are walking down the street and a criminal mugs you with a gun, but to when the forces of the state are used. It refers to a military state, to MARTIAL LAW, where whoever disobeys the Curfew will first be arrested and one day will be shot.

Ihoshua repeated over and over again that this would not be the end, and that they should not be afraid or despair because it was NECESSARY for these things to happen FIRST. Let them endure, because only those who resisted this psychological war until the end would be saved. By stating that in this series of events they would be saved if they did not give in, it is because it is not just that they are locked up, threatened or punctured, but that this pressure will be the prelude to something worse. Those who inject the poison into their blood will not be saved, and no one can say that they are forced, because it is false. No one can force you, EVEN, only pressure you, coerce you and threaten you. Both the one and the other are a crime - and no one is above the law -, so if there are constitutional laws, whoever wants to appeal and denounce the facts, and if they don't want to, it is a question of not depriving themselves of losing social benefits or feeling pointed out or criticized, but that is not obligatory, it is a personal choice, the consent of an anti-constitutional principle that violates human rights and the Nuremberg agreements of 1945 and the Bioethics codes of 2005 (Universal Declaration of Human Rights).

"...whoever resists UNTIL THE END" of these things, "THOSE will be saved." (Ev. Matthew 24.13). With those words Ihoshua warned of the period that is developing as a prelude to the world events that will give rise to the public appearance of the Antichrist in the subsequent years. This is just the beginning, and for now it is just a mental fight that you must win.

Phases of the COVID Agenda towards the 2030 Agenda

What is the COVID agenda? A plan to push the government of the Antichrist. Oppression and reinforcement of dictatorial imperialism, a detail especially mentioned in the prophecies of Ezra and Baruch. There were isolated dictatorships, and they have still been seen, true or not, in Cuba, Venezuela, North Korea, Russia, China, Chile, Italy, Germany, Spain, Iraq, Libya... however, none of that compares to the new communism , Nazism, Marxism, fascism, Francoism and other "isms", which has emerged globally since quarantines were announced in almost all countries in the world in March 2020. According to another ancient text, the Antichrist would dominate the world for 1,332 days, but a series of events would have occurred before his appearance. I will divide these events into 3 sections. Gathering a multitude of information, especially prophecies, I will explain below what this sequence of 3 series of events would be like that will give rise to the manifestation of the Antichrist. Although, for years I have warned about this 3rd phase of events, and I have also given various presentations of the 2nd, but this time I will give it a reinterpretation with new data.

First of all, if you don't know yet, the word COVID is not the name of a disease. If you want to be deceived and led like a sheep to the slaughter, believe the news, the politicians and the pharmaceutical industry. If you don't want to be fooled, do your own research and turn off the television. 'COVID 19' is the acronym for 'Digital Identification of Vaccination Certificate with Artificial Intelligence'. This is not a virus that came out of bat soup and mutated into more harmful versions. This is a global control program that has been centuries in the planning. You must know that this world is not run by politicians. They are pawns who obey the corporate system, the banking system and, above all, an aristocratic elite and their oligarchic minions. We are talking about families that control the entire world. For centuries they have been making alliances with the aim of creating a global government, which will ultimately be led by artificial intelligence. It is a planetary dictatorship, a police state, with all people in a transhuman state controlled by digital technology, wave weapons and mass surveillance systems.

The COVID-19 phase was designed in 1989 as the key tool to achieve a Coup d'état against humanity, eliminate its rights and freedoms and modify the law to create an all-powerful supranational state. To achieve this without the mass opposition of the people, we worked with two of the 7 basic fears of man: Fear of Illness and Fear of Death. Previously, in 2001, a first phase had begun to carry out this globalist plan, with the story of Terrorism, but it did not achieve its full objectives. The COVID-19 program includes Agendas 201 (or Agenda 2030) and ID2020. Let's see a brief review of prophecies that place us in the now.

1. Isaiah 9:11 prophesied 9:11 (attack on the Twin Towers), the beginning of a series of wars in the Middle East and awakening the Islamic "enemy."

2. Much of the prophecies, both biblical and parabiblical, describe that there will be a time when deceit and lies will reign. The context of this is applicable to today because of how politicians lie, the media manipulates information and how all things are presented to society distorted, retouched and biased. This is a component that persists and will be the master key of the Antichrist, who will use deception to achieve his ends. This is something unique that has never before been possible to do because of the dark power over all of humanity at the same time, especially because they did not have the technologies and resources that exist today.

3. Apostasy is also referred to, and is clearly seen. The value of religion and the principles that were maintained are degraded. Decidedly before WWII you were still a heretic if you contradicted the Catholic Church, however, the tendency to attack the figure of Jesus, for example, was more of a fashion that began to be seen in the mid-90s. It is Freemasonry that has led this trend, and the Rockefellers who have weakened religious faith due to their multiple social brainwashing campaigns.

4. Colossal advance in technology and science, mentioned by both the Jopi Indians and the prophet Daniel.

5. In line with deception is ignorance of the truth and failure to understand what is happening. Daniel also said it in this order of things, arguing that, furthermore, those who do understand would be those who would be chosen for the future kingdom.

6. People who call themselves Christ, or the return of Jesus, or the reincarnation of Jesus, or the one sent by Jesus, as savior. Definitely, if someone had come out with this story several centuries ago, it would end up in hell.

Now let's look forward to events to see, according to social behavior, the consequences of the crisis caused by the COVID-19 Agenda, added to the COVID-21 Agenda. Although I am writing these lines on Wednesday, February 17, 2021, these words and their application must be recorded at the moment you may be reading this chapter. There is a first element that is present in the prophecies that Yeshua (Jesus) provides about what they define as "signs" of the "end" of this era, to invite the return of the Lord. Revelation and Yeshua's references are, without a doubt, the most extensive and clear when it comes to reporting on these events. Yeshua begins his warnings by announcing that there will be "false Christs," that is, pseudo messiahs, false saviors, who would say they come in the name of Jesus, or they themselves are Jesus.

Well, this has been seen for several years, and it would not be surprising if it were seen more frequently, especially because "in the country of the blind the one-eyed is king", and in a time of crisis, fear and uncertainty, inventing That you are a savior puts you on a pedestal and many people after you. Some think this matches the description of the White Horse of Apocalypse and the Q movement, or supporters of Donald Trump. True or not, or to some extent false or not, is something that will become evident in due course. However, it is true that we can find ourselves faced with a bad translation and misinterpretation of the biblical passage.

Let's see, the verse says, <<Take heed that no one deceives you. For many will come in my name, saying, I am the Christ; and they will deceive many.>> (Matt. 24:4-5, RVA 60). To begin with, anyone can say, "I come from Jesus," whether well-intentioned or not. You can believe what you are saying; You may be right, or lying. But if you say that you come from Jesus, it does not mean that Jesus appeared to you and said, "come from me", or it may be, it is enough that you have an ideal based on a Christian concept, for example, such as principles ethical, moral, spiritual or religious. On the other hand, saying that you are "the Christ" refers to a conception of a Greek word. He is actually saying "I am the Chosen One," "I am the Anointed One," "I am the heir to the Throne," "I am the Messiah," "I am the Deliverer," or "I am the Savior."

So here the case of Donald Trump fits in like a glove, who might not be lying in his statements and intentions, but in reality he is just a man. However, people could later become disillusioned or disappointed by their trust in him. The meaning of the word used in the Greek text, Planísousin, fits here, relating to erring, making mistakes, getting confused, getting lost, being deceived, becoming disillusioned, disappointed, losing focus or failing. It would not be strange if Trump left a military legacy, to say the least, and his former generals began a series of maneuvers to "reestablish," at least, the United States. That would fit the description of the White Horse, as it also fits very well. good with Trump's victory in the 2016 elections. However, this barely receives any room in the prophecies, because the Red Horse follows directly.

Ergo, the next element that accompanies these indications is war. Here, like a funnel, all the "end-world" prophecies meet. Let's see, according to the COVID-19 Agenda, there would be about 18 months to achieve mandatory vaccination implementation. If this started with the 2020 World Quarantine, everything would be ready, according to your plans, by approximately September 2021. In the worst case scenario, few people would have time to escape such a macabre plan. At best, the White Horse "helps us out," but only to slow things down, giving us a short window of time, while simultaneously allowing more people to open their eyes. How do you achieve it?

It seems the only way that is plausible under the circumstances: war. It is notorious that the scenario of the global war confrontation is the hidden agenda of the Illuminati. It is my assumption that the world leaders who are participating in this, having allowed themselves to be bought off by Soros and his henchmen and bosses, have not been informed of this move. They believe that they will receive a paradise plot somewhere in the Caribbean while their country enters the gears of the Illuminati's planetary dictatorship, and they will simply give people mandatory vaccines, let's say chips, and a strong police state. I think they were not told about the "Trojan horse" trap. One of the reasons that lead me to this deduction are other prophecies, such as those of Baruch, Enoch, Ezra or Billy Meier, about the perplexity and bewilderment of world leaders when military tension increased and the outbreak of a thermonuclear conflagration became evident. .

What ties this together perfectly – from my personal point of view – is in the description of this programming. In accordance with the COVID Agenda, in March 2020 the implementation of concentration camps was accelerated from January 2021; Labor Reform would be promoted and Universal Basic Income was presented as a solution to the economic crisis since February and March 2021, when the story of Covid-21 infections would begin; Between April and June, food would become scarce in supermarkets and there would be great economic instability; between April and July new confinements would begin; and from July riots would begin, and local governments would begin to withdraw while military controls in the cities increased. This business of "riots" and "military control" actually translates into civil unrest in the streets.

This was also prophesied by Enoch, Baruch, Ezra and Yeshua, among others, and, clearly, in its context. Yeshua would have said – according to the description of the doctor Luke – that this would be the second thing to happen: <<And when you hear of wars and seditions, do not be alarmed; because it is necessary that these things happen first; but the end will not be immediately.>> (Luke 21:9, RVA 60) Social unrest would increase. This translates into what is also defined in the Greek text as riots, commotion, tumult or disorder. It is logical that many people end up getting tired of the nonsense, their economy is about to completely fall apart, they find themselves incapable of dealing with expenses and commitments, and hunger squeezes and clouds reasoning.

With the precedent of the 2020 Quarantine, this time people will take to the streets outraged, with more than compelling reasons, and in all parts of the world. This, from my point of view, is the outbreak of civil wars that will be unleashed, propagated and expanded from now on throughout the planet, until the Blue Beam Agenda has been completed, or at least, to a large extent achieved. to complete. I will include another element: covid-21 vaccine. Operation LockStep is designed to put such pressure on society to accept mandatory vaccination, and while in the first phase people were locked up, 5G antennas, which are the key to why graphene is injected into the world, were withdrawn around the world. people. It is the main part of the agenda of the 2020 and 2021 lockdowns. Weaken the minds of the people so that they crave this vaccine, and if there is resistance, also exhaust it everywhere and by all plausible means. The covid-21 vaccine would be presented in July, precisely, and the vaccination wave would already be a fact by August of this year.

This would only further stress the people, especially those who refuse to be poisoned. To appease this there would be the idea of Universal Basic Income, which additionally allows the elimination of all debt, even if you must abdicate your property rights. This idea, proposed for September 2021, coincides with 50 years of the inflationary petrodollar financial system that allowed the banksters, masters of all the banks, to create money from nothing and put nations in debt. According to the prophetic scenery of 'I Pet Goat II', Barack Obama's work is followed by the fall of the Statue of Liberty, which in turn is followed by the monitor (screen) where a reptilian brainwashes the youth (while being intoxicated with drugs and injections) and finally the markets collapse to break out nuclear war.

The hour will come when all who do iniquity will receive what they have sown. We, who faithfully believe in reincarnation, are aware of the law of cause and effect, and that no one escapes it. In the last decade, doctors, virologists, scientists, and other experts in self-healing, natural medicine, and expensive treatments have been murdered all over the world. Because? At this point the answer is more than obvious. They will return in their next incarnation, and continue their path of growth. Others are now repressed, but they fight, despite everything and the high level of censorship.

All of us who are speaking are the prophets of this generation, no longer with rags, beards, disheveled hair or words from a biblical vocabulary, but we prophesy, we predict, we announce, we declare the truth, we say what is necessary so that many can know the truth. TRUE. We are the voice that cries out today from the networks and the web, although they censor us, delete our posts and our videos. We talk in the street, although we are prohibited from approaching others. The level of deception and brainwashing on neutral brothers in the world is so serious that they hear us and are confused, disconcerted, misplaced, because they have been presented with a false world, and they have believed it.

I have had face-to-face discussions with state officials and doctors, and they themselves, after agreeing with me, remain silent and confused. There is no holistic knowledge, however, they do not see the image in perspective, they do not know what is behind it or imagine it (and they will not even want to know when they find out how deep the "rabbit hole" is). The mere question of pedophilia is shocking. The first time I heard about this was back in 2008. I was affected for at least 3 days. The pain I felt in my heart and soul bathed my cheeks with tears. I couldn't believe it, but something inside me told me that it was true. More of that came to me about two years later, with Abdullah Hashem's YouTube series, 'The Antichrist-Dajjal will be a Metamorphic Reptilian'. This made me understand the depth of the rabbit hole, and the very creepy, well-crafted and titanic program of mind control directed by the CIA, in turn motivated by the usual ones.

It was with the quarantine of the "bug" that I saw many prophecies and words of the Bible different, in light of events, and I understood that we were already at the beginning of the Great Tribulation. The prophet David, who was king of Israel about 3,000 years ago, spoke of the beginning of this in his 91st psalm, and Yeshua did too, but neither announced this "pandemic" because it is not a pandemic. What they did say was that we would be in a time of DECEPTION. That is the beginning of everything, <<For this reason God sends them a deceptive power, so that they believe the lie...>>> (2 Thes. 2:11, RVA 60). They said what would be true, such as the deprivation of rights and the dictatorship, such as <<a lot of oppression>> (2nd Ezra and 2nd Baruk). Likewise, Daniel said in chapter 12 that "many would be cleansed and purified and made white," and "the wicked will act wickedly, and none of the wicked will understand, but those who understand will understand." (verse 10, KJV 60) .

This is the time of inner purification, of awakening, of awareness, of inner perfection, of demonstrating who we are. We understand what is happening, and we must be a light on those who do not understand, because they have fallen into the web of deception and lies. That is our mission, <<those who are wise will shine like the brightness of the firmament; and those who teach righteousness to many, like the stars forever and ever.>> (Dan. 12:3, KJV 60) We are the prophets of the present, of whom Joel said, <<I will pour out my Spirit on all flesh, and your sons and your daughters will prophesy; Your old men will dream dreams, and your young men will see visions. And also on the male and female servants I will pour out

my Spirit in those days.>> (ch. 2:28-29, RVA 60). What are these visions and prophecies about? In warning what is happening and where it is headed: the New World Order.

This is what Yeshua was referring to when he stated that this gospel would be <<preached, as a testimony to all nations, and then>> is when <<the end>> would come (Matt. 24:14). Yeshua was not speaking of the kingdom of heaven at that time, but of the kingdom of Belial. He spoke of a message, or news (gospel) that would be made known everywhere so that it would remain a record, that would be a testimony to all humanity. As in this passage and in Joel 2:28, other verses remind us of this current mission, and the consequences, where many will be persecuted and killed for speaking the truth: <<Because they shed the blood of the saints and the prophets, You have also given them blood to drink; because they deserve it.>> (Rev. 16,6, RVA 60) And he points to the source of evil on our planet, as guilty of this: <<And in it was found the blood of the prophets and saints...> > (Ch. 18,24). Saints and prophets? We have to see things according to the proper prism. Whoever announces and predicts falls into the category of prophet.

He who has innocence and inner purity is a saint, and that includes little children: <<See that you do not despise one of these little ones; because I tell you that his angels in heaven always see the face of my Father who is in heaven.>> (Matt. 18,10, RVA 60). And just as the murder of prophets – whether today or yesterday – will bring divine "revenge", in the same way the mortality, abuse and exploitation of the innocent will bring its retribution: <<And whoever causes any of them to stumble For these little ones who believe in me, it would be better for them if a donkey's millstone were hung around their neck and they were drowned in the depths of the sea. Woe unto the world because of offenses! for stumbling blocks must come, but woe to that man through whom the stumbling block comes! Therefore, if your hand or your foot causes

you to offend, cut it off and throw it away from you; It is better for you to enter life lame or maimed, than having two hands or two feet to be thrown into eternal fire.>> (Matt. 18,6-8, RVA 60)

Before the so-called Rapture there will be a great persecution against those who follow the truth, although it will not be as terrible as that which will come after that event. At that time those who are connected to the Light, vibrating in the Truth, guided by the Holy Spirit and his angels will be protected. However, many have been suffering from the attack of tyrants and will continue to fall before the hunt of the masters of the world: <<When he opened the fifth seal, I saw under the altar the souls of those who had been killed because of the word of God. God and for the testimony they had. And they cried with a loud voice, saying, How long, Lord, holy and true, will you not judge and avenge our blood on those who dwell on the earth? And they were given white garments, and told to rest for a little while, until the number of their fellow servants and their brothers, who also were to be killed like them, was completed.>> (Rev. 6,9- 11, RVA 60)

Although some have been killed, both these and those who remain alive will be taken, as I have already explained in my other books regarding the theme of the Rapture. And in the meantime, those who are attuned to the Spirit and his messengers will be protected, as noted in Psalm 91 of David. It is certainly irrefutable that they are cornering humanity, "if anyone has understanding, let him understand." Those who understand, they see what happens. Those who are deceived do not see, or do not want to see. You fill their hearts with fear because they see the world from fear. Therefore, they do not see the love that is in everything that happens and the need for it to happen. They believe that they are a body and that their current experience in a body is everything, so they protect it with fear and trembling. Indeed, the Antichrist "will receive power to prevail over the perfect and defeat them," as current laws and the police state are demonstrating, but for all who vibrate in the light and synchronize with the Truth there is always a way out.

Do you have understanding? If you have an open mind, if you search, if you do not fear, if you have love in your heart, if you use your intelligence to connect the dots, then, and only then, you are not a victim, even when you are pressured. When you walk in the Light, the Spirit guides you towards the path of protection, the way of escape. You have nothing to fear. If you are one of those, however, you understand, and the prophecy said about you, "he who has understanding must analyze the figure of the Beast, for it is the figure of a man," and he added "here is wisdom." Wisdom, numbering? In the Greek manuscript it says "sophias" and "arithmos". Let's look at the etymology, because Aritmos also means "that which does not have fluidity", "that which has no rhythm". For its part, curiously, Sofia is the name of the image of the artificial intelligence that goes around the world promoting the consciousness that a robot has received, as the passage says, "and spirit was given to the image of the Beast to that I could speak..." Every person is registered as a code, with a numerical system, and that Sofia could end up being the "friendly" face of the Super State.

If you understand the background of the message of this book, don't be silent. It is our moral responsibility, to ourselves and our fellow human beings, to tell them what is happening. This is the "gospel" of this time that is being preached. Gospel means good 'news', or the 'good news'. It refers to news or message. Like English, new is news, reports or reports, and identifies newscasts. The current fake news, or promulgators of false news, are, however, the new "evangelists." Jesus said that the "gospel" of the Great Tribulation would be preached, and then the end of this era would come. However, it referred to the promulgation of reports and news, but by whom? Not from the news, but from the "knowing ones," as the archangel Gabriel called them in a vision of the prophet Daniel.

Jesus said about this that whoever "endured" (persevered) until the end would be saved, which I interpret as referring first to social pressure, since those who do not get vaccinated are socially coerced and cornered.

Apocalypse said that those who worship the Beast and have his number, name or chip will not have rest, but not because they worship him, but because they all have the same thing in common: they have all been injected with poison. Every time they put their arm to be inoculated with the components that the Antichrist has moved to be inoculated, the less human they are and the less time they have left to live. With your patience you will save your souls (life) and with perseverance and endurance we will protect our life and integrity, due to social pressure. As evil increases, the love of many grows cold, injustice increases. Things get worse and worse and society loses its human warmth; They pressure them so much that even police officers who had great ideals and intentions become the new Gestapo. Believe, when it was said: “I saw those who had achieved victory over the beast and their image standing before a sea of glass,” because this will not last long.

Jesus prophesied the Plandemic

For years I have carried out biblical revisionism, searching for new manuscripts and versions of original texts and carrying out corrections of passages of said scriptures. From the beginning of the “plan-demic” I was convinced that what was happening must be hidden in ancient Hebrew texts, since the most important events in our history have been prophesied in advance. Ihoshua (Jesus of Nazareth) has been the greatest prophet on record. His warnings about how Ihudeah (Judea) was devastated by the Romans in 66 AD. C., thirty years before the events that occurred, was very precise. Although, Ihoshua had reported that another prophet, Daniel, had already warned about this event before, but he reiterated his words and announced that this would be about to happen soon, adding details about how the Romans would attack Ihudeah and Irushalim (Jerusalem) and massacre the people . Hebrew with several wars in a row and with large armed troops.

The Essenes had also warned that this would happen at that time, but Ihoshua had also added that his followers would be put on trial before synagogue courts, sent to prison, and several of them would be murdered for speaking his message, which which is what happened, just like the family fights over ideological issues between the defenders of the teachings of Ihoshua and those of Mashah (Moses). However, Ihoshua announced future things, not only of impact for the Hebrew people, but for the entire human race. We know the popular story of Ihoshua's life – or at least some facts based on real events – thanks to various sources, but roughly most of the information was referred to in the so-called Bible. It is considered that the texts that speak of Ihoshua were originally written in the Greek language. However, Ihoshua and his followers were Hebrews, and at that time their mother tongue was Aramaic.

Unlike Ihoshua's supporters, the Sanhedrin (main assembly of the Jewish people), had several important opponents, among whom were the president of the assembly and his son-in-law. These people, apart from being honorable members of the Sanhedrin, represented the heavyweights of the Jewish aristocracy of that time. Debates between Jewish supporters of Ihoshua and Jewish deniers who claimed that Ihoshua was a bastard witch – literally – have continued to this day. Both Yakob ben Iosef and Shimon ben Iosef - both brothers of Ihoshua (Jesus of Nazareth) - were presidents of the original Judeo-Christian community, which resided in Irushalim (Jerusalem). Shimon took over when Yakob was assassinated by opponents of the Sanhedrin in 62 AD. C., but the theological debates about the figure of Ihoshua remained.

To carry out serious open debates, both parties had writings of the events that occurred and the words of Ihoshua, so that it could be verified whether what Ihoshua said and did corresponded with the guidelines that the expected Messiah had to comply with. In that respect, the events that occurred were copied equally for both parties. The versions of the Judeo-Christians became the copies that the Gentile Christians (non-Jews) translated, first into the Koine language (popular Greek of the time). The detractors and deniers had, for their part, versions in the Hebrew language. As the centuries passed, the translations suffered alterations, and the Catholic Church deliberately altered many parts of the manuscripts. The best-known complete versions were therefore those of the Byzantium empire, but a Hebrew version remained, that of Rabbi Baal Shem Tob, analyzed by Hebrew-speaking Jews.

When the followers of Ihoshua (Jesus) were with him in Irushalim (Jerusalem) in the days before his crucifixion, they called his attention to the magnificence of the Second Temple, the reconstruction of Solomon's temple, to which Ihoshua told them that everything What they saw would be turned into ruins. This intrigued them and hours later they asked him several key questions to understand various past, present and future historical episodes.

<< *And when he sat on the Mount of the Olive trees in front of the Temple, Petros and Yochanan and Andreah asked him in secret: "When will all those things be and what will be the sign when all these matters will happen, or when they will begin and when will the end of the world and your coming be* ?>>
(Ev. Matthew, from Baal Shem Tov, chapter 24, verse 3)

There were various questions here, very different topics, that most eschatologists and theologians have failed to understand, because they have seen them all as one, instead of several questions on several different issues. Consequently, Ihoshua responded to them on all these topics, although the references appear mixed after the various translations of the texts. First Ihoshua spoke to them about the Antichrist, mentioning 2 keys to know when in history he would appear. The first has been overlooked historically speaking:

<< *And Yeshua answered them:*
"Be careful that no one misplaces them,
because many will come in my name
saying: "I am the Mashiach", and the
they will lead you astray .>> (verses 4-5)

This is said out loud all of a sudden, but until after the Second World War no one would be so bold as to claim that he was the reincarnation of Jesus Christ, because he would have been lynched, and in the Middle Ages he would have been sent to the stake. It is, therefore, notorious that Ihoshua (or Yeshua, as his friends called him), was leaving a first guideline to know when the Antichrist would appear. A time where claiming that you were the reincarnation of Jesus of Nazareth not only would not be a reason for persecution, but many people would believe it. I think we are all aware of how many people have been appearing around the world for decades saying that they are the return of Jesus Christ, or his reincarnation. But there was a second guideline that Ihoshua left to know when the time was.

<< *And you, when you hear about*
wars and a company of armies,
Be careful that they don't get stupid, because
all this will happen, but it will not yet be the
end .>> (verse 6)

Here Ihoshua says that one would hear talk, both of various wars and of movements of military groups of large units (which in light of the Hebrew word, 'Tzabaot', does not have to be only military but of massive agglomerations of people, such as concentrations en masse due to protests and demonstrations). It must be considered that until 1941 television did not exist, and as telecommunications have advanced, the more we are quickly informed about events taking place anywhere on the globe. The news bombards us with information on issues of war conflicts all over the planet, especially since the Cold War.

However, wars as such have increased since the Deep State began the so-called "war on terror." Ihoshua not only talks about the fact that we would learn of many armed conflicts on the planet, but also about the mobilization of large troops and people. Before, only spies could have that knowledge. With social networks, information does not run, it flies, and you find out what would have been impossible to know even thirty years ago. But Ihoshua adds something interesting, warning those in the know, "do not be foolish," in the sense that all these things must happen, that they must take place first, but despite everything the end would not have yet begun. By "final" he refers to what he later revealed to his apostle Iojanan (John) on the Greek island of Patmos, and which we know as the book of Revelation, or "Revelation."

The book of Revelation recounts the beginning of the events of the end of this era with the appearance of 4 horsemen, 3 of them predicting serious events before the public appearance of the Antichrist. A red one speaks of a war of terrible proportions, a black one of a world famine that would immediately follow, and a brown one, which announces a genocide caused by an "invisible enemy." Ihoshua also mentioned it back then, as the beginning of the end.

<< *And nation will rise against nation and kingdom against kingdom; and there will be great tumults, severe famine and earthquake in (several) places* .>> (verse 7)

Unlike the other translations, Ihoshua says that "goi" would rise above "goi." The translator puts "nation", but in the Hebrew language the idea does not simply refer to countries, but to non-Jews. Elsewhere the doctor Luke wrote that Ihoshua would have said that first the nations of the Gentiles would end their reign, understood through a world conflict that could possibly end up weakening them, something worse than the Second World War. Here we see the same example of the red horse, and then the black one, when saying "burdensome hunger." Revelation speaks of this "hunger" as a situation where the cost of food will skyrocket and will be seriously rationed, to the extent that as the problem spreads, millions will die of hunger because there will end up being no supplies, already in industrialized countries. This responds to a previously known repetitive principle, which is the systemic collapse of markets, which leads to cuts in transportation and food supplies, and armed uprisings to restore the economy in each country.

But let's not forget the key to "tmults" or "agglomerations", which other translations and scrolls outline as "seditions", "social unrest" or "civil mobilization", which is currently on the rise. Furthermore, here we add a component that, like the previous ones, appears in all the prophecies around which this matter revolves: earthquakes. This is not the time to talk about that, but for years many of us have warned about the use of scalar wave weapons by certain governments to alter the climate, and the master strategy that would come to aggravate the "plan-demic", with environmental disasters that force new quarantines and curfews, with the deployment of the military apparatus with the true purpose of stopping the uncontrolled and massive global protests that the current situation is unleashing. Thus, Martial Law would be imposed by order of a State of Emergency, calling for a State of Siege. But let's not get ahead of ourselves, because Ihoshua was only explaining the context, since he then explained to them what would definitely be the prelude to the beginning of those apocalyptic events, called "the Antichrist", and which today are known as the "Illuminati New World Order." ".

In Jewish eschatology there is a great coincidence with Christian eschatology. Both speak that for the appearance of the Chosen One, the Messiah, there will be a severe worldwide tribulation, and an anti-messiah will manifest at a certain time. The Jews call him Armilius, and the Muslims know him as Al-Dajjal. But Judaism and Christianity curiously use the expression "birth pains" to refer to these events, although the expression comes from very different visions that were never connected. The "birth pangs of the Messiah," according to Jewish eschatology, are delicate world events that will take place before the Chosen One is revealed. The beginning of those "birth pains" Ihoshua referred to as that great world war and that global famine added to protests at a planetary level and tremendous environmental disasters (mostly earthquakes) everywhere. This period is also known in Christianity as 'the Great Tribulation'.

<< *All these are the beginning of suffering* .>> (verse 8)

But now things get even more interesting. Ihoshua not only gave two guidelines to know when in history the apocalyptic events would be located, or what the beginnings of those "birth pains" would be to begin the Apocalypse. To the surprise of those of us who study Kabalah, the words saved by Baal Shem Tob hit squarely with the international events that currently afflict us. Reviewing the following contributions from Ihoshua, it is clear that he announced the so-called "pandemic", just as I have also found in the Greek passages of Revelation chapter 13. Within this conversation with his disciples Ihoshua let us know what would happen between the historical sign (the false Christs) and the beginning of the Apocalypse (World War III and global hunger). I will do it first with a conventional translation and then I will explain it in the light of the Hebrew language and its equivalent in the modern Spanish language.

<< *Then they will bind them for tribulation and*
They will kill you, and you will become a
reproach all people for me
name .>> (verse 9)

Here Ihoshua mentions three things, two of them general and one specific. In both the Greek and Hebrew versions it speaks of a confinement, whose purpose is to socially destabilize the population. The word used is "tribulation", which is the most accurate to define the context of the "Health" Dictatorship that we have been seeing since 2020. Quarantine in Hebrew translates as "house for prison", yes, people forced to not be able leaving their homes, lost jobs, closed companies, business bankruptcy, fines for going out after hours, prohibition of access to beaches or parks, social pressure, mandatory wearing of muzzles, pressure to use alcohol and censors of temperature, among so many draconian measures that have taken away freedoms and rights from humanity and have troubled the world. This tribulation is not only one of social and psychological pressure, economic pressure and freedom, but of permanent fear. However, Ihoshua's words were very true, the confinement (confinement, quarantine) had as its first rule to be a measure designed to create social tribulation. But there was more behind it.

Ihoshua adds that the next thing after the lockdowns – the social tribulation agenda – would be mass genocide. When referring to the fact that widespread murders would be carried out, we must move to the next phase. 2020 was the year of confinement, and 2021 was the year of mass genocide. The mass media, being bought, do not inform but misinform, lie and deceive (the Agenda of Deception, which I have already talked about and will talk more about, since it is what the apostle Paul said would be the key to success. of the Antichrist). So you learn the truth starting with rumors and suspicions, until you slowly learn the truth and, finally, as time passes, you know the entire agenda and what has been happening. This was prophesied by another Jew before Ihoshua, named Irmiahu (Jeremiah), saying: <<And do not let your heart faint, nor be afraid because of the rumor that will be heard in the land; In one year there will be rumor,

and then in another year rumor, and there will be violence in the land, ruler against ruler.>> (Jer. 51:46)

Before continuing with Ihoshua I want to emphasize the words of the prophet Irmiahu, as he encourages us not to despair, as Ihoshua also stated, "persevere to the end", endure, do not give up, because of the psychological and emotional war that this tribulation entails. The prophet Irmiahu spoke of a year of unofficial information (2020), and then another year of the same (2021), spreading the truth underground, through social networks and by word of mouth for two years throughout the planet (already (that the Hebrew word used here is Shmuah, which is something that is heard, something that is reported). After those two years, the prophet maintains, there will be violence all over the planet, using the Hebrew definition 'Never'. That definition - which you will already know because it is the name of an Islamic terrorist group - has been translated as error or violence, but its etymology comes from the idea of crying out for help, suffering, complaining, expressing responsibility due to a violent act, which in current terms translates as global waves of protests and demonstrations that will increase.

This is warned by Ihoshua in other passages and is referred to by other prophets, speaking of civil rebellion against the state, uprising and sedition of the population against their governments taking to the streets, ending in civil war in all the great cities of the world, which Iermiahu defines as 'Mashal' (great nations, powers). The first phase, the lockdown of the world, as it appears in the Baal Shem Tob text, 'Yeesrou' (they are going to lock you up), is followed by the genocidal agenda of vaccination, leading millions of people to start a campaign of protests. anti-system that will continue and increase. But returning to Ihoshua, he seems to warn that before – and after – the outbreak of these brawls and waves of civil clashes against the state there will be genocide of many.

We can see a close relationship between this attempt to reduce the world's population by the elite with civil movements everywhere, to protest and join in shouts and banners against the tyranny and death agendas planned by the Illuminati. You clearly know that this is about pseudo-vaccines, which were designed both to chip people and to wipe out the largest number of people in less than 3 years. The mandatory nature of certificates for these false vaccines is increasing demonstrations in the streets, starting with large nations, such as Israel, France, Australia and England, which are being followed by Germany, Belgium, Spain, Italy, several states in the United States. USA, South Africa, Argentina, Greece, Denmark, Japan, and others.

Although this is not counting on national revolutions for other reasons, which have been added, such as in Colombia, Algeria or Cuba, the fact is that it was warned that this would be something that will begin to be seen more and more and would be part of the "Pain of Birth". We must add to this the phrase of Ihoshua: you will be social disgrace because of my name. Your name? In Hebrew culture the name referred to what something or someone represents. In his case, Ihoshua represents the Truth. Those who fight against tyranny, genocide, deception and apartheid will be considered a threat.

Since 2020, activists have been called deniers and conspiracy theorists, and they have progressively been referred to as terrorists, which means that in due course they will fall under the law modifications that send "terrorists" to prison. " without the need for legal processing. If they call you a terrorist, they just have to put you in a vehicle and take you to a concentration camp indefinitely, without the right to any trial. This "anti-denialist" propaganda is increasingly gaining strength, penetrating the minds of people indoctrinated by the mass media bought by the state to divide society just as the Romans and Nazis did with the Jews at the time. .

<< And then many will be disturbed,

They will act treacherously towards each other, and
They will be angry with each other .>> (verse 10)

The word here can be translated as both getting angry and stumbling, or erring. The brainwashing work will turn many people against each other, seeing them as enemies, as a threat, first and foremost, as dangers. This label of "potential dangers" is used to define those who do not allow themselves to be injected with the poison of Bill Gates and the Rockefellers – along with DARPA (advanced technologies area of the US Department of Defense) – with their industries (Pfizer, Moderna, etc.). Healthy people who can supposedly infect people who have been vaccinated, precisely so as not to become infected. So why did you get vaccinated?

Brainwashing is essential to cloud reason. That is why when someone pricked gets sick or dies, indoctrinated people do not associate that it was due to allowing poison to be inoculated into their blood, but rather they believe what governments and the purchased media tell them: that a bug mutates and has a predilection for those who have been vaccinated. The highest level of human stupidity when he stops using his intelligence. But these idiotic people persecute, and will persecute, those who defend truth and freedom. To achieve this we have been programmed for years with Mind Control Technologies that come from the Cold War. These strategies are used in the body language and vocabulary used by reporters from pseudo-news networks, and by official spokespersons. Of them, and of the corrupt and sold-out world leaders, it was also prophesied.

<< *And false prophets will arise and*
They will lead many astray ....>>

Ihoshua could not have been more right with these words. A prophet does not have to be that individual from centuries past, dressed in rags, with a long beard, shaggy hair, living in a cave and eating grasshoppers. Today's prophets are heralds of the 21st century with the resources and dispositions of the 21st century. It is the same as the "gospel" of today, it is not that of two thousand years ago, but it adjusts to current circumstances: denouncing the Antichrist. Ergo, every time someone turns on a television, hordes of preachers of deception and fallacies come out, from politicians, world leaders, television presenters or spokespersons for pharmaceutical companies. All of them, as a whole, are aligned with the pharmaceutical mafia and the agendas of the Antichrist (Illuminati, New World Order, Agenda 2030, Agenda ID2020, etc.). Just look at its keynote speakers: Bill Gates and Anthony Fauci. It is this propaganda that is leading millions of people around the globe to the slaughterhouse – seeking their lives, losing them, while those who deprive themselves of their benefits save them – to fulfill the following.

<< *And when iniquity multiplies,*
The love of many will grow cold .>>

Those "evils" that come as a result of so much political-corporate deception appear in the Greek text referred to as Anomies, or injustices. You should know that the Greek word Anomis is an epithet of the Antichrist that was used since the time of the ancient prophets of Israel (using the Hebrew word 'Belial'). The apostle Yochanan (John) said that the Antichrist was not simply a person but a collective consciousness, a grouping, a system, an agenda, a spirit, a society, a machinery . The increase in machinations or conspiracies that are set in motion increasingly corners people and chills them socially. Social Distancing has two reasons for being: 1) efficient control from satellite and drones over individuals at a distance; 2) cool interpersonal relationships based on human warmth and integration and interaction. By distancing individuals and preventing them from "crowding" or "gathering" – and conditioning them to wear a muzzle – they relegate them to the non-emotional contact that social media represents, where there are no hugs, kisses, smiles, sharing and strengthening. personal and family ties. Thus they manage to weaken humanity in what most makes us special living beings: love.

<< *And he who waits until the end will be saved .*>>

As I have already said, the pressure of the tribulation of the plan-demic will increase, mentally and psychologically exhausting individuals, because in addition, the sad component of apartheid is added for those who do not accept being injected with the Illuminati poison. This pressure in schools, jobs and companies increases, cornering free-thinking people who want to advocate for their rights and the privacy and integrity of their body. As I have already said several times, this agenda is going to monopolize more and more areas to achieve its main goal: to implant under the skin of the back of the right hand of its followers a device for centralization and transmission of data in a large part of the population.

Consequently, without this device or the numbering of the inoculation certificate, no one will be able to shop in a supermarket, collect a salary, receive an economic benefit, pay rent or carry out any type of banking transaction. We have been talking about this for decades and more is being preached, mostly by non-religious people, as another Jew prophesied more than twenty-five centuries ago, saying that in a time humanity will begin to prophesy these things, from children to the elderly, and it would be known to everyone. the planet, before the great moment was unleashed, with "fire, blood and columns of smoke" (Joel 2.29), the same columns or thermonuclear mushrooms referred to in other prophecies from various cultures.

<< *And this good news will be proclaimed*
(this is euvangueli) all over the world
for a testimony about me to all
Gentiles, and then the end will come.
That is the Antichrist ...>> (verses 14-15)

Having said this, Ihoshua concluded this part of his exposition, which continues later explaining what Revelation defines in the so-called 'Seals', or beginning of the end of this era. In the Gospel of Ammonius this theme is summarized by stating that he "announced the Antichrist to them, that he would come with wars, and pestilences, and famines, and earthquakes..." (ch. 13.4). We must understand that the concept of "plague" is something invisible that kills on a large scale, but, as I have said many times – and many others around the world are also clarifying – it is not primarily a question of biological microorganisms, that is, It is not about bacteria, viruses or germs. But I will leave that topic for another time, since up to this point I have explained this, concluding with the quote from the source of Baal Shem Tob, the prelude to that Great Tribulation that will bring humanity to its knees to accept the Antichrist.

The Martyrs

The book of Revelation talks about many things that fit perfectly with today's description of what the U.S. is about, but some argue that this association is meaningless compared to the phrase that blamed the harlot (Babylon) of being a murderer of the faithful: "I saw the woman drunk with the blood of the saints, and with the blood of the martyrs of Jesus..." (Rev. 17:6, KJV 60) The root of the great Babylon is not limited to the establishment of the USA; It seems to go further back in time. The apostle John describes that "in it was found the blood of the prophets and the saints, and of all those who were slain on the earth." (Verse 18:24, KJV) How can that be possible? There is no kingdom that has prevailed since the time of the prophets of ancient Israel, much less "all those who have been" murdered on Earth. The only thing that could explain this is that it was a non-visible government, a power in the shadows. We can document this with many records and sources, and it does indeed come from further back than the founding of the US and the Illuminati, further back from the Jesuits, further back from Rome, further back from the Macedonian kingdom of Alexander, further back of Persians, Babylonians, Assyrians and Egyptians... it is the root of power in all these kingdoms.

What would happen if instead of seeing the prostitute described in Revelation sitting on the 4th beast we had seen her before on the 3rd, before on the 2nd and before on the 1st? The harlot is not the 4th beast but the one who has been over the beast itself, who has controlled and directed it. If that harlot (Babel) is so ancient, wouldn't she also have been the one who raised up and/or led the previous beasts? The prophet Daniel spoke about 4 beasts that would arise from the Earth until the coming of the kingdom of the Eternal God, and the Oahspe (from the year 1882) describes these 4 beasts as the human system and its main religious beliefs carried into the realm of conflagration and bloodshed. Other records, such as those of Ezra and Baruch, define these beasts as kingdoms that came after Babylon (Persia, Macedonia, Rome and what would be the current one). Consequently, we would not only be talking about one, but about the root of all of these. If so, there must have been vestiges of this, and there are: the elite from which Freemasonry emerged.

The majority of society believes that the world is run by its respective government, and that is why they waste time voting or with false hopes of changes pushed by others, without understanding that everything is controlled by a shadow government through banks. and all the networks that depend on money, that is, those who are in everything. From the records of ancient Sumer, the Egyptian mystery cults, the Eleusinian mysteries, the Mithraist sect, the assassin order (or 'Nizaris'), the orders of knights (Maltese, Templars, etc.), the European monarchies, cabalistic occultism, etc. Hermetic and initiatory systems have been the secret behind-the-scenes networks of power in every empire and nation up to the present. All of them have structured schemes of ascension levels, appointments, ceremonies, have used specific symbols and have kept their actions out of public knowledge. The most important thing about bringing all this to light is that all of them have had in common the cult of disembodied, extraterrestrial or astral entities. It is thanks to the favor received, according to them, from these entities, that the plans of these hidden institutions have been successful.

Although the workers are dying, the ideals have not been lost. They have changed their name, country, clothing and language, but their symbols are still present, and it is through them that this dark network - which operates clandestinely and with Luciferian and demonic help - directs the threads of the world and seeks a World Order based on totalitarianism, complete control of the people and the resources of the planet, drastic reduction of population, promotion of fear, need, dependence, slavery, nullification of conscience, apathy, absolute and irrefutable submission and obedience, transhumanism, drug dependence, mental programming and control, destruction of the family unit, genetic alteration, satanism, anarchy, theistic irreligion, sexual, moral and spiritual degradation, annulment of civil rights and liberties, martial law, the plutocracy of a petty aristocracy, eugenics, euthanasia, false peace at the cost of nuclear paroxysm, military imperialism, the deception of the material senses, ignorance, disease, hunger and poverty, and the worship and idolatry of a single sovereign dictator. It is basically a devilish beast on Earth.

No system can progress with opposition or without the cooperation of others. For this reason, these organizations are structured as clubs, hermetic societies or secret guilds that progressively ally themselves with others, whether similar or with other general interests, but with whom a link and reinforcement can be made to achieve greater influence and better achievements. For many historians, the role of the Jesuits in the history of the founding of the United States is key. The year of the founding of the USA, 1776, is precisely the year of the founding of the Bavarian Illuminati, created by a Jesuit, Adam Weishaupt. This leads to the belief that the US $1 bill does not evoke the founding of "America" but rather that of the Bavarian Illuminati order. Since Martin Luther's Reformation in Germany, the splits in the Roman Catholic Church have been increasing. It was no longer just the separation of the Greek Orthodox Church but that of the Anglican Church and the rest of the Protestant movement, Lutheranism and Calvinism. Rome's mortal wound had to be healed, so Ignatius of Loyola proposed to Pope Paul III in 1540 a better idea than returning to the Inquisition or the persecutions and wars of the Counter-Reformation.

This consisted of creating an organization of global influence infiltrated into every government apparatus, every monarchy, every economic system, every religious movement, every social and civil revolution and, subsequently, every means of influence: music industry, film industry, media, etc This network created these mass media and directs them. This initiative was a successful strategy that achieved the planned objectives, and has remained completely silent in the popular idea: except for a few researchers and historians, society ignores this more than less. The oracles of the Greek Sibyl are just some of the texts that present a painful outcome for Rome and for the new Babylon: "Who will be the only one [who will] dominate the entire earth because of honor, who was first assigned to the Lord Poseidon ; then a great star will come from heaven into the terrible sea and burn up the vast depths, and Babylon itself, and the land of Italy, since, of whom there are many [who] perished faithful holy men among the Hebrews and a people TRUE." (Book V. vers. 210) What relationship is there between the US and the Vatican? The jesuits.

Many times I have explained about the prophecies that announce the fall of two asteroids almost simultaneously on Earth within a short time, the first of which would fall into the sea - possibly north of the Atlantic -. This, according to ancient warnings, would be before the absolutist reign of the Antichrist and the war of Har-magedon, so the sibyl's omen could not have referred to ancient Babylon: The city of the past disappeared under Medo-Persian power , and Rome did not yet exist; Conversely, when Rome began, Babylon was no longer a great empire. As in many other cases, this prophecy announces an asteroid falling into the ocean and affecting "Babylon", but the historical city that bears that name is south of current Baghdad, in Iraq, and there is no ocean there. Furthermore, an impact in the North Atlantic would affect, not only the United States, first, but also Portugal and Spain, which would shelter Italy (where Rome is located) from the shock wave and tsunami.

So, what does this warning mean? The sibyl speaks almost all the time of the future destruction of Rome (who devastated the Hebrews in the 1st century AD) in various ways, one of them by fire. For many, that Rome refers to the global power of the Vatican, which controls our world through many branches, such as the Jesuits and the USA (with the Jesuits being within the structure of the USA itself). Consequently, what these passages seem to say is that at almost the same time a Babylon other than ancient Babylon, and a still-living Rome, whether together or separately, will be destroyed.

In other words, the set of prophecies evoke the great biblical Tribulation, which will bring misfortune to the United States while sinking the world economy, unleashing a nuclear war, bringing hunger and pandemics to every corner of the globe, and triggers waves of crime, terrorism and civil war, including some of these hotspots in the Vatican. In an interview with researcher John Phelps, speaking on this topic, they commented that the Antichrist would be responsible for ending the entire "mother" or Great Babylon (which would be the elite of Roman Catholicism), as it is the axis of Christianity worldwide. and historical; so that the power structure would be cleansed of all Christian influence at all levels. This takes us back to Revelation, to the phrase that speaks of the martyrs in the 5th seal, coinciding with the words of Yeshua (Jesus) about the persecution that there will be to Christians before his coming (or 'parousia', the advent of Christ). In this way, one of the few allusions that seem to contradict the substantial fact that the US is the main candidate to be the great Babylon described in the Apocalypse, is rejected.

But not only do these passages allude to this issue, but also the verses themselves that speak of the great Babylon, who is blamed for the blood of the just and martyrs. In previous articles and in 'Remote Viewing', I talk about the elite's plan to persecute Christianity, and the use of martial law in the US with the beginning of a "purge" on evangelicals and other Christian groups during the Great Tribulation that is at the doors. The existence of a last world government before the arrival of the true Messiah is referred to in many present and ancient religious teachings of many peoples, and former Satanists, former Freemasons, former witches and many other traitors of the dark side always speak of the headache. which represents the Protestant world for the Catholic-Jesuit New World Order. It's not that they are saints or their teachings are pure, but it's what they represent, and as long as Protestants exist, the elite will not be able to carry out their great plan, so they must eliminate the resistance.

In the case of Oahspe, it speaks of Guatama as the last government that will exist on Earth, and that will fall resoundingly before the beginning of the new era of the world. Precisely, the book calls Guatama the American continent, and implies that this "America" will be the last global power of an era of 75,000 years, which includes the period of modern man. The US is something like the current "body" of Rome (not Italy, but of the Roman empire, Vatican, the Jesuits, the opus dei, etc.). It is drunk with the blood of saints, witnesses (in Greek "martyr") and envoys (in Greek "apostles) in many contexts:

1. The elite (USA-New York-Illuminati) murders the lights of this world (I recommend in this sense studying this topic especially, since all those who see against the elite are destroyed), finances terrorism (that kills Christians in Africa and Asia, be they people with their churches or missionaries) and wars (where another pretext is to use Islam to cut the throats, rape and burn Christians); 2. Since the days of Yeshua (Jesus) in Yhudeah (Judea), Rome – directly or indirectly – was behind the deaths of Christians (Jesus, Peter, Paul and the others who threw to the lions, crucified, hanged or sent to the pyrrha). 3. To this day there are still saints and prophets, and since they are killed by today's elite, God will punish today's elite (he will not punish today's people for what their 30th generation ancestors did): " Because They shed the blood of the saints and prophets, you have also given them blood to drink; Well they deserve it. » (Rev. 16:6, R60)

The nation of the United States, although appearing to be just another country or dependent on the UN, has really been the greatest superpower (for some the only one), and is where the modern Babel is located (the building and headquarters of the United Nations, which when it falls will be transferred to Europe, to the city of Brussels (Belgium), from where the Antichrist will operate); The current UN building in Manhattan was given by the Rockefeller bankers, the same ones who financed and supported Harry S. Truman's rise to power, so that he could found the United Nations, so that there would be a false appearance of democracy and diplomacy. international beginning in the 1940s, which would really be the global unification (Babel) that would begin the Global Government of the Antichrist (it would be the first entry structure for it, but it must sacrifice the US, where it rests, to bring the world to the paroxysm of chaos, so that they accept and even demand something better, or New World Order and a world savior).

Some very simple examples, the Statue of Liberty, in the middle of the waters is a hermaphrodite sculpture, combining Isis with Apollo, but secretly evoking the Masonic goddess 'Columbia', whose Greek meaning is "she who is in the pond." (which is the scientific name given to 'pigeons' (Columbidae)), that is, the one that sits in the middle of a pool or in the middle of the water: "I will show you the sentence against the great harlot, the one that sits on many waters; with which the kings of the earth have committed fornication" (Rev. 17:1-2, KJV 60) The name of the statue 'Liberty' is from the Roman 'Liber'. Liber or Líber ("the free", also known as Liber Pater, "Free Father"), in Roman mythology, was a god of fertility, viticulture, wine and freedom. She was a patron deity of the plebeians of Rome and was part of the Aventine triad along with Ceres and Libera. His holiday, Liberalia, which was celebrated on March 17 (which is still commemorated today as 'Saint Patrick's Day', the day of drunks), came to be associated with freedom of expression and the rights inherent to the majority of age. Her cult and functions became progressively associated with those of Bacchus (Dionysus, Greek god of wine and drunkenness): « I saw the woman drunk with the blood of the saints, and with the blood of the martyrs of Jesus; and when I saw her, I was amazed with great amazement. » (Rev. 17:6, KJV 60)

Many have defined the Statue of Liberty as the Roman goddess Liberta or even the Babylonian Ishtar, while others believe that it is really a symbol of the Great Whore or Beast disguised as justice and freedom (that would explain its 7 rays on the head, evoking his 7 heads and the 7 mountains, and the base of the 11-pointed star: 10 kings and the Antichrist): « And he took me in the Spirit into the desert; "And I saw a woman sitting on a scarlet beast full of names of blasphemy, having seven heads and ten horns." (Rev. 17:3, KJV 60) .

Just remember Louis Lefebvre's video, 'I Pet Goat II', where you can see the breakup of the Statue of Liberty with the progress of the

New World Order, once the twin towers were destroyed. According to that sequence, it is precisely with the destruction of the Statue of Liberty that the frames of children's programming come, the collapse of the markets, the destruction of an important Islamic center possibly in Turkey and the start of nuclear war. Does the US fall only because of immorality? No, also by the pawns of the elite, like Donald Trump, in charge of finishing putting together the pieces for the beginning of martial law in the United States. The era of the United States would be about to collapse, and with it the Roman Catholic influence of the Vatican, so that the UN (later controlling NATO) becomes the new great global government, but this time from Brussels, Belgium (Europe). But would Russia and China allow it? Precisely for this reason there has been so much talk that the fall of the United States as a nation will go hand in hand with the use of its army abroad, to fight Russia and China in a thermonuclear conflict that reduces power, influence, capabilities and energy of these three powers, leaving Europe and the government in the shadows to raise up the Antichrist, who from Europe will be able to present himself as heir to a Merovingian-Arthurian-Davidic royal lineage.

«Inebriated heart (in love with beer) Rome, you who from Olympus will be set on fire with Macedonian spears; But God will make you completely unknown, When you want to appear to stand much firmer in sight. So to you those things that I am going to cry out. Then you must perish screaming and boiling in pain...." (Sibylline Oracles. Book VII. Verse 145) The degradation of religion and the calamities to come go hand in hand with the end of the US and the Vatican: "...Three times then to Rome the Almighty brings regrettable luck..." (Sibylline Oracles. Book 8. Verses 225) In turn, religious degradation is also accompanied by moral degradation and despicable values that are promoted and legalized daily. Those who promote iniquity, injustice and social rot will be the main affected, but before the effects of these created, maintained, developed and applauded causes come, the elite has determined that Christianity be eliminated, and for this they seem to have established a series of guidelines. One of them, deceive them with a Christian president, with supposed Christian values, with a strong hand to oppose anti-Christian or anti-biblical criteria, feed the people's hatred again towards religion - but directly Protestant religion -, control the sermons of churches, control the capacity of churches, control mass gatherings of Christians, humiliate their convictions and principles by subjecting them to arbitrary laws.

Once Christian influence falls in America, the rest will be "a piece of cake." This is because Christianity is actually an influence on the American continent, not the rest of the world, where it is a large minority. IN Europe, atheism is increasing, and the Christian values of the elderly have been disappearing to accept the new "modernist" ideas. This way, when the New Babel of Antichrist rises in Europe as ruler of the world, with Israel as second in command, there will be no religious opposition against them. The pope will have completed his ecumenical work of mixing all religious aspects into a "Thelema", or philosophy where everything is valid and you can take whatever you want from any religious aspect to create each person's own personal vision, which will later be integrated. in the religion of Antichrist. The New Babel in Brussels will then replace the Great Whore, the UN Babel in the US, and from there it will rule the world.

You can already see the example in how the European Parliament building – in Brussels – has the shape of the Tower of Babel from the old descriptive portraits of it, and how the network of European Commission complexes has also been installed in Brussels for decades. , the Berlaymont, where several floors interconnect the most powerful computer in the world (called 'The Beast'), from where the AI (Artificial Intelligence) of 'the Beast', presented as a slogan, 4D logo (holographic projection) or icon (image), will control the entire planet, as Yochanan (John) predicted: "and he was given life to the Image of the Beast so that the Image of the Beast could speak and order to kill all those who did not worship the Image of the Beast" (Rev. 13.15).

EPILOGUE

Elijah must return

Here you can see an example of what we are talking about: https://www.elperiodico.com/es/entre-todos/participacion/la-union-europea-es-la-torre-de-babel-moderna-63544 [1]. It is not our war to fight against the system, nor should we be afraid to tell the truth. The wars fought at each level have their corresponding opponents. We must be vigilant and prudent in preparing our time outside the system, because the Antichrist will have to face several asteroids, serious earthquakes, waves of solar radiation, the trial of the Galactic Confederation, and, just before, the propaganda battle in his against, duly supported, by two returning prophets of ancient Israel. The Bible speaks of two olive trees representing two individuals who will come to fight the Antichrist. In Greek they appear as "duo elaiai", or "duo Elijah". The correspondence of the name Eliahu (Elijah) with the word Elaia (olive tree) is no coincidence. Olive tree (ZIT = 39 / 417) is a symbol of peace (state of consciousness), anointing (election and transcendence), wisdom-prudence. Olive (olive) produces oil analogy of gold analogy of light (three states of matter). Those 2 olive trees (zeitim) or 2 lampstands (menorot: providers of light) are defined as his "2 witnesses" who "stand before God", also as his "2 anointed ones" (Zech. 4:11). The only individuals who have gone up to those rooms and remained there, according to Hebrew knowledge, are Janoch (Enoch), Elihu (Elijah) and Yeshua (Jesus).

1. https://www.elperiodico.com/es/entre-todos/participacion/la-union-europea-es-la-torre-de-babel-moderna-63544

It is a fact of Jewish knowledge that Elijah must return "and restore all things," unifying the "relationships of fathers and sons," according to his call for the Ministry of Reconciliation. They even consecrate a cup of wine to him every Easter, longing for his return because the Messiah comes with him; That is, when Elijah appears it is because the Messiah will be about to manifest himself. Both Enoch, Jesus and Elijah were taken alive and physically to heaven: "And it came to pass, as they went and spoke, behold, a chariot of fire with horses of fire separated them both; and Elijah ascended into heaven in a whirlwind." (2nd Kings 2:11) And as Luke narrated about Jesus: "And when he had said these things, when they saw him, he was taken up, and a cloud met him and hid him from their sight." (Acts 1:9) We know that Jesus is referred to as a lamb in Revelation, but the other two witnesses are those of the promise.

It is said that in total Enoch was away from Earth for 300 years (Gen. 5:22) and then he was left with his family for an entire year to teach his message; After this they took him back to Heaven (Heb. 11:5): "So Enoch walked with God, and was gone, because God took him." (Gen. 5:24 and multiple explicit references from the book of Enoch himself). Enoch is the other witness, as he himself testified to Rabbi Ishmael: " — Because I am Enoch ben Yared. When the flood generation sinned - because with their works they had corrupted themselves - saying to God: " Depart from us, for we do not want to know your ways", then the Holy One, blessed be He, took me out from among them to serve as a witness against them . before all the inhabitants of the world..." And verse 5 reiterates: "For this reason the Holy One, blessed be He, caused me to ascend into the high heavens while they were still alive, and before their own eyes, to serve as a witness against them in the world to come, and named me prince and sovereign among the ministering angels." (3rd Enoch 4:2-3)

Then, in 3 Enoch 48 c, verse 2, it mentions the following: "And I took him: Enoch, the son of Yared, from among them and elevated him, with the cry of trumpets and with shouts, to the heavens, so that he might serve as a witness along with the Jayot who are next to merkabah in the future world." This is also how the Introduction to the 2nd book of Enoch begins: "There was a wise man, a great craftsman, and the Lord conceived love for [him] and received it, for he must contemplate [the] dwellings of the Most High and be a witness." eye of the Wise and Great and the inconceivable and immutable Kingdom of Almighty God..."

The Book of Jasher, recovered from the caves of Qumran, tells us: "When Hanoch had spoken to the people, the Lord sent darkness upon the Earth, and there was darkness, and it covered those men [who were] standing with Hanoch. , and they carried Hanoch up to the highest Heaven, where the Lord is; and he received him and placed him behind his face, and the darkness departed from the Earth, and the light came again. And the people saw and did not understood how Hanoch was taken away, and they glorified God." The Gospel of Valentin also testifies that Yeshua told his disciples that Enoch was in high heaven, "So that Enoch might write in paradise, when I spoke to him about the tree of knowledge and the tree of life." (ch. 49.22)

In the gospel of Nicodemus, it is said, in chapter. 15:1, "And Nicodemus stood up and said, You speak rightly, children of Israel. You have heard what those three men said, who swore on the law of the Lord that they had heard Jesus speak with his disciples on the mountain of the Olive Trees, and saw him ascend to heaven. And the Scripture teaches us that the blessed Elijah was transported to heaven, and that Elisha, questioned by the sons of the prophets about where his brother Elijah had gone, answered that he had been taken from them. And the sons of the prophets said to him, "Perhaps the spirit has taken him away from us and placed him on the mountains of Israel. But let us choose men to go with us, and let us go through those mountains, where perhaps we will find him." And thus they besought Elisha. , who walked with them three days, and they did not find Elijah. And now, listen to me, children of Israel. Let us send men to the mountains, because perhaps the spirit has taken Jesus away, and perhaps we will find him, and we will do penance. !

These are examples of writings from thousands of years ago that reflect the point of view of that time... "And the Lord, taking Adam by the hand, put him in the hands of the archangel Michael, whom all the saints also followed. And he brought them all into the glorious grace of Paradise, and two men, very old, stood before them. And the saints questioned them, saying, Who are you, that you have not been in hell with us, and who have been brought bodily to Paradise? And one of them answered, I am Enoch, who has been transported here by order of the Lord. And he who is with me is Elijah, the Thesbite, who was carried away by a chariot of fire. To this day We have not tasted death, but we are reserved for the advent of the Antichrist, armed with divine ensigns, and lavishly prepared to fight against him, to receive death in Jerusalem, and to, after three and a half days, be raised alive again. in the clouds." (Ev. Nicodemus 26:1-4)

[]

About the Author

Israeli writer, researcher, disseminator, documentary filmmaker and influencer. He is the writer of more than 35 books, mostly research and dissemination theses.

Read more at https://www.frederickguttmann.com.

www.ingramcontent.com/pod-product-compliance
Lightning Source LLC
LaVergne TN
LVHW090316210926
848480LV00001B/266